OPERATING SYSTEM ELEMENTS

Prentice-Hall Software Series
Brian W. Kernighan, advisor

OPERATING SYSTEM ELEMENTS

A User Perspective

PETER CALINGAERT

Department of Computer Science
University of North Carolina at Chapel Hill

PRENTICE-HALL, INC., Englewood Cliffs, New Jersey 07632

Library of Congress Cataloging in Publication Data

Calingaert, Peter.
   Operating system elements.

   (Prentice-Hall software series)
   Bibliography: p. 220
   Includes index.
   1. Operating systems (Computers) I. Title.
II. Series.
QA76.6.C338   001.64'25   81-10617
ISBN 0-13-637421-2   AACR2

©1982 by Prentice-Hall, Inc., Englewood Cliffs, N.J. 07632

Printed in the United States of America

10 9 8 7 6 5 4 3 2

Editorial/production supervision and interior design: Nancy Milnamow
Cover design: Judith A. Matz
Manufacturing buyer: Gordon Osbourne

PRENTICE-HALL INTERNATIONAL, INC., *London*
PRENTICE-HALL OF AUSTRALIA PTY. LIMITED, *Sydney*
PRENTICE-HALL OF CANADA, LTD., *Toronto*
PRENTICE-HALL OF INDIA PRIVATE LIMITED, *New Delhi*
PRENTICE-HALL OF JAPAN, INC., *Tokyo*
PRENTICE-HALL OF SOUTHEAST ASIA PTE., LTD., *Singapore*
WHITEHALL BOOKS LIMITED, *Wellington, New Zealand*

ACKNOWLEDGEMENTS

Sections 2.1.4 and 4.7 are reprinted with minor changes from Peter Calingaert, *Assemblers, Compilers, and Program Translation* (1979), by permission of Computer Science Press, Potomac, MD.

Figure 4.19 is reprinted from P. J. Courtois, F. Heymans, and D. L. Parnas, Concurrent Control with "Readers" and "Writers", *Comm. ACM* **14** (October 1971), 667-668, © 1971, Association for Computing Machinery, Inc., by permission.

Figures 4.20 and 8.1 are adapted from Alan C. Shaw, *The Logical Design of Operating Systems,* © 1974, p. 83, by permission of Prentice-Hall, Inc., Englewood Cliffs, N.J..

Figure 4.21 is adapted from C. A. R. Hoare, Monitors: An Operating System Structuring Concept, *Comm. ACM* **17** (October 1974), 549-557, © 1974, Association for Computing Machinery, Inc., by permission.

The discussion of the RC 4000 system in Section 4.4 is adapted from Per Brinch Hansen, *RC 4000 Software Multiprogramming System* (1969), by permission of A/S Regnecentralen, Copenhagen, and from Per Brinch Hansen, The Nucleus of a Multiprogramming System, *Comm. ACM* **13** (April 1970), 238-241, 250, © 1970, Association for Computing Machinery, Inc., by permission.

Figure 4.23 and the accompanying discussion of deadlock are adapted from E. G. Coffman, Jr., M. J. Elphick, and A. Shoshani, System Deadlocks, *Comput. Surveys* **3** (June 1971), 67-78, © 1971, Association for Computing Machinery, Inc., by permission.

The discussion of multiprocessing system reliability in Section 8.2.3 includes material adapted from Anita K. Jones and Peter Schwarz, Experience Using Multiprocessor Systems — A Status Report, *Comput. Surveys* **12** (June 1980), 121-165, © 1980, Association for Computing Machinery, Inc., by permission.

CONTENTS

Chapter 3   PROCESSOR MANAGEMENT   53

Chapter 4   PROCESS MANAGEMENT   79

Chapter 5   DEVICE MANAGEMENT   122

Chapter 6   FILE MANAGEMENT   146

Chapter 7   SYSTEM MANAGEMENT   174

PREFACE

The present book is a text about operating systems, and the control programs they comprise, for persons who are studying programming systems for the first time. Of the many students, even in computer science, who study control programs, relatively few will ultimately design and implement an operating system. Only a somewhat larger number will modify a control program, but virtually all will use the facilities provided by operating systems. They will benefit, therefore, from knowing the assumptions underlying operating system design, the goals for which an operating system exists, and the techniques used to achieve those goals.

When time to study such engineering artifacts as operating systems is limited, an important question is whether to examine one system in depth or several systems less deeply. Different instructors have different preferences. Moreover, they usually have little control over the availability of reference material that describes appropriate systems in suitable depth. The availability of such materials and the appropriateness of different systems will vary with time. This book is intended to present the principles of control program function and operation that will illuminate, and be illuminated by, the parallel study of one or more specific operating systems. Because the many facets of control program function are interrelated, multiple passes over the material are a great aid to understanding. A technique employed by one of my colleagues is to make two concurrent passes, one pass examining the major issues and the other considering selected complete systems. An alternative to such concurrent passes is to make sequential passes, treating all topics once at least lightly, before undertaking a more detailed examination. This book is designed to serve for either the first of such sequential passes or for the concurrent pass that examines issues.

The book makes a single pass over operating systems, at a level that is intended to be neither trivial nor deep. Principles take priority over engineering details, and complete implementations are not discussed. A few algorithms are expressed in a bastard Pascalgol that should tax no one able to read Pascal, PL/I, or Algol programs. An Appendix summarizes the notation used. Examples are drawn from real systems, both commercial and non-commercial. Although I have attempted to present information that is current as of the date of writing, there is no guarantee that the descriptions will continue to match the most recent version of each system. Exercises are chiefly analytic rather than synthetic, requiring the identification of problems and the suggestion of solutions.

The text emphasizes resource management as the central feature common to all control programs, and takes pains to distinguish management policies from the mechanisms used to implement the policies. It attempts to give balanced coverage to the different resources, irrespective of how much is known about managing each type of resource, or how well that knowledge has been systematized. The focus is on principles rather than on example systems, and I hope that the treatment is not colored by excessive attention to particular systems or schools of thought. By following an approach that is descriptive rather than analytic, and practical rather than formal, the student is directed toward understanding what operating systems do and how they do it, rather than how to design an actual operating system.

It is widely accepted that data structures should be studied before control programs. I believe that some knowledge of translators as well is helpful in the study of control programs because (1) issues of binding time, which are important in control programs, are often more readily learned in the context of translation, and (2) certain demands upon an operating system, particularly in storage management and name resolution, are direct consequences of source-language requests and of translator function. Translator knowledge is important also because the mechanisms of generation and interpretation are widely used in control programs, and the designer needs to know the advantages and costs of using each in a particular situation. Nevertheless, because design is not the central focus of this book, prior formal study of translators is not necessary.

Communication-based systems and computer networks, despite their increasing prominence, are not covered, primarily because control programs for such systems are affected by the requirements and facilities of communication subsystems to the extent that the latter should be studied before the former. In a book of this length there is no room to present the required material in sufficient depth.

No sequence of presentation of operating system elements is ideal. The reasons for the choices I have made are stated briefly in the following summary of the content of the book. Chapter 1 presents an overview of the resources to be managed, thus both establishing the central theme and providing an initial mini-pass over operating systems. Chapter 2 is about main storage, because that is the resource whose management is perhaps the most simply described, and because it serves as a point of connection with translators, among which the linker and loader also serve in part as control programs. Chapter 3 might have been called "time management"; the resource is the evanescent stream of instruction cycles. Its position next to Chapter 2 emphasizes the space–time tradeoff. Moreover, allocation of the instruction counter does depend on which programs reside in that storage from which execution is possible. Consideration of multiple processors is deferred until later. In Chapter 4, attention is turned from the processor and focused instead on processes, which contend for it. Issues of concurrency, deadlock, and invocation are raised in the context of uniprocessing. Chapter 5, on device management, describes interrupts, covered in Chapter 3, as one mechanism for handling input/output. It also relies on notions of concurrency developed in Chapter 4. Chapter 6 is concerned with management of information files. Since files occupy storage and use devices, it is convenient to have encountered those two topics earlier in the book. Several issues that apply over-all are grouped in Chapter 7 on system management. Chapter 8 opens with a brief chronicle of operating systems, showing their present state as a consequence of historical developments. It continues with some design issues that serve as a bridge to further study, and concludes with an examination of system configurations that are either specialized from, or generalized from, the basic configuration assumed in the preceding chapters. In particular, multiprocessing systems are treated here only after the student has been exposed to all of the resources involved.

The book is written primarily for third- and fourth-year undergraduate students. More advanced students who have had little or no prior exposure to control programs will find that it provides a rapid survey, which can complement a more advanced treatment. Because of the book's descriptive orientation, many technical managers and computer users will also find it appropriate. The readers are assumed to have some experience in programming in an assembler language and in a programming language, and to be capable of reading short programs in an Algol-like notation. They should be familiar with such elementary data structures as arrays, queues, stacks, and trees. The readers should also understand how the various hardware components of a computer system work together. Although queuing theory is important to a thorough analytic study of operating systems, it is not used in the book. Reference is occasionally made, however, to such elementary descriptive statistics as mean and variance.

In writing about operating systems, the choice of terminology often presents difficulties. Competent writers disagree on important definitions, such as that of *process*. Proprietary usages often conflict: IBM's "job" is Univac's "task", IBM's "task" is Univac's "activity", and Honeywell's "activity" is IBM's "job step". Words well-defined in other contexts are misused, as in describing a "job queue" that is not really a queue. Introducing new terms sparingly, I have attempted to use terminology that is, at worst, not misleading and, at best, reasonably acceptable. Common alternatives are usually indicated. Apologies are offered to the reader who is unhappy with my choices. Apologies are also offered to the reader who is unable to accept my grammatical use of the masculine gender as in no way implying personal reference to the male sex.

The book is designed as a self-contained one-semester text. For some classes and instructors, even one quarter may be long enough. The text can, but need not, be supplemented with system descriptions. The following list of systems that I would currently suggest as candidates for study reflects a number of personal biases, and does not imply endorsement of any commercial product. Historical: Atlas, T.H.E., M.I.T. Multics, IBM OS/360, TENEX, Venus, C.mmp HYDRA. Contemporary: Bell Labs UNIX, Burroughs B7000/B6000 MCP, CDC Kronos, Honeywell GCOS6, IBM VM/370, Prime PRIMOS V, Univac EXEC.

The course for which I envision this book as the text is similar to, but less demanding than, course I4, "Systems Programming", of Curriculum 68. The three most significant differences are the following. First, I have no predisposition to "devote most of the course to the study of a single system". Second, the depth of this book is restricted to permit its being finished in one semester. Third, this book, unlike I4, is designed to capitalize upon whatever prior exposure to translators the readers may have. Although the Curriculum 78 courses CS 6 and CS 10, "Operating Systems and Computer Architecture", differ from the one I have in mind, the book could nevertheless serve as a major resource for those courses.

Conventional wisdom dictates that a first course in operating systems be quantitative and design-oriented, encompassing detailed algorithms and offering evaluations of system performance. I believe that operating systems are inherently more complex than translators, and much more complex than the application programs likely to have been written by a first-time student of operating systems. Consequently, I hold the view that the operating systems courses of Curricula 68 and 78 are too design-oriented to serve as first courses for most students. A more descriptive course offers the background that enables a student to derive maximum benefit from a subsequent design-oriented course. It also provides sufficient basic information for the many students who have no need for a more advanced course.

The original inspiration for this book was dissatisfaction with the textbooks available for a course, entitled "Programming Systems", that I taught in 1973 and 1974 at the University of North Carolina at Chapel Hill, introducing students to both translators and operating systems in one semester. Because of necessary differences in the levels of the introductions to subjects of unequal difficulty, I decided to write separate books on each subject. One of the sequels to the programming systems course was a semester course in control program design, which I also taught, and the two courses convinced me of the need for a brief descriptive introduction to operating systems. In mid-1977 I taught a course from the first draft to third-year undergraduate students at the University of the Witwatersrand (Wits) in

Johannesburg, and in late 1977 from a revised version to third- and fourth-year students at North Carolina State University. Further revision of the material has led to the present text, which has continued to be used by undergraduates here. The book on translators has taken shape meanwhile as *Assemblers, Compilers, and Program Translation* [1979]. The two books contain some material in common, because loaders and linkers function both as translators and as control programs, and because issues of process invocation are relevant to both.

It is a pleasure to record my debt to Hans Messerschmidt, not only for detailed suggestions developed while teaching the course at Wits after my departure, but also for his encouragement. Among others who urged that I complete the book are J. Craig Mudge and Trevor Turton. For many insights I am indebted to lectures by, and conversations with, my colleagues Frederick P. Brooks, Jr., and David L. Parnas. A number of anonymous reviewers were collectively most helpful in suggesting improvements to earlier versions of the manuscript. I thank them, and I especially thank Karen Dwyer, who examined with a critical eye what I had thought was the final version. I accept full responsibility, of course, for any deficiencies that still remain. The students in Computer Science III at Wits in 1977 contributed perhaps more than they realized; to them, too, I am grateful. Finally, I thank Kristine J. Brown for typing the original text into data files and Kathy Yount for entering the substantial and seemingly endless revisions.

Peter Calingaert
Chapel Hill, North Carolina

Chapter 1

OVERVIEW

In this chapter we begin by explaining why operating systems exist, what goals they are intended to accomplish, and how they are related to user programs. We continue by examining the variety of computer resources that operating systems make available to users, and discuss the effects of adopting different philosophies for the design of an operating system. Finally, we describe a technical distinction that recurs in the more detailed consideration paid to specific resources in subsequent chapters.

1.1 PROGRAMMING SYSTEMS

A user who enjoys exclusive access to a computer facility commands all of its resources. He can use those resources, with no concern for any other users, in whatever manner best suits his specific needs. The user can tailor programs precisely to his requirements, and can choose whichever language translators offer the most satisfactory compromises among language and processing features. If the user can afford exclusive access to a computer that has the capabilities required to process his most demanding application, he need look no further. Computer installations, including most microcomputers and many minicomputers, are often operated in just this fashion.

Not infrequently, however, a user's resource needs are ill-matched to his computer's capabilities. This occurs, for example, when the user has much greater need for one system resource than for another, as in an application that is heavily processor-bound, that is, uses much less than the available input/output (I/O) capability, while keeping the processor busy nearly all the time. Another type of mismatch results from a user's having a peak demand for computer service that is much greater than his average demand. A common example is an interactive service, which the user requires only during isolated periods separated by intervals of "think time". Needs can vary over brief time intervals, whereas facilities and costs (rental, or amortization of purchase) stay fixed over long intervals. When mismatches occur, the cost of providing the computer service may exceed the benefit to the user.

The cost can often be lowered by giving up exclusive access, and *sharing* the computer with other users. If a way can be found to run an I/O-bound job concurrently with a processor-bound job, the total cost of executing both can be made lower than the sum of the costs of executing each in succession. Similarly, a computer that accommodates two interactive users, serving each while the other thinks, can cost almost as little as a computer that accommodates only one. This manner of use is widely known as *time sharing.* Similarly, a computer used part of the day for one application and part for another can cost less than two computers, one used for each application. The foregoing modes of sharing, whether concurrent or sequential, can readily be extended beyond two users, and lead to the concept of a community of users of one computer facility. It is not necessarily the case that different users are different persons. In fact, a single person may have multiple requirements for computer service that make it appropriate to think of the person as several users, one for each requirement.

The functions desired by the individual members of a user community, whether distinct persons or not, are embodied in the *application programs* prepared by the users. Although the requirements of the various users differ, they typically have common elements, which can be met by providing common programs to facilitate the preparation and use of application programs. These common programs, intended for all the users who share the computer hardware, are called *system programs*, and can be thought of as constituting three major subsystems, the *language system*, the *operating system*, and the *utility system.* To help place operating systems in broader perspective, we begin by looking briefly at all three subsystems, realizing that the boundaries between them are not sharp.

Following Habermann [1976], we use the term "language system" to connote the system programs related to issues of language. These are the *translators* and their *run-time routines.* Translators, or *translation programs*, have as their principal goal a transformation of the language in which an algorithm is expressed. The content is by and large preserved, but the encoding is changed, often from a form oriented to human communication to a form oriented to machine communication. Common examples are assemblers, compilers, interpreters, linkers, and loaders. Run-time routines (e.g., mathematical subroutines) are pretranslated programs specified by the user at compilation time and made available at execution time.

The system programs that constitute operating systems (see Section 8.1 for the origin of the term) are *controllers*, or *control programs.* Their object is to facilitate the sharing of a computer system by several users, either sequentially or concurrently. Examples include storage allocators, disk access schedulers, job dispatchers, and interrupt handlers. Linkers and especially loaders are not only translators but control programs as well. Some input/output control programs can also be used as components of the language system's run-time routines.

We use the term "utility system" for the collected *utilities*, or *utility programs*. Their chief actions are to convert the medium, sequence, or layout of programs and data. Medium converters preserve content but change form in that one medium of representation is substituted for another. They include card-to-tape and key-to-disk conversion, and printing from disk; their function is essentially an input operation concurrent with an output operation. Sequence converters, or *sort programs*, perform rearrangements. Their function may or may not involve input and output, but always includes the changing of addresses, whether implicit in the medium or explicit. Layout converters are assuming increasing importance among system programs, although their function is often also a desired end use of the computer. They include both *editors*, which facilitate editorial changes in program or other text, and *formatters*, which control printing or composition of text in a specified manner. Other layout converters include those that change the encoding of data, both to reconcile application programs that use different encodings, and to encrypt and decrypt sensitive material. Recorders of system usage statistics for accounting can be classified either as utilities or as part of the operating system, as can program and data library management routines.

To the extent that the system programs cooperate harmoniously, they constitute a *programming system*. It is possible and often fruitful to study programming systems in their entirety, but in this book our attention is focused on operating systems. Unlike translators and utilities, which can usually be thought of as serving users, even multiple users, *individually*, operating systems generally serve users *collectively*. Among the services that operating systems may provide for the user community are the loading of arbitrary storage locations with programs to be executed, the apparently concurrent execution of two or more programs by a single processor, the meeting of time constraints of real-time response or deadline scheduling, the protection of one program from interference by another, the securing of data against loss, and the maintenance of reduced service in the face of partial system failure.

Although each user is a member of a community, sharing system resources with other users, he is nevertheless competing with those other users for a share of the resources. Operating systems provide their services to the users chiefly by allocating resources to users and perhaps by withdrawing resources from users. This *management of resources* is a central function of operating systems, and that about which this book is organized.

1.2 RESOURCES

Before delving into the details of how the system resources are managed, it is important to examine briefly what resources are offered by a system. Space and time are two basic resources; viewed simply, in the context of a computer system, they represent storage space and processor instruction cycle time.

Among the principal characteristics of storage are its random-access time (time to access an arbitrarily located datum), serial-access time (time to access the spatially adjacent datum), capacity (usually in bits or words), cost per unit of capacity, and volatility (loss of data if power is removed). Computer storage is typically provided in a hierarchy of levels, with speed of random access, speed of serial access, and cost per bit normally decreasing with decreasing level. Following Lowe [1969], we shall call *executable* any storage from which a processor can execute instructions. An important characteristic of executable storage is that serial- and random-access times are equal. Executable storage always includes *main storage*. This is the highest level* under programmer control. For two decades, main storage was nearly always realized with coincident-current magnetic core memories, and is therefore often referred to as "core" or "fast core." We shall avoid that usage, however, and employ the more general "storage" without implying a particular physical realization.

A second level of executable storage is available in some older systems. Its access time is usually within an order of magnitude of that of main storage. An example is IBM's Large Core Storage (LCS).

After executable storage comes *backing* storage, often also called "secondary" storage. Random-access time of backing storage is typically longer than serial access time, perhaps by several orders of magnitude, and both are usually longer than those of the slowest executable storage. Diskettes (on smaller computers) and disks provide the most frequently used backing storage media, but magnetic drums and tapes are also common, and paper tape and cards are still encountered. Some storage devices incorporate removable storage media, such as disk packs, diskettes, and magnetic tape reels and cassettes. Each individual removable unit, such as a reel of tape, is called a *volume*. Timely mounting of the correct volume is essential to the proper use of this so-called *mountable* (also "demountable", "dismountable", or "removable") storage.

For either mountable or permanent backing storage, a distinction must be drawn between storage *space* and storage *access*. The former refers to the

---

*Facilities such as instruction pipelines and cache memories, although they can constitute a vital part of the design of the computer hardware, are typically not under programmer control, hence not directly accessible to the operating system, and will be ignored in this introductory treatment.

amount of storage occupied by data, whereas the latter refers to the act of accessing the data. Space and access are distinct resources, for it is possible to be permitted either without the other. Both resources are needed if full use is to be made of backing storage.

What we have called backing storage devices have long been called *peripheral* devices, or "peripherals", because they originally stood at the periphery of the computing system, arrayed about the once centrally located and physically large central processing unit. They are also called input/output devices because, when viewed from main storage and an associated processor, transfer of data from backing storage constitutes input, and transfer to backing storage constitutes output. Nowadays, the term "input/output" is becoming restricted to refer to "true" input/output, where the source or destination of the data is human or operated by a human being. Examples include terminal keyboards and screens, mark sense readers, optical character recognition (OCR) readers, card readers, voice answer-back units, computer output microform (COM) recorders, and card punches. The many devices, both for backing storage and for true I/O, are usually connected to a computer system by means of units that may vary from programmable peripheral processors to simple I/O channels. Between the devices and these units may lie controllers, concentrators, multiplexors, or other intermediaries.

The processor itself is an important resource. It becomes available to the machine-language programmer if he can cause instructions to be executed. The key to processor use is therefore the instruction counter. The principal time resource is the increment of service represented by an instruction cycle, rather than merely elapsed time. In a system with multiple processors, each unit is a resource to be allocated. Processors are allocated to *processes*, which can be thought of for now as instances of a program execution. (Further definitions appear in Chapters 3 and 4.) It is possible for multiple processes to be active at the same time, even if all must share a single processor. Then it becomes necessary to manage these processes, especially if they need to share other resources, such as programs or data. If not in main storage, these data may be *on-line*, either on permanent backing storage or on a mounted volume, or they may be *off-line*, on an unmounted volume. An off-line volume may or may not still be known to the operating system.

The foregoing resources differ in the manner in which they may be shared. A few are actually divisible, and portions can be allocated to different users truly *simultaneously*. The best example of a simultaneously sharable resource is the storage medium, in either main or backing storage. Different areas of main storage can be assigned to different users, as can different cylinders of a disk volume. Most resources, however, are not divisible. They can be allocated to different users one after another at such speed that the users appear to be using the resources simultaneously, when observed over the duration of program execution. Such *concurrently* sharable resources include disk volume accesses and reenterable[*] program code. A few remaining resources are not sharable even concurrently, but only *sequentially*. Among them are printer use, processor cycles, serially reusable[*] program code, and both space on and access to volumes of magnetic tape (except such pre-addressed varieties as DECtape).

Sometimes the apparent sharing mode of a resource can be changed, the apparent extent of a resource enlarged, or the identity of a resource disguised. This is accomplished by the provision of a *virtual* resource, whose appearance to the user differs in sharing mode, in extent, or in identity from that of the underlying *real* resource that is used to provide it. A virtual printer can be allocated to a user to prevent his output from being interlarded with lines of output for other users whose programs are executing concurrently with his. This change from sequential to apparently concurrent sharing of the printer requires the provision of storage space to accumulate all the print output from one user before starting to print any of it. Virtual processors, which appear to operate concurrently, can be allocated to several users of a single sequentially sharable processor, at the cost of increasing the elapsed time required to execute any one of their programs. Virtual storage, in at least one of its forms, is an example of resource enlargement in which backing storage is disguised as main storage, again at a cost in elapsed time for program execution.

Just as the provision of virtual resources does not come free of cost, neither does the straightforward sharing of real resources. The control programs that manage the resources must themselves occupy storage space, require execution time, and demand other resources. Their needs compete with those of the very users they are intended to serve.

1.3 DESIGN PHILOSOPHIES

What philosophies guide the operating system designer in attempting to provide facilities for the management of the various resources? Different operating systems are based on different philosophies, but there appear to be three assumptions common to all. One is that the goal of the operating system is to maximize the productivity of the community of users rather than that of any single user. A second is that it is sufficient to provide general solutions to user needs rather than specific solutions tailored to individual users. The third is that the user is willing to pay substantial costs for the services provided. Included are costs of main storage for the central portion of the operating system, of backing storage for the remainder, and of time

---

[*]Serially reusable code incorporates the initialization of values changed by the code. Reenterable code is serially reusable code that incorporates no modification of itself during execution. For a fuller explanation, see Sec. 3.1 of Calingaert [1979].

for control program execution. The costs can be defrayed by spending money for more storage, for a faster processor, or for both.

The name generally applied to the resources used by the operating system itself is *overhead*, a word that to some persons connotes waste, but is better viewed in the operating system context as a neutral technical term. A user may indeed consider the overhead of a particular operating system to be excessively high, but he may find that of another quite acceptable. In practice, it is usually a computer facility manager, acting as agent for the users, who chooses the operating system and its features.

Other aspects of design philosophy are debatable and indeed debated, with different assumptions being reflected in different operating systems. Some of these aspects are the following.

How is productivity of the user community defined? One candidate is *throughput*, the amount of nonoverhead computation performed per unit time. The use of throughput does not consider the users' off-computer work to be productive, whereas *response time*, or *turnaround*, considers only off-computer productivity.

Should the user be permitted to perform any operation of which the computer hardware is capable, or should the operating system provide only selected facilities? The latter choice, if carefully implemented, may make it harder for the user to write efficient programs while making it perhaps easier to write correct ones. With a limited menu, the user has fewer choices to learn and less likelihood of choosing badly.

What is the extent of the resources to be managed? A typical decision is whether to include or exclude off-line data.

Should the operating system serve as a substitute for the computer operator, or as the operator's assistant? The former choice may reduce potential for operator error, but it forgoes applying execution-time human intelligence to the problems of resource management.

What degree of control program function and what extent of control program service should be provided? Many aspects of resource management are optional. These include deferring specification of backing storage or I/O devices until execution time, providing virtual storage, and dynamically changing the execution priority of different users.

Should extra resources be devoted to equitable allocation of the overhead cost to the several users? Careful accounting can be very expensive. It is said of Howard Hughes that he would encourage a prospective purchaser to make an offer for one of his companies, as a way of obtaining an evaluation of its worth at someone else's expense.

How general should the operating system be? At one extreme is the computer utility that caters to a large variety of demands for service. More modest is a system designed to facilitate only one type of use, such as program development.

A community of users who do not find the benefits of a shared large computer with its attendant control programs to be worth the cost are free to opt instead for multiple small computers, including minicomputers and microcomputers. Until recent years, this freedom has been more theoretical than real. Now that economies of scale in hardware have decreased, and more and more powerful programming systems are offered for small computers, the choice has become very real.

1.4   POLICIES AND MECHANISMS

The choice of design philosophy leads to the adoption of *policies* to be embodied in the operating system. Consider, for example, a computer with enough main storage for several jobs, I/O (true and backing) whose operation can be simultaneous with that of the processor, and means for signaling both the completion of an I/O operation and the end of a specified time interval. Let there be submitted a stream of jobs, of which a fixed number are at any time resident in main storage. The single processor is allocated to a job, which runs until it terminates, or until the operating system withdraws the processor from that job, or until the job requests input, in which event it cannot resume running until completion of the input operation. Many different policies are available to govern the choice of job to which the processor should next be allocated. Here are three. Policy A is to provide job terminations in as nearly as possible the same sequence as job initiations. Policy B is to maximize throughput. Policy C is to impose less delay on a shorter job than on a longer one. Policies A and C are clearly contradictory. The extent of compatibility of policy B with either of the other two policies is less immediately obvious.

To implement a policy it is necessary to provide a *mechanism*. For example, either of the two following mechanisms might be used to implement policy C. Mechanism 1 requires each user to estimate the total execution time for a job, and it keeps track of the amount of time used by each job. It allocates the processor to that job with the least remaining estimated time, and permits it to run to completion or until it requests input. Mechanism 2 allocates the processor to each of the jobs in turn, but restricts the time of each to a fixed interval on each turn. Although both of these mechanisms impose less delay on short jobs than on long ones, they differ in their costs and in their effects. Mechanism 1 must keep time records for all jobs; mechanism 2 must set a timer to interrupt the currently running job. Under mechanism 1 there is no guarantee that any long job will eventually start, let alone terminate, because it may wait indefinitely as short jobs keep arriving. Mechanism 2 switches the processor more frequently from one job to another, but it does guarantee that each job will start and eventually terminate. On the other hand, if mechanism 2 is used with a large collection of jobs, even the shorter jobs will suffer long average delay.

It is important to distinguish policy from mechanism. The policy states what is to be achieved; the mechanism is the means whereby it is achieved. Put more simply, policy is *what* and mechanism is *how.* Policies for different resources cannot be adopted independently and combined at will, because the various resources are interrelated. For example, the disk management policy of minimizing total arm movement time can be shown to be incompatible with the main storage policy of holding as few jobs in storage as can coexist, with at least one of them not waiting for I/O.

The choice of mechanism for implementing one policy is largely independent of the choice of mechanism for another policy, although implementation costs can sometimes be reduced by choosing mechanisms with similar features. The choice of mechanism does affect the cost of adherence to a policy, as we have seen in the different number of job switches required by processor allocation mechanisms 1 and 2. The choice of mechanism may also affect the quality of adherence to a policy. For example, a policy might be stated in terms of mean response time, and different mechanisms could yield the same mean but with widely different extents of deviation from the mean.

Although the many resources of a computer system are interrelated, it is both possible and practical to consider in turn specific areas of resource management. Each major area is the topic of a subsequent chapter, which examines the problems and describes some solutions, outlining both policies and mechanisms.

FOR FURTHER STUDY

Two good overviews of operating systems are those in Sec. 1.2 of Habermann [1976] and Chap. 1 of Tsichritzis and Bernstein [1974]. The seminar paper by Hoare [1972] offers interesting insights, but does not consider interactive systems. The chapter by Warwick [1970] emphasizes *why* we have operating systems. Watson [1970, Secs. 1.1 to 1.4] stresses interactive systems, whereas Kurzban, Heines, and Sayers [1975, Secs. 1.2 and 1.3] describe chiefly batch-oriented systems. Graham [1975] offers an introduction to programming systems in Chap. 1, an overview of a simple batch operating system in Chap. 2, and a brief discussion of interactive operating systems in Chap. 13. The distinction between policy and mechanism is propounded by Levin et al. [1975].

Chapter 2

STORAGE MANAGEMENT

Main storage, or at least executable storage, is a resource without which no program can execute. It is true that at any given moment all but a very few storage locations are passive, merely retaining information for later access. Yet the importance of the one or more locations that are active is so great that there is scarcely a program that is not more easily written or more rapidly executed when use is made of more main storage. Programs waiting for the main storage resource are normally held in backing storage, but backing storage plays a more vital role as well. Mechanisms are often provided for using backing storage as an extension of main storage, thus causing the latter to appear larger than its actual physical size. This provision of even a virtual resource enhances ease of programming, by freeing the user from concern for how much storage actually is available. As we shall see in Section 2.3, it often increases the efficiency of use of the underlying real resource, although generally at the cost of decreased speed of execution.

A portion of main storage must be occupied by what is known as the nucleus (or "kernel"*) of the operating system. The nucleus is that set of control programs that must be resident in main storage to ensure that the entire system will be able to function without unwarranted delay. We shall defer until later an examination of what the nucleus must include, but do need to note here that some storage must be set aside at all times for the control programs themselves.

A potential problem is protection of programs and data against loss or contamination caused by other programs. The operating system nucleus is presumably correct, however, and can usually be counted on not to attack the user's program. The latter, on the other hand, may be in the initial stages of debugging, or perhaps embody a design flaw that becomes apparent only for rarely encountered input data. In such an event, the user program

---

*In at least one system (C.mmp HYDRA) "kernel" is used to refer instead to a basic set of facilities upon which the users can build their own operating system. See Wulf et al. [1974].

may destroy the ability of the control program to operate correctly. The only serious loser, however, is the current user, because only he is being served at the moment by that control program. Other users will have to wait a bit, of course, to allow the nucleus to be reloaded. Means for that operation must be provided, not only for such restarting but also for getting under way initially. They are discussed in Section 7.5.

In this chapter we explore first the storage management policies that allocate to each job a contiguous area of main storage, and then policies that allocate a collection of areas that are not necessarily contiguous, but that collectively satisfy the job's storage requirements. For each policy we examine the extra assistance provided if backing storage is furnished as a concomitant to the main storage. Finally, we explore techniques for keeping track of what storage is available, applicable both to interprogram competition for storage and to intraprogram utilization of storage.

2.1 SINGLE CONTIGUOUS ALLOCATION

One policy for storage management is to keep the cost of implementing it as low as possible. This is readily accomplished by requiring users to share main storage sequentially. Only one user program is admitted at a time.

2.1.1 Storage Layout

A single user is allocated the entire storage, except for a fixed area reserved for the nucleus. To leave the largest possible area for user programs, the nucleus typically occupies an area at one end of storage. Because of the widespread availability of different sizes of storage for a given computer, it is often more convenient to assign the lower end to the nucleus than the higher. Then the nucleus occupies the same locations regardless of storage size.

All succeeding locations constitute a single contiguous allocation available to the user program, which can then be guaranteed that each time it runs it will occupy storage locations having the same addresses. Consequently, the user program can be written to be executed from fixed physical locations. This requires a less powerful translator than if the locations to be used are not known at translation time. User-written subroutines, too, can be written to be executed from whatever locations the user chooses. The computer installation may also provide a collection of subroutines. These and other programs offered to users constitute the *library*. If a library subroutine has also been designed to run in fixed locations, the user must know what storage is to be reserved for that subroutine. If the library of subroutines is large, and they are desired in different combinations, it may not be possible to fit the required ones simultaneously. One solution is to prepare

multiple versions of the most frequently used subroutines, each version encoded to be run in different locations. Other solutions are discussed in subsequent sections.

Successive user programs that are awaiting execution under single contiguous allocation are kept on a *job queue* on a true I/O device or in backing
storage. This queue can be as simple as a stack of punched cards sitting in
the hopper of a card reader, maintained by the computer operator, or as
elegant as blocked program text occupying successive cylinders of disk
storage, and maintained by a control program. In either situation, a control
program must be available to sense the termination of one job and call for
loading of the next. Because of the card stack, the original name of this program was *stacked job monitor.*

Single contiguous storage allocation presents two major costs. First is
the inability to use the processor while the user program is waiting for completion of an operation such as reading data input. Time is thus lost because
there is no other user job to take up the slack. Second is the waste of all
storage beyond that required by the nucleus and current user together, as
illustrated in Fig. 2.1.

Despite the time and space cost of single contiguous allocation,
its implementation is inexpensive and storage protection can be forgone.
The implementation cost is only a simple job monitor and an equally simple
absolute loader program. It is but a step beyond running one self-loading
program at a time, with no resident control program, and was for many years

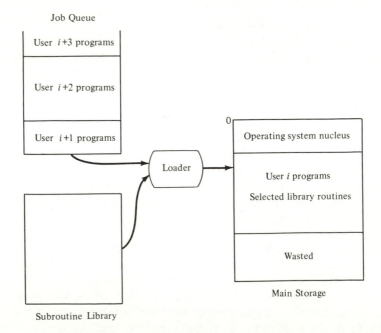

Figure 2.1 Single Contiguous Allocation

the normal mode of operation. It is still widely used with smaller computers, for which the space waste is not serious.

2.1.2   Loading

The mechanism for effecting single contiguous storage allocation is implemented by the *absolute loader*. The function of this simple control program is to read text that contains program and data, to store it at addresses specified with the text, and upon completion to transfer control to a specified location. Because all of the necessary information has been prepared by the user, normally with the assistance of a translator, the loader's task is trivial. It need merely maintain a work area to hold one input record. Each input record except the last contains text to be loaded and the number of a storage location. If the text items are of variable length, the record also contains the length. The text records need not be presented to the loader in any particular order. After each record is read into the work area, the loader moves the fixed or stated length of text into storage locations starting at the location specified. The last input record prepared by the translator contains a code that distinguishes it from the preceding text records, together with the number of a storage location. On finding that final record in its work area the loader executes an unconditional jump to the specified location.

The three storage accesses required for the text (one for reading and two for copying) can be reduced to one by first reading only the length and starting location. The loader then reads the text directly into its final location. The number of read operations needed can be reduced by preparing the text in large units, each of which will occupy consecutive storage locations. Language translators are normally provided that produce program text in the form required by the loader. (Some translators, termed "load-and-go", generate machine code directly in the storage locations from which it is to be executed. In a sense, they incorporate their own loader.)

The loader reads each job from the job queue after the preceding user job has terminated. When the job terminates, it does so by executing a jump to the job monitor. Once loading is complete, the loader is of no further use to the current program, and could be discarded. The next user program, however, could not be started unless the loader were available. Consequently, a loader is part of the operating system nucleus. Many parts of the nucleus are required because loading them as needed would cause intolerable delay. A loader, on the other hand, is required because nothing else can be loaded without one.

2.1.3   Relocation

The constraint of fitting the user program and selected library routines in the required storage locations without a conflict can be met by preparing the library routines in such a form that the specification of which storage locations they require can be deferred until loading time. The specification is so made at that time that the selected library routines interfere neither with each other nor with the user program that requires them. This flexibility is achieved by preparing library routines whose address fields do not specify physical storage locations directly, but are intended to be mapped later into physical locations. A program prepared in such a form is said to be *relocatable,* and the control program that performs the mapping is called a *relocating loader.* Of course, if a relocating loader is provided, not only the library routines but the user program and subroutines as well can be made relocatable, and such is usually the case. The resulting convenience to the user is great enough that relocating loaders, rather than absolute loaders, have often been used to implement single contiguous allocation.

The program to be loaded and relocated is a unit of what is termed *object code,* produced by a translator. A relocatable unit of object code is generally known as a *segment.* Address references made by the object code to the main storage locations that it will occupy after loading must be adjusted by the addition of a *relocation constant* before the access is made. Instruction and data fields that require this adjustment are termed *relative,* because their values are relative to the segment origin. Fields that do not require adjustment are termed *absolute.* Within an instruction, the operation code is absolute, as are register addresses. Operand fields may or may not be absolute. Immediate data and shift amounts are absolute; many address fields, although not all, are relative. Constants generated by the translator are absolute, except for address constants. The value of an address constant, typically written in source language as A(PLACE), is defined to be the number of the execution-time storage location corresponding to the symbol named. Clearly, such a field is relative.

The *relocatability attribute* of each field (i.e., whether it is relative or absolute) is determined by the language translators and incorporated in the object code. The function of the relocating loader is to load the text starting at an arbitrary location (typically specified by the job monitor), and to replace all relative address fields by the physical location numbers appropriate to the specified origin.

Implementation of relocation depends upon the principal mode of specification of main storage locations by address fields of machine-language instructions. Three ways are common.

1. The address field is a single number that refers directly to the storage location. This is *direct* addressing, encountered on many small computers.

2. The address field is a single number that specifies the value of the difference, or *displacement,* between the physical location being referenced and the location of the origin of the program segment. Before execution of the program begins, the value of the origin, known as the *base address,* is

placed in a *base register* by the operating system. During interpretation of the instruction at execution time, the hardware automatically adds the displacement to the base register content. The sum, known as the *effective address,* specifies the storage location. Because the instruction does not refer explicitly to a base register, this is *implicit-base* addressing. Often associated with the base register is a *limit register,* which holds either the maximum storage location, or the maximum displacement, allocated to the segment. Implicit-base addressing is used in a number of computers, including the DEC PDP-10, Univac 1100 series, and Honeywell 6000 series.

3. The address field is a pair of numbers, of which one designates a base register and the other constitutes the displacement. This is *explicit-base* addressing. The programmer and translators, not the operating system, bear the burden of ensuring that the value of the origin is loaded into the appropriate base register. The DEC PDP-11 and the IBM 360-370 use explicit-base addressing.

We examine relocation for a direct-addressing computer first. The relocating loader, having no access to the source text, cannot determine from inspection of the generated text whether a field is absolute or relative. It cannot even distinguish instructions from data. The translator must therefore specify for each field whether it is relative. One way to specify these relocatability attributes is to emit with each line of text one *relocation bit* for each field. In Fig. 2.2(a), which shows object code generated for a hypothetical machine, the convention is that bit value unity indicates that the associated field is relative. The relocation constant to be added is the location of the origin of the segment, and is normally specified by the operating system.

The algorithm executed by the relocating loader is simple. It reads lines of object code one at a time. It copies the text of each line to locations

	Object Code				Machine Code	
Disp	**Len**	**Reloc**	**Text**		**Disp**	
0	2	01	12 17		40	12 57
2	3	011	13 17 15		42	13 57 55
5	2	01	12 17		45	12 57
7	3	011	13 17 13		47	13 57 53
10	2	01	03 18		50	03 58
12	2	00	07 99		52	07 99
14	2	00	00 99		54	00 99
16	1	0	11		56	11
17	1	0	99		57	99
18	1	1	16		58	56
	(a) Before relocation				(b) After relocation	

Figure 2.2 Use of Relocation Bits

formed by adding the relocation constant to the indicated addresses. For each relocation bit equal to unity it also adds the relocation constant to the corresponding text field. This second addition can be performed either before or after the text is copied. If the relocation constant is 40, the resulting content of storage is as shown in Fig. 2.2(b). Despite its name, the relocating loader does not really relocate code. Instead, it makes the code executable from an arbitrary location in storage.

The displacement values can be omitted from the object code if the lines are presented in serial order with no gaps, as they are in the figure. In that event the loader runs a physical location counter initialized to the origin location. Some translators provide for the use of multiple origins. The loader must know how much space is required for each, and to which origin each relative address is relative. The space requirements are given in a header to the segment. The origin identification can be embodied in a multibit relocation code or encoded separately.

Interleaving relocation bits and length fields with the program text precludes reading the text directly into the storage locations it is to occupy. Moreover, it requires that the text be handled in small units, often of variable length. These disadvantages can be avoided by collecting all the relocation bits into a single contiguous *relocation map,* which follows the text of the object code. Such a map is readily prepared by the assembler (or other translator), which produces a segment of relocatable text followed immediately by the associated relocation map. The segment and map are read as a unit into storage locations beginning at the segment's assigned origin S, resulting in the status depicted in Fig. 2.3(a). The assembler is required to furnish the lengths of the segment and of the map. Consequently, the loader can determine the location M at which the map begins. The loader scans the map and adjusts those addresses that correspond to bits that signify relocation. The segment origin S for the first segment is specified by the job monitor. For each succeeding segment it is redefined by performing the assignment S ⟵ M prior to reading. Figure 2.3(b) shows the status after the first segment has been relocated and the second one loaded.

A rather efficient compromise between line relocation and segment relocation is to divide the text into fixed-length chunks having precisely as many potentially relative fields as the machine word has bits. One chunk of relocatable text is loaded, together with one word of relocation bits. The relative addresses in the chunk are relocated before the next chunk is loaded. This approach captures much of the I/O efficiency of the map method, without requiring extra storage for the last segment map, and permits the use of fixed-length units throughout.

For a machine with explicit-base addressing, any program normally incorporates instructions to load appropriate segment origin locations into base registers at execution time. Relocation is then performed even later

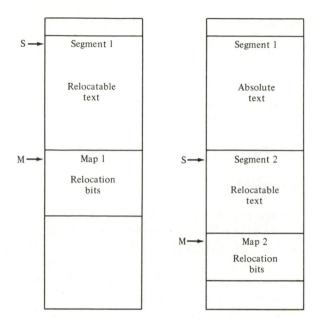

(a)   Before relocation of Segment 1   (b)   After relocation of Segment 1

Figure 2.3 Use of Relocation Map

during execution time by the machine's calculation of effective addresses for
each instruction that references storage. Although this relocation applies to
address fields of instructions, it is not performed upon address constants,
because they are not interpreted as instructions. Address constants must be
relocated in much the same manner as are all addresses in a direct-
addressing machine. Because address constants typically constitute a very
small portion of the text of a program, it is wasteful to supply relocation bits,
all but a few of them zero, for all fields of the program text. Instead, the assembler appends a *relocation list,* which specifies the adjustments to be made.
Figure 2.4 shows a program fragment in a typical assembler language. Ir-
relevant details have been suppressed, and displacement values appended.
The object code assembled at displacement 71 for the address constant
A(SIGMA) is the number 38. The relocation list entry specifies the address
(71) to be modified. The loader merely scans the relocation list after loading
the text and makes the indicated adjustments.

     For a machine with implicit-base addressing, all relocation is performed
during the machine's calculation of effective addresses. The segment origin
is placed in the base register not by the user program, but by the loader.
Although address constants could be handled by the mechanism described
in the preceding paragraph, they are normally not used when programming
machines with implicit-base addressing.

Displacement	Label	Operation	Operand
0	PROG3	START	0
0	..	LOAD	POINTER
	..	..	..
38	SIGMA	..	..
	..	..	..
71	POINTER	CONST	A(SIGMA)
72	TWO	CONST	2

Figure 2.4 Program with Address Constant

2.1.4 Dynamic Loading

If a job's main storage requirement exceeds the space available to it, execution requires the provision of more powerful mechanisms. This is possible if the programs and data can be subdivided into segments not all of which need be present simultaneously in main storage. They can share main storage sequentially, each using a given portion of space in turn. A segment that is not currently needed can be held in backing storage until it is required, at which time it is loaded into main storage, *overlaying* one or more segments that are needed no longer, or at least not until some time reasonably far in the future. This process of loading a segment is known as *dynamic loading,* because the decision to load is made dynamically at execution time.

If a reference is made to a segment that is not in main storage, execution must be delayed to allow that segment to be loaded. The resulting decrease in execution efficiency can often be held to a tolerable level by careful selection of the segments to be resident simultaneously. The translator has no practical way of identifying the groups of segments that should be resident simultaneously to prevent unacceptable loss of efficiency. Consequently, this information must be specified by the programmer. If the writer of the program can predict in what combinations different program segments will be required, the segments can be replaced dynamically in a predetermined spatial pattern. This overlaying may be performed under direct control of the programmer, who incorporates the requisite I/O instructions into his program. Alternatively, the programming system may provide facilities to perform overlaying as required.

Most programming systems incorporate a translation program known as a *linker,* whose primary function is to resolve intersegment references in separately translated segments, thus linking them into a single program. In some systems, the linker can accept a specification of what dynamic loading is to be performed and generate the necessary execution-time calls to the loader. The specification customarily takes the form of a static *overlay structure* in the form of a tree, which may be multiply rooted. Each node of the tree represents a segment. The tree has the property that two segments that are to be in main storage simultaneously lie either (1) on the same path from a root to a leaf or (2) on disjoint paths from a root to a leaf. An example is presented in Fig. 2.5. The unorthodox representation of that tree facilitates the visualization of storage use. Each node is drawn as a vertical line of length proportional to the size of the corresponding segment. The arcs to descendant nodes are drawn as horizontal lines from the bottom end of the parent node. Thus vertical position anywhere in the diagram is in direct correspondence to location in storage. Each segment is labeled by its number and by its storage requirement. Segments 1 and 5 are both root segments; of the others, only segment 3 is not a leaf. Segments 1 and 6 may be co-resident because they lie on the same path (1,3,6). Segments 2 and 6 may not be co-resident because they lie on different paths (1,2 and 1,3,6) that are not disjoint. Segments 1, 3, 4, 5, and 8 may be co-resident because segments 1, 3, and 4 lie together on one path, segments 5 and 8 lie together on another path, and the two paths are disjoint. The storage required for those five segments is 78K,* the maximum needed for any set of segments that may be co-resident. It would require 132K, on the other hand, to store all nine segments simultaneously.

Segments with a common parent are never co-resident, and in fact are assigned the same origin just beyond the end of their parent's allocation.

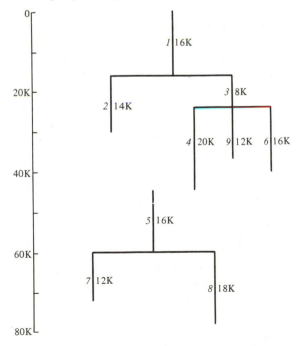

Figure 2.5 Static Overlay Structure

*K is used as the customary abbreviation for 2^{10}, or 1024, which is approximately equal to 1000, traditionally denoted by the Greek prefix *kilo*. The units are typically words or bytes, and will be specified if appropriate.

One such segment *overlays* another when it is loaded. A root segment, of course, is never overlaid.

The use of an overlay structure to save space requires the linker and relocating loader together to ensure (whether they are combined or not) that references external to a segment result in the correct execution-time accesses. In examining this requirement it is helpful to distinguish two classes of external references, those to a segment that is permitted to be co-resident (*inclusive* references in IBM parlance) and those to a segment that is prohibited from being co-resident (*exclusive* references). For example, an instruction in segment 1 that loads a word from segment 6 makes an inclusive reference; a call of segment 8 by segment 7 is an exclusive reference. An inclusive reference upward in a path presents no problem, because the referenced segment is necessarily in storage. This is true, for example, of a reference from segment 6 to segment 3. Other inclusive references, such as from segment 3 to segment 8, may require that the referenced segment first be loaded. This action can be effected at execution time only if a description of the tree structure is available and if the loader can be invoked as needed.

The linker must therefore generate a description of the static overlay structure. This description is often called a *segment table*. To ensure that the segment table will be available at any time during execution, it is placed in a root segment, thereby increasing the length of that segment. The segment table also indicates for each segment whether it is loaded or not. At execution time, a control program called the *overlay supervisor* interrogates the segment table for every external reference other than an upward inclusive reference. The overlay supervisor calls the loader if the referenced segment is not resident. It also updates the segment table entries of the overlaid segment(s) and of each newly loaded segment.

If a segment about to be overlaid has been modified since it was loaded, it is necessary first to copy that segment to backing storage, unless it is known that the segment will never subsequently be reloaded. This rollout of an overlaid segment is obviated if the segment is serially reusable and the overlaying occurs between successive uses, or if the segment is reenterable. The same is true of a segment of read-only data.

The linker must generate code for execution-time calls to the overlay supervisor. The moments at which these calls will be issued are, of course, not predictable. It is therefore hardly worth preparing and using an overlay structure if the overlay supervisor is not permanently resident in storage during execution of the overlaid program. This, too, somewhat reduces the space saving.

An exclusive external reference presents the further problem that the segment that makes the reference is overlaid before the segment to which reference is made becomes available. For this reason, some systems do not permit exclusive references. Those that do usually limit them to procedure calls and returns, because unrestricted communication between segments that overlay each other is intolerably inefficient. The linker generates a table of all symbols to which an exclusive reference is made. The overlay supervisor can interrogate this exclusive reference table to discover to which segment an exclusive reference is made, and then consult the segment table as before.

Dynamic loading permits a program to exceed its space allocation. It is applicable not only to single contiguous allocation, but also to the various multiple contiguous allocation methods presented in Section 2.2. Although the loading is dynamic, the overlay structure is static, being unchanged from one execution of the program to the next. Sometimes, however, the selection of required segments cannot be determined prior to execution, because it is data-dependent. Such dynamic overlay structures are characteristic of transaction-oriented interactive systems, such as airline reservations or banking. The nature of the transaction dictates which processing programs are required, and they are loaded as appropriate and linked with the using programs. Because the translators are no longer available, they cannot provide overlay management, and the operating system is called upon to perform this *dynamic linking*. Techniques for handling a dynamic overlay structure are discussed in Section 2.3.2.

2.2 MULTIPLE CONTIGUOUS ALLOCATION

To decrease the time and space waste due to single contiguous allocation, *multiprogramming* was devised. In this mode of operation, several programs reside simultaneously in main storage and execute concurrently. The basic policy underlying multiprogramming is to keep the processor busy. Time is saved by having a program ready to enter execution as soon as another needs to wait. Space is saved by more nearly filling storage, although more total storage space must often be provided for multiprogramming than for uniprogramming. The real storage saving is not so much absolute as relative. The fraction of storage that remains unused is, typically, considerably smaller than under single contiguous allocation.

To accommodate multiple programs the storage is subdivided into multiple areas. In one version of the IBM OS/360 operating system those areas are called "regions" but in another, "partitions". The latter usage conflicts sharply with the usual architectural notion of a partition as a dividing wall. We shall therefore use *region* to denote the area of storage and reserve *partition* for the boundary between adjacent areas.

The first question raised by any form of multiple allocation is protection. The earliest multiprogramming systems ran several system programs for I/O but still only one user program. In these so-called "spooling" systems (see Section 5.5), it was necessary to protect the system programs from the user program. Reliance was placed to great extent on the use of compilers that would guarantee not to generate code that accessed the regions known to be reserved for the spooling programs (or for the nucleus). To permit true user multiprogramming stronger guarantees are required. It is necessary to protect not only the system programs occupying reserved regions, but also other user programs sharing the nonreserved regions. Even such seemingly innocuous transgressions as having an array subscript out of bounds could overwrite a neighboring program or its data. Some form of protection enforced by hardware is typical. In an implicit-base machine each user can be held under "house arrest" by the use of base and limit registers. In other machines he can be "locked out" of forbidden storage locations by the use of locks and keys. Attempted transgressions can be detected and used to initiate corrective action by the operating system.

The next question to consider is that of the number and sizes of the regions. Ideally, a heavily processor-bound job and a heavily I/O-bound job, each of which requires the same execution time under uniprogramming, should require about that same length of time if run concurrently. In practice, the two jobs will probably both need the processor simultaneously part of the time, and will both have some simultaneous I/O waiting. Moreover, only rarely are jobs so well matched. As a result it often requires a *multiprogramming ratio* (the number of jobs being executed concurrently) of four or five, and therefore that number of regions, to keep the processor busy as much as 90% of the time. An important decision is whether the regions and the partitions between them should be fixed or movable.

2.2.1 Fixed Partitions

The simplest mechanism for multiprogramming fixes the number, size, and location of the regions. From a different point of view, the partitions are stationary, and we shall refer to this form as *fixed-partition allocation.* The average region size is determined by the number of regions and the total storage available. Because no job can be run that does not fit in the largest region, it is customary to make some regions larger at the cost of having others smaller, and hence capable of handling fewer of the jobs. In some systems it is possible for the operator to reconfigure manually the number and sizes of the regions. This is a much more flexible solution than requiring the preparation of different versions of the control programs.

Figure 2.6 illustrates two types of storage waste that can still occur under fixed-partitioned allocation. The first is the fact that 6K of region 1 and 24K of region 4 lie unused. The second is that even if the four jobs were repositioned to make the unused areas the last 6K of region 2 and the first 24K of region 3, the allocation mechanism does not permit the resulting contiguous 30K of storage to be used for another small job. Each of these types of storage waste is characterized by the presence of unusable fragments of storage and is therefore often called *fragmentation* or, more particularly, *external fragmentation* to distinguish it from another form to be discussed later.

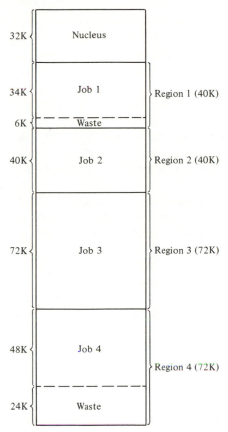

Figure 2.6 Fixed-Partition Allocation

How is fixed-partition allocation implemented? One method is to associate with each region its own queue of jobs. The assignment of a job to a queue is typically based on the user's time and space requests, and perhaps on other resource needs. If, for example, the user can characterize a job as processor-bound or I/O-bound, the job can be enqueued with others of the same class to present as balanced a job mix as possible. If the job class can be determined at translation time, the physical locations at which each job will run are known at that time, and one absolute loader could serve in principle for all the regions. The storage allocation process is then equivalent, for n regions, to n parallel instances of single contiguous allocation. Of course, a single job monitor, rather than n, can control all n regions.

The foregoing approach is rarely used, for it is not wise to bind at translation time the identity of the region in which a job is to be run. This is because to do so would prevent reconfiguration and, more important, because it is generally not possible to know at translation time what will be the most desirable allocation of storage at execution time. In particular, there may be a temporary lack of jobs in the queue associated with a particular region, and it may be more efficient to run in that region a job of a different class than to lower the multiprogramming ratio. The deferral of storage allocation to loading time is made possible by the use of a relocating loader. There is no need to assign physical locations in advance, and any free region of sufficient size can be used. This also makes it possible to replace the multiple job queues by a single queue, although the retention of multiple queues still offers the advantages of job class balancing.

The foregoing pair of approaches illustrate the concept of choice of *binding time,* the time at which an entity is specified literally. In this example the entity to be bound is the set of storage locations to hold a job. The first approach binds storage locations at translation time. Such early binding offers simplicity, here an absolute loader, at the cost of the inability to make effective use of storage at execution time. The second approach binds storage locations just prior to execution time. Such late binding offers flexibility, but at the cost of complexity, here a relocating loader.

Regardless of the choice of binding time, however, fixed partitions cannot be readily adapted to the requirements of a varying job stream. Moreover, the attendant storage fragmentation is very wasteful. Consequently, fixed-partition allocation has fallen into disfavor since its use in IBM's OS/360 MFT (Multiprogramming with a Fixed Number of Tasks), which incidentally calls regions "partitions".

2.2.2 Movable Partitions

To provide an initial attack on fragmentation, the policy can be adopted of holding in main storage as many jobs as will fit in their entirety at a given time. Various mechanisms can be used; they share the principle of variability in job location, hence require relocation. The fragmentation caused by a job being smaller than its region can be eliminated by tailoring the region size to fit the job exactly. Some computers provide storage protection only for fixed units of storage (e.g., 1K or 2K bytes). On such a computer the region size is set to an integral number of units, and there may be some attendant waste. When a job is about to be loaded, a control program we shall call the *space manager* finds a storage area large enough to satisfy the job's space request, and sets the partitions that delimit the region. Typically, one of the partitions will be an existing partition, thus avoiding extra fragmentation. A relocating loader is sufficient; it receives the segment origin from the space manager. Among the movable partition systems is OS/360 MVT (Multiprogramming with a Variable Number of Tasks).

The space manager needs to maintain a pool of available storage, reserve a region for each job to be loaded, and liberate the region released by each job that has terminated. This appears to be a simple table maintenance operation, but in fact it raises important issues. A few of the many possible techniques will therefore be discussed. Because these techniques are applicable to other storage allocation problems, discussion is deferred to Section 2.4.

The result of the process can be understood, however, from a study of Fig. 2.7. In Fig. 2.7(a) the system has allocated space to jobs 1 through 4 in sequence, and 42K words of storage are free. In Fig. 2.7(b) job 3 has terminated, freeing 50K words, which are coalesced with the previous free area to yield 92K. Job 5 has been allocated 62K of that space in Fig. 2.7(c), and in Fig. 2.7(d) job 1 has terminated, freeing its 26K. Total free storage is now 56K, large enough for job 6, which needs 38K. It is not possible to load job 6, however, because the largest single block of free storage is only 30K. Nor will termination of job 2 help because its 24K is not adjacent to either block of free storage. Eventually, in Fig. 2.7(e), job 5 has terminated and in Fig. 2.7(f) job 6 has been allocated its request, as has job 7.

It is possible for a job to request and release space dynamically during execution, thus occupying its maximum space requirement only during the interval of maximum need, and making that space available to other jobs at other times. The partitions could, in principle, be moved in and out to satisfy the changing space requirements. This mechanism was proposed for OS/360 MVT but subsequently abandoned. If the maximum size request is

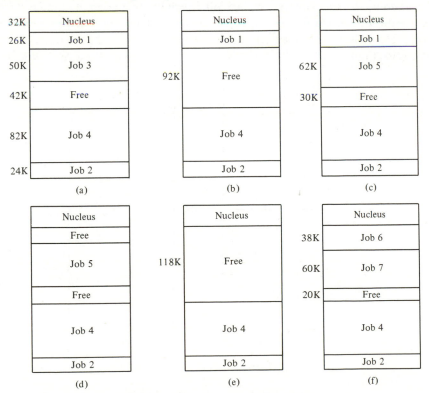

Figure 2.7 Movable-Partition Allocation

not known at loading time, there is no guarantee that each partition will not stand hard against another occupied region. If the maximum size request is known at loading time, two jobs can occupy adjacent regions with a movable partition between them. When one job requests more storage it may have to wait for the other to release it. This increases the job switching overhead, and also increases the multiprogramming ratio required to attain given utilization of the processor.

Movable-partition allocation can be thought of as a mechanism for seeking local optimization. The best allocation is sought for each successive job individually, but no account is taken of the jobs as a collection.

2.2.3 Movable Regions

In Fig. 2.7(d), it is clear that enough space is available to hold job 6, which needs only 38K, but that the space is fragmented into blocks that are too small. The two free blocks are separated by job 5. If that job could be moved up to be adjacent to the nucleus, or down to be adjacent to job 4, the free blocks would coalesce, as shown in Fig. 2.8, and job 6 could be loaded without waiting for a further termination. This *compaction* of storage is easily handled by the space manager, but job 5, originally loaded in storage starting at location 58K, cannot be expected to run correctly at location 32K. Why not? The relative addresses in job 5 have been modified for origin 58K and the relocation bits have been thrown away. There exist some software-based

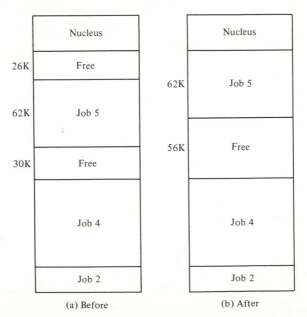

Figure 2.8 Dynamic Relocation of Region 5

solutions to this problem, but their cost in time is rarely less than the gain in not having to wait for another job to terminate.

Relocation of a running job, called *dynamic relocation,* is generally practical only on a computer that provides implicit-base addressing. The segment origin is placed in the base register by an otherwise absolute loader each time the segment is loaded. If the segment is moved, the new origin must replace the old. For the example of Fig. 2.8, job 5 is relocated from 58K to 32K. The addition of −26K to the base register content will preserve correct execution of the job. Address constants, which do not appear as instruction address fields, are not relocated by this means. The chief use of address constants, however, is to supply values for explicitly addressed base registers, and they are not normally used in conjunction with an implicitly addressed base register.

Movable-region allocation can be thought of as a mechanism for seeking global optimization. Allocation is performed by taking into account all the jobs currently in main storage.

A major problem of region relocation is that the addresses that need to be adjusted are not limited to the region to be relocated. They may be found in processor registers, and they may have been passed to subroutines. If I/O has been invoked for the job to be relocated, the I/O routines will hold addresses. It is normally necessary to wait for outstanding I/O to complete and to suspend execution lest new I/O be initiated. If the job has spawned any subsidiary tasks (see Section 4.7.1), it may be necessary to await their completion also.

A major cost of region relocation is the obvious one of time for copying the program from one storage area to another. There is also a monetary cost for the base-register mechanism. Whether these several costs are cheaper than that of buying extra main storage is a technology-dependent question. Another important question is whether the extra cost of the base registers should be invested instead in backing storage.

2.2.4 Swapping

A variant of region relocation is often encountered in time-sharing systems. The utilization of main storage can sometimes be improved, for multiple allocation as well as for single allocation, by providing backing storage as an extension of main storage. In its move from one region to another, a job may be copied not directly, but to backing storage first. This action is known as *roll-out.* The corresponding reloading of the job from backing storage is called *roll-in,* which normally requires relocation hardware. Roll-out and roll-in together constitute *swapping,* which can be viewed either as one job changing regions or as one region changing jobs (and perhaps position and size). Swapping requires not only the provision of backing storage for inactive jobs, but also maintenance by the space manager of lists of what jobs are where.

Swapping is useful in allowing a job's storage allocation to be reclaimed without requiring that job to be restarted from the beginning. Such reclaiming of a previously allocated resource that is still in use is called *preemption,* and may be required to serve higher-priority jobs or to prevent the phenomenon known as *deadlock,* which is discussed in Section 4.6. Preemption of storage may be advisable for any of a number of reasons. A major one is to permit the convenient execution of many more low-activity jobs than will fit into main storage at once. This situation arises often with users seated at terminals spending seconds thinking between demands for milliseconds of service. Another reason is to free the storage occupied by a job that requires intervention by the operator, such as mounting a magnetic tape or disk. A third reason for swapping is to permit more effective use of resources other than storage. For example, if the normal job selection process has loaded a number of processor-bound jobs and the I/O subsystem is relatively idle, the arrival of an I/O-bound job in the queue may warrant rolling out a processor-bound job to make room for the new arrival and thereby to increase system throughput. A simple reason for swapping is to make room for a job of higher priority. The same problems of addresses in registers, outstanding I/O operations, unterminated subroutines, and subsidiary tasks can occur as for region relocation.

A limited form of swapping is possible even in the absence of relocation hardware. This constraint requires that a job be rolled in to the same region from which it was previously rolled out. An absolute loader can perform this roll-in.

The need for swapping can be diminished for many users who are using the same program by providing that program in reenterable code. Then all users can share a single copy of the program. Each user has a private data area, to be sure, but total space requirements are much reduced. If swapping is still necessary, only the user data areas need be swapped. This is the key to serving many users concurrently on an interactive system, and has been widely implemented.

2.3 NONCONTIGUOUS ALLOCATION

A different attack on external storage fragmentation relaxes the requirement that each job be allocated one contiguous area of main storage. Fragmentation is reduced by making productive use of what would otherwise be gaps. Either with or without backing storage as an extension of main storage, the increased flexibility in storage allocation can greatly enhance the efficiency of main storage use. Moreover, noncontiguous allocation offers important mechanisms for implementing the policy of freeing the user from any concern with knowledge of physical storage locations. Before examining the principal techniques of noncontiguous allocation, it is instructive to compare the characteristics of the physical main storage of a computer with a programmer's requirements for naming and accessing the entities of a program.

2.3.1 Storage Spaces and Mappings

The *physical* (also "absolute", "actual", or "real") storage of a computer is a fixed-size collection of *locations,* each referred to by a unique number of fixed length, and collectively ordered as a vector. The set of usable physical locations is invariant, even predefined, and constitutes what we shall call the *physical location space* (or *location space*) of the computer. Other terms in common use are "absolute address space" and "real address space."

The programmer refers to storage (except in raw machine language) by means of an unfixed collection of *logical names,* which are symbolic rather than numeric and which have no inherent order. The length of the names can vary for two reasons. One is the freedom permitted in the source language. The other is name qualification, which is explicit in subscripting and in variables such as COBOL group items and PL/I structures, and implicit in the use of block structure. Although the symbolic names used by one programmer are unique, nothing prevents different programmers from using the same name to refer to different quantities. For the community of users, therefore, logical names are not unique. Moreover, the set of names in use is not predefined and it changes with time. We shall use the term *name space* to refer to the set of names associated with a single user.

The programming system must associate each user-supplied symbolic name with a machine-provided physical location. For the collection of user programs, the system must therefore provide a *mapping* from the union of the name spaces into the location space. In general, this mapping is performed in two stages, the first by the language system and the second by the operating system, particularly the storage management control program. At the interface between the two mapping stages is a form of storage reference known as a *virtual address.* The set of virtual addresses available describes the *virtual storage* of the system, which is in general defined neither by the using programs nor directly by the computer hardware, but rather by the programming system. The latter is dependent, of course, on the underlying hardware. Virtual addresses, depending on the system, may be symbolic, numeric, or mixed. The set of virtual addresses is often referred to as the *virtual address space.* In keeping with our two-word designations, we shall simply call it the *address space.* Figure 2.9 shows the relationship among the three spaces that concern us.

One extreme choice of address space is to make it identical to the location space. The entire mapping is then performed by the language system, which generates absolute code. The operating system merely provides a fixed, contiguous storage allocation. Load-and-go assemblers exemplify this choice.

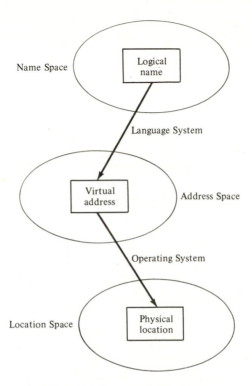

Figure 2.9 Spaces and Mappings

The opposite extreme choice of address space is the name space. The entire mapping is then performed by the operating system, which makes extensive use of symbol tables and directories (see Chapter 6) at execution time. Because this mapping must be repeated for each occurrence of a name, and is particularly time-consuming for qualified names, it is not widely practiced. It is sometimes encountered with interpreters, for which the distinction between translation time and execution time has become blurred. An example is provided by the microcode-assisted APL interpreter for the IBM 370.

We have already seen one compromise between the foregoing extremes. This is the provision by the translator of a relative address as the virtual address, followed by the operating system's relocation of the program into one of several contiguous regions. In that mapping, performed by the relocating loader, the size of the address space is necessarily limited to that of the location space. A particularly important characteristic of this form of relocation is that, after loading, the virtual address is lost and storage accesses are made directly to physical locations.

A more flexible compromise results when the translator provides as the virtual address both a relative address and the identification of an origin, and the operating system performs the second mapping not just once, but for each access. The term "virtual storage" is in fact commonly restricted to systems that preserve the virtual address during execution. A consequence of this deferral of the second mapping is that physical locations can be changed as execution proceeds. Properly performed, such changes can improve storage utilization while relieving the programmer of much of the burden of detailed storage management. The following sections describe *segmentation* and *paging*, the chief virtual storage methods.

2.3.2 Segmentation

The user need not be constrained even to think of his entire name space as being contiguous. Instead, he can be permitted to think of his job in terms of its logical parts, or *segments,* each of which might be a data area, procedure, or collection of procedures. The user refers to any location by means of a segment name, which by execution time has been translated to a number, and a *displacement* from the origin of the segment. The segments do not need to be of the same length; indeed, the length of a segment can be changed dynamically, thus making the segment a particularly attractive means of accessing a data area whose size varies during execution. Although addressing within a segment is contiguous, one user's several segments need not be contiguous, nor need they even all be in main storage. The mechanism underlying segmentation is to perform the second-stage mapping, that from virtual address to physical location, for *each* storage access.

If all the segments for one user are constrained to be held in main storage, then segmentation takes the form of movable regions, and one relocation register per region being accessed performs the required mapping. If the number of segments is limited to one, this is essentially the dynamic relocation mechanism described in Section 2.2.3. Computers with more than one relocation register also exist; for example, the Univac 1100 series has two, one for instructions and one for data.

A more general form of segmentation permits segments to be copied between main and backing storages, thus providing implicit overlaying effected entirely by the operating system without explicit programmer specification of an overlay structure. Among the operating systems that provide this form of segmentation is the Burroughs B7000/B6000 MCP. The mapping performed by segmentation is illustrated in Fig. 2.10.

The implementation of segmentation uses for each job a *segment table* similar to the one used for overlay management. A hardware *segment table register* points to the start of the segment table for the current job. A storage reference has the form (s, d), where s is the segment number and d the displacement. By adding s to the content of the segment table register, the computer determines the physical location of the segment table entry for the referenced segment.

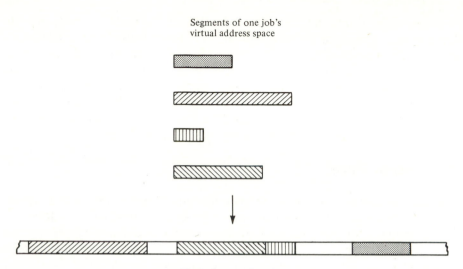

Figure 2.10 Address–Storage Mapping under Segmentation

Each entry includes three items. First is a flag to indicate whether the segment is currently in main storage. If the segment is in main storage, the next item gives the physical location of its origin. Addition of the displacement to this origin yields the desired location. The two-stage mapping process under segmentation is depicted in Fig. 2.11. For simplicity of exposition, main storage is assumed to consist of decimal locations 00000 to 49999. The virtual address (s, d) is (15,01326). Addition of s (15) to the current job's segment table origin (00400) yields the location of an entry with flag 1 (present in main storage) and segment origin 47293. Addition of d (1326) to that origin produces the required location of word 1326 in segment 15.

The third item in the segment table entry is the current length of the segment. If the displacement is as large as the length, as it might be in building a growing array, an interrupt is generated to signal to the space manager that more storage is needed. Because the referenced storage location might lie within a different segment, access must be suppressed until after more space is allocated, and the length item updated. If, as will sometimes be necessary, the segment needs to be moved, the segment origin item will also be updated. If, as has been assumed, the segment table is held in main storage, *two* storage accesses are required for each address specified by the programmer. The first access is to the segment table; the second, to the segment itself. The provision of special hardware to hold segment tables can mitigate the speed reduction due to these multiple accesses.

If the segment is not in main storage, a *segment fault* is said to have occurred. The hardware then generates an interrupt, which invokes the *segment fault handler*. This is a control program whose tasks are (1) to load the

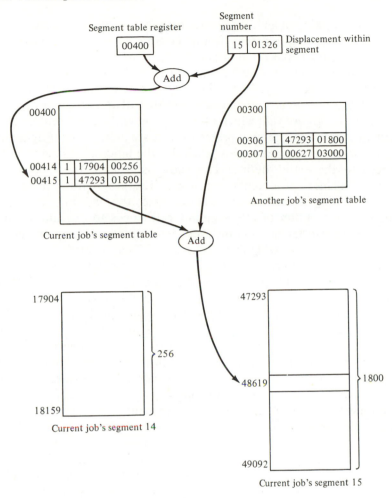

Figure 2.11 Implementation of Segmentation

desired segment from backing storage, perhaps after having rolled out one or more other segments to make room, and (2) to release the processor to another job, one that does not have to wait. Each time a segment is loaded, the flag and origin in the segment table entry must be set. In determining where to roll segments in, or to what area to move a growing segment already in main storage, the system uses techniques such as those discussed in Section 2.4. The choice of which segment(s) to replace, should that be necessary, follows considerations similar to those discussed for paging, under the heading "Replacement Policy" in Section 2.3.3.

One advantage offered by segmentation is that it provides overlaying, including interuser overlaying, with no intervention by the user. A linker is not needed at translation time to set up an overlay structure, nor is a relocating loader or overlay supervisor needed to implement overlaying.

The static linking of an overlay structure is possible only if the programmer is able and willing to specify at linkage time which sets of segments are to be co-resident at execution time. There exist situations, however, in which the programmer may prefer to, or need to, postpone the specification until execution time. An error routine, for example, may very well not be invoked in the course of a particular execution of the program. Although the programmer knows with which other segments the error routine is to be co-resident if invoked, he may prefer to allocate storage for it dynamically only if and when it is invoked. This precludes the binding, at linkage time, of references to the error routine. The same is true of the indeterminate number of instances of a recursive routine. The programmer must choose between allocating a maximum amount of space that *might* be required and deferring the resolution of intersegment references to execution time. In many transaction-oriented systems, the determination of which segments must be co-resident is highly data-dependent. There is often a large collection of processing routines, almost any small subset of which may be needed at a given moment, but hardly enough main storage to hold all. Dependence on a static overlay structure could cause intolerable service delays. A solution is provided by performing dynamically not only the loading, but also the linking. The language system's linker does not attempt to resolve intersegment references beyond translating each into a virtual address (s, d).

A second advantage of segmentation is thus that it simplifies linking. In an intersegment reference, the name of the referenced segment can still be used at execution time. A simple table lookup at that time can yield the segment number of a separately translated segment. The mapping of all addresses of the various modules into a single linear address space is obviated. Moreover, whereas translation-time linking requires the resolution of intersegment references regardless of whether those references will actually be made at execution time, the *dynamic linking* provided by segmentation does not even occur if the instruction that contains an intersegment reference is not executed. Hardware assistance can be provided to indicate whether an intersegment reference is to a segment that has already been linked.

A third advantage is that segmentation facilitates sharing. Often, several users desire access to the same compiler. If the compiler program is reenterable, all users can access a single copy of it concurrently, each with a private work area. Otherwise, a personal copy of the compiler would be needed for each user. Sometimes several users need access to the same data base. (If more than one writes into the data base, serious problems of synchronization can arise. These are discussed in Chapter 4.) Whatever the need for sharing, its implementation is simple. The segment to be shared is given an entry in the segment table of each sharing user. All of these entries contain the same origin address. Care must be taken to update all copies of that address if the segment is rolled out and back in or is otherwise moved. This sharing capability is but one aspect of the use of segmentation in the management of information as well as in that of storage. Information management is considered primarily in Chapter 6.

Segmentation, as described thus far, forces the space manager to deal in allocations of variable length both in main storage and in backing storage. Although each segment fits its region (by definition), the arrival of new segments and departure of old ones continues to cause external fragmentation. Compounded by overlaying and compacting, this requires often time-consuming dynamic storage control techniques. Much of the pain disappears when segmentation is combined with paging. Before discussing the combination, however, we examine paging alone.

2.3.3 Paging

A different mechanism for mapping virtual addresses leads to *paging,* which prohibits external fragmentation by the simple expedient of dividing main storage into units of equal size and allocating each one either in its entirety or not at all. The virtual address space is divided into *pages* of a fixed size. Storage references have the conceptual form (p, i), where p is the page number and i an index within the page. For convenience, page size is normally fixed at a power of two (in a machine with binary addressing). Then a single number serves as the virtual address, with the high-order bits specifying p and the low-order bits specifying i. The physical location space is divided into page *frames* of the same size as the pages. Thus the high-order physical location bits specify the frame f, and the low-order bits, as before, specify the index i within the frame. The execution-time mapping performed by the system is reduced to that of p to f; the addition of d required under segmentation is replaced by the catenation of i to the high-order bits.

It might appear that paging is just segmentation with fixed-length segments, and it is sometimes so described. This is an oversimplification, however, because the division of a program into segments is logical and performed by the programmer, whereas the division of a program into pages is arbitrary and performed by the translator. There is no guarantee in general that pages will correspond to logical groups of instructions or data.

The number of frames is a consequence of main storage size and frame size. The number of pages need not be restricted to the number of frames, because extra pages can be accommodated in backing storage, which then serves as a main storage extension. The storage devices most attractive for this purpose are those with no arm access motion, hence no access motion time (e.g., magnetic drums and the logically equivalent head-per-track disks). Moving-head disks are nevertheless also used. If the entire device is dedicated to holding pages, as it is on some systems, it is common to qualify its name by the designation "paging", as in "paging drum". Each of a job's pages is either in a frame in main storage or on the paging device. Contiguity within each page is still required, but contiguity of the several frames that hold the different pages is not. If consecutive page numbers have been assigned, paging maps contiguous virtual storage into noncontiguous real storage, not all of which is necessarily even main storage. The mapping performed by paging is illustrated in Fig. 2.12.

Although most paging systems use backing storage, some systems (e.g., XDS 940) restrict the paging to main storage only. If, however, backing storage is incorporated in the paging system, pages that are not needed at a given moment need not tie up the valuable main storage resource. Moreover, the programmer is permitted to program for a storage much larger than the one physically provided. In this situation, the virtual storage is sometimes called a *one-level store,* because the provision of paging can give the programmer the illusion of using a large store on one physical level.

Implementation. The implementation of paging will be described under the assumption that backing storage is used. The simplifications for the opposite case are straightforward. The correspondence between the pages of a given job and the frames that store them is specified in a *page table* associated with that job. The page table has one entry for each of the job's pages. Each entry contains two items. The first is a flag that indicates whether the page is in main storage or on the paging device. If the page is in main storage, the second item is the identification (high-order location bits) of the frame that holds it. If the page is not in main storage, the second item is information to identify its location in backing storage. A hardware *page table register* holds the physical address of the start of the page table for the currently running job. For each address reference (p, i), the computer adds p to the register content, obtaining the location of the page table entry for the referenced page p. It then checks the flag in that entry. If the page is not in main storage, a *page fault* is said to have occurred. The hardware then generates an interrupt, which invokes the *page fault handler.* This is a control program whose tasks are (1) to bring the desired page into main storage and (2) to release the processor to a job that does not need to wait. Each time a page is loaded, the flag and frame location in the page table entry are set. If, on the other hand, the page is already in main storage, the frame location f

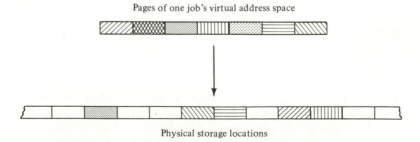

Pages of one job's virtual address space

Physical storage locations

Figure 2.12 Address–Storage Mapping under Paging

in the page table entry is catenated to the index *i* and the result is used to access the storage location that corresponds to the virtual address issued by the user job.

Figure 2.13 represents the two-stage mapping process. Main storage is again assumed to be addressed decimally from 00000 to 49999, and also to have 50 frames of 1000 words each. The virtual storage address (p,i) is 71638. Addition of p (71) to the current job's page table origin (00550) yields the location of an entry with flag 1 (present in main storage) and high-order location 24. Catenation of i (638) to 24 produces the required storage address of word 638 in page 71. If, as has been assumed, the page

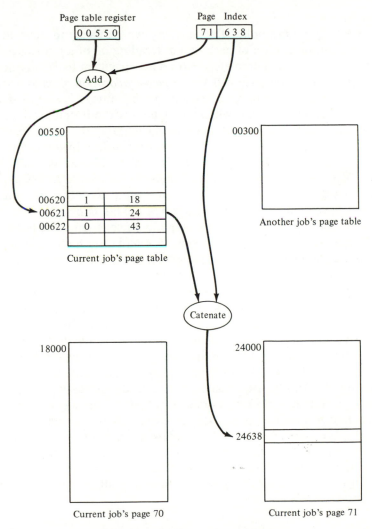

Figure 2.13 Implementation of Paging

table is held in main storage, *two* storage accesses are required for each address specified by the programmer. As for segmentation, the provision of extra hardware to hold page tables can mitigate the speed reduction.

The more of a job's pages are in main storage, the lower the multiprogramming ratio, because there is less space for other jobs. The fewer of its pages are in main storage, the longer it will occupy storage and the more paging I/O traffic will be generated, because more page faults will normally occur. Over-all effectiveness of a paging system is therefore responsive to the policies used for deciding what page to *fetch* into main storage and what page already in main storage the newly fetched page is to overlay, or *replace*.

Fetch Policy.   One policy for choosing which pages to have in main storage is the minimization of page faults. Loading *all* of a job's pages prior to beginning execution completely eliminates page faults. Consequently, this approach, which we shall call *simple paged allocation,* does not use the backing store as a main storage extension. Its advantage is simply that free storage is immediately usable wherever it lies, without compaction. Multiprogramming capability can be maintained without the need to relocate one job after another terminates. Moreover, an absolute loader can be used, because relocation of storage references is performed automatically by the paging mechanism. This mode of allocation is used in the XDS 940 system.

Another policy is to minimize page faults while accepting the constraint that not all pages can reside in main storage. This constraint is a consequence of providing a larger virtual storage to a user than there is real main storage in the system, or of the decision to maintain a high multiprogramming ratio with large jobs. *Prepaging* is a mechanism based on the prediction of program behavior. If it is known what pages will be required, they can be fetched before they are needed, thus eliminating page faults. In those few situations where page needs can be predicted, prepaging can reduce paging traffic from the drum. It can be shown, however, that the cost of prepaging one page that is not referenced is much greater than the gain in prepaging one page that is indeed referenced.* Because the prediction of program behavior is difficult, dynamic prepaging is rare. Static prepaging is exemplified by the simple paged allocation already discussed. Prepaging is mandatory, of course, if backing storage is not part of the paging subsystem.

The common mechanism is to fetch pages only on demand. In *demand paging,* all pages are fetched as the consequence of page faults. It is guaranteed that every page fetched is indeed needed and will be accessed. With a suitable replacement policy, an effective paging device, and an appropriate page size, demand paging can be very satisfactory in raising the multiprogramming ratio.

---

*See Tsichritzis and Bernstein [1974, p. 105].

The first demand paging system was Atlas [Kilburn, Payne, and Howarth, 1961], implemented on the Manchester University MUSE around 1960. The virtual address space was 1 million words; main storage was a magnetic core store of 16K words organized into 32 frames of 512 words each. A 96K drum served as the paging device.

A more recent example is the TENEX system for the DEC PDP-10 [Bobrow et al., 1972]. This system has the uncommon property that each user's virtual storage is smaller than the 1-megaword physical storage. An 18-bit virtual address specifies one of 256K words, organized into 512 pages of 512 words each. Each user's page table therefore has 512 entries and can fit in a single page. The main storage is divided into 2048 frames, requiring an 11-bit frame number, although the virtual address embodies only a 9-bit page number.

Replacement Policy.   If there is a vacant frame, a newly fetched page can be stored in that frame. If no frame is vacant, room must be made by replacing a page currently in main storage. Many policies exist for choosing which page to replace. Under demand paging, all fetches are necessary, and the goal that all of the replacement policies attempt to satisfy is the minimization of paging traffic, hence of page faults. If a read-only page can be recognized as such, the traffic represented by recopying it to backing storage can be eliminated. We have seen similar savings under swapping and under segmentation.

It has been shown by Belady [1966] that the optimal replacement policy is to replace that page the next reference to which is the furthest away in the future. In the absence of knowledge of future references, however, this policy is impossible to implement. It does, however, serve two purposes. One is to serve as a standard of comparison with other policies; comparisons can be made in retrospect. The other purpose is to justify the intuitive feeling that pages that are unlikely to be referenced soon should be replaced in preference to those that are. Many policies have been devised, analyzed, and measured. A few of the more important ones will be described.

Two policies that are easy to implement are cyclic progression through all frames and random selection. Clearly, they frequently remove useful pages. Other policies attempt to remove less useful pages.

The first-in-first-out (*FIFO*) policy replaces the page that has been in main storage the longest time. If storage references were truly sequential, that page would have high probability of not being needed again in the immediate future. In practice, however, FIFO often removes useful pages. Its chief attraction is ease of implementation. The space manager needs only to maintain a queue of all frames, ordered by time of fetching. Because the number of frames is fixed, this is easily accomplished in a small contiguous storage area.

The least-recently-used (*LRU*) policy replaces the page to which no reference has been made for the longest time. The underlying principle is that of locality of storage reference: a reference to a given storage location is likely to be followed by one to a nearby location. Once there have been no references to an area for a while, further references are unlikely. The LRU policy works well in practice and is among the most widely used, having been adopted for Atlas, TENEX, and many commercial systems.

The chief disadvantage of LRU is cost of implementation. Time is divided into intervals, usually fixed, and a list is maintained of only those frames that were not accessed during the most recent time interval, together with the number of consecutive intervals during which each was not accessed. Whenever a new page is read into a frame, that frame is deleted from the list. At the end of each interval, any frame accessed during the interval is removed from the list and any frame not accessed has its count incremented by unity, after having been placed on the list if not already on it. To learn which frames have been accessed during an interval, another table can be maintained, with one bit for each frame. All bits are reset to zero at the start of the interval. Each time a frame is accessed, its bit is set to one. At the end of the interval, nonaccessed frames are those with bit still zero. Sometimes these bits are included in the page tables. Often, hardware is provided to turn them on and off.

The least-frequently-used (*LFU*) policy replaces the page to which the fewest references have been made in a given interval. Like LRU, it is based on locality of reference. Implementation is similar to that of LRU. Recently loaded pages should be exempted from replacement until they have resided long enough in main storage for the frequency of their use to become measurable. Otherwise, the most recently loaded pages will be the first to go, and they will keep replacing each other at high cost in paging traffic.

It should be observed that delay in fetching a demanded page may be reduced by keeping one frame free at all times. This does not preclude the need for a replacement policy. It merely postpones application of the policy from prior to loading the new page until after loading, because another frame must be freed immediately to allow for the next page fault.

A given policy can be applied either *globally,* to all pages in main storage, or *locally,* to the main storage pages associated with a given job. In the latter event it is necessary to use a mechanism to select the job whose pages are to be considered. The most obvious candidate is the job for which the new page is being fetched. This tends to maintain indefinitely the amount of real storage available to each job in the system, and fails to take into account changing patterns of activity. Another candidate is the job that was assigned the lowest priority for execution. A disadvantage of the latter choice is that too much of main storage can become filled with low-utilization pages of high-priority jobs.

Behavior. Demand paging offers two principal advantages to the user. One is to free him from main storage limitations. The other is to simplify and broaden overlaying. As under segmentation, the users themselves need no longer plan overlaying; the system takes care of it. The costs of paging are not inconsiderable. Extra hardware, execution time, or both are required to perform the address translation. Fault handler time, and perhaps hardware, must be invested in implementing a replacement policy. The need to move pages between main and backing storage induces an artificial need for substantial I/O traffic beyond that requested directly by the users. Elapsed time to execute a job can be delayed by waiting for pages to be fetched.

A fruitful view of paging is provided by the *working-set* model due to Denning [1968]. This defines the working set $W(t, T)$ of information of a job at time t as the collection of information referenced by the job during the last T time units [i.e., during the time interval $(t-T, t)$]. The *working-set size* is the number of pages in the working set. Observations of program behavior have shown that even for intervals whose length T is the duration of the entire job, the working-set size is often smaller than the total number of pages of the job. This is not unreasonable when we consider the provision of error routines that might not be invoked during a particular run. It is often the case, too, that some portions of a job, such as initialization or the phases of a compiler, are active only once. For even a substantial duration T, the working-set size of such a job can be significantly less than the total number of pages. A job's working set is often a good predictor of the job's information requirements in the immediate future. It follows that if enough main storage is allocated for the working set, there should be relatively few page faults.

The TENEX system uses the frequency of page faults as a measure of how the working set size compares with the number of frames allocated, and raises or lowers the allocation accordingly. Its target is to have the mean time between page faults for any given job equal to two revolution times of the paging drum, approximately 67 milliseconds. This approach has been carried over into DEC's successor operating system, TOPS-20. Similarly, the MPE III system for the Hewlett-Packard 3000 minicomputer maintains a working-set list for each program and attempts to maintain a constant inter-fault time.

If the working sets of several jobs are all substantially smaller than the jobs' total size, main storage can effectively hold more jobs under demand paging than under prepaged or nonpaged allocation, thus raising the multiprogramming ratio. For interactive users, demand paging can be used to achieve a very high degree of multiprogramming.

Paging is not, however, a panacea. If too few frames are allocated to each job, most pages in main storage will be useful pages, and nearly every page fault will cause the replacement of a page that will itself be needed

shortly, causing another page fault. This chain of induced page faults can occur even if only one job has too few frames and the replacement algorithm
employs a local policy that selects the page to be replaced from the same job.
The resulting phenomenon is known as *thrashing,* a state in which the system spends most of its time handling page faults. The rate of useful computation can be degraded by a factor as large as 100; the system runs full tilt ac-
complishing nothing. Thrashing is an excellent illustration of the principle
that provision of a virtual resource, although it may ease the user's burden,
is only a virtual provision, and the user is not getting something for nothing.
There is no storage like real storage.

The effectiveness of paging is dependent upon page size. Because all
pages have the same fixed size, no part of main storage need ever go unallo-
cated, nor is relocation of storage areas necessary. There still remains, however, one form of storage fragmentation, that due to fitting jobs of arbitrary
length into an integral number of fixed-size pages. This is known as *internal
fragmentation,* or page *breakage.* If all job sizes are equally likely, the average
breakage per job is half a page. The larger the page size, the greater the total
breakage. Moreover, large page sizes mean fewer pages in main storage,
therefore perhaps fewer jobs. On the other hand, small pages mean more
space consumed by page tables and more page faults. The total volume of
pages transferred may be slightly less for small pages than for large, but each
transfer will require the same average rotational delay, and there will be
more transfers. Page size must therefore represent a compromise between
the two extremes. Typical sizes are in the range 2^8 to 2^{10} words, although
Venus [Liskov, 1972] uses 2^8 bytes and OS/370 MVS uses 2^{12} words.

2.3.4 Paged Segmentation

Paging can be used in the implementation of segmentation to alleviate the
problems of fragmentation and compaction, and to simplify the use of backing storage. The combination seeks to offer the benefits of both paging and
segmentation, at the cost of an extra level of indirection. The displacement d
within a segment is treated as a page-index pair (p, i). The user's virtual address (s, d) then appears to the system as the triple (s, p, i). Each user's segment table has, as before, an entry for each segment. This entry no longer
points to the segment directly. Instead, it points to a page table for the segment. Its two items are the origin of the segment's page table and the
current length of the segment, measured not in words but in pages. Segments may still be of variable length, and can have different numbers of
pages. An attempt to access a page beyond the number allocated causes an
interrupt that invokes the creation of a new page for the job. A segment can
be shared by placing, in the segment tables of the sharing job, the same page
table origin in the entries for that segment.

The mapping performed by paged segmentation is illustrated in Fig. 2.14. Page number p and displacement i are used to access storage as explained in Section 2.3.3. Segment number s is used as in Section 2.3.2 to access the segment entry in the current job's segment table, whose origin is held in the segment table register. The three-stage mapping process is depicted in Fig. 2.15.

Three main storage accesses are now required, first to the segment table, then to the page table, and finally to the page. Without substantial hardware assistance the delay would be intolerable. For most storage references, the two table lookups in storage can be replaced by a single lookup in faster circuitry. The component used for this is a *content-addressed storage* (CAS), also called "associative memory" or "associative registers".

When a standard storage is presented with the number of a storage location, it searches only that location and delivers the data held there. A simple content-addressed storage, in contrast, is presented with a data value and delivers the number of each storage location, if any, that holds that value. The usual CAS hardware typically implements the following variant. Each location, typically called a *cell,* holds what we shall view as two data values, an *argument* value and a *function* value, each of fixed length. The CAS is presented with a *key* value of the same length as the arguments. It performs a parallel search over all cells, looking for matches between the one key and the several arguments. For each argument that matches the key, the CAS delivers the corresponding function value. Because such a storage is expensive to build, it is usually small, but it can be made to operate very fast.

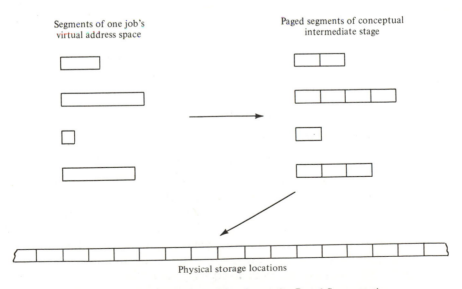

Figure 2.14 Address–Storage Mapping under Paged Segmentation

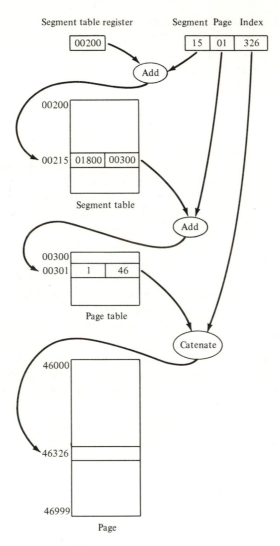

Figure 2.15 Implementation of Paged Segmentation

To accelerate the operation of a paged segmented storage system, each cell of a CAS holds, as argument value, the pair (s, p) of a page resident in main storage and, as function value, the origin of that page. The pair (s, p) of the desired page is used as the key, and only one main storage access is required instead of three. If the pair (s, p) is not found, the normal three-step sequence is performed, and the resulting page origin address is then inserted together with the key (s, p) into the CAS, overwriting an older entry. Thus table entries for the most recently used pages are maintained in the CAS. To save time in the event of an unsuccessful CAS search, the normal sequence can be started at the same time as the search.

Even for a single job, the number of pairs (s, p) can be rather large, whereas a CAS is practical only if small, typically 8 or 16 cells. To a great extent, however, storage references are concentrated in a small number of heavily accessed pages, whose entries become those held in the CAS. The over-all speed degradation due to paged segmented access can often be kept as low as 10%.

The performance of paging without segmentation can also be enhanced by the use of a CAS. Each entry in the storage contains a page number and the associated origin. The search is performed using the desired page number as key, and the page origin is immediately available if the search is successful.

Paged segmentation combines the advantages of segmentation with those of paging. True, page breakage reappears, but the other problems of storage allocation do not. The costs are substantial, both in execution time and in provision of the extra hardware for segmentation and paging. Nevertheless, paged segmentation has become probably the most popular implementation of virtual storage.

The classic example is M.I.T.'s Multics* [Corbató and Vyssotsky, 1965], originally implemented on a Honeywell 645. The virtual storage encompasses 2^{34} words, addressed by 18-bit segment numbers and 16-bit displacements. Each segment, which can therefore attain 64K words in length, is paged in units of 1K words.

Even minicomputers can be provided with paged segmentation, as in the Venus system, for which the underlying Interdata 3 had special microprograms installed to support segmentation and other operating system features. The virtual storage is somewhat smaller than that of Multics, being 2^{31} bytes (not words), addressed by 15-bit segment numbers with 16-bit displacements within segments of maximum length 64K bytes. The page size, as previously mentioned, is 256 bytes. Consequently, a segment may contain 256 pages.

Commercial system examples are provided by the VS/1 and MVS versions of IBM's OS/370, which are the virtual storage cognates of OS/360 MFT and MVT, respectively. For either version each user's virtual storage extends 2^{24} bytes in segments of 64K bytes. Segments in VS/1 have 32 pages of 2K bytes, whereas in MVS they have 16 pages of 4K bytes. A more recent example is the Prime 500, under the PRIMOS V operating system. Each user has 128K-byte segments, half of which are available for user programs and half for the operating system. Each segment has 64 2K-byte pages, managed under the LRU replacement policy. The virtual address includes a 12-bit segment number, a 6-bit page number, and a 10-bit index to the 2-byte word within the page.

---

*This system should not be confused with the more recent commercial Honeywell Multics system.

2.4 SPACE CONTROL TECHNIQUES

In managing movable partitions, relocatable regions, and unpaged segments, it is necessary to keep track of what main storage space is available and to allocate it in blocks of different sizes. We shall see (in Chapter 6) a need for similar control of backing storage space for filing systems. The function that provides this service is generally known as *dynamic storage allocation,* although that set of words could be applied to most of the techniques presented in this chapter. When a storage area is no longer needed, the space manager may or may not be notified explicitly. If notification is explicit, the storage area is said to have been *freed* or *liberated.* Proper handling of liberated storage, and the liberation of unneeded storage, are functions concomitant with allocation. The literature offers many dynamic storage allocation and liberation algorithms. The underlying ideas will be presented here to indicate what is involved in controlling space dynamically.

2.4.1 Dynamic Storage Allocation

The space manager must keep track of what storage is available, the so-called *pool* of available storage. Space to hold this information could be specifically allocated to the space manager. It is more economical, however, to use the pool of available storage itself for that purpose. Three principal techniques are available. One is to *chain* the blocks of available storage into a linked list, each node of which resides in a different block of available storage, states the size of that block, and points to another block. A second is to *mark* each word in the pool with a value reserved for that purpose. A third is to implement multiple lists, as in the *buddy system.*

Chained Pool. With a chained pool, the list of available blocks is searched to satisfy each request for storage. One of two criteria, *best fit* and *first fit,* is used to reserve a block. Best fit selects the smallest block that is large enough to satisfy the request. First fit selects the first block encountered that is large enough. The best-fit criterion may require a search of the entire list, and its use increases the number of very small blocks. It has the merit of saving the larger blocks for use in satisfying the larger requests. The first-fit criterion may cause premature breakup of larger blocks, but it is less likely to create many small blocks, and the search is often much shorter. Moreover, first fit sometimes works, surprisingly enough, when best fit does not. For example, let the available storage consist of two blocks, of sizes 6100 (first on the list) and 5800. Successive requests for blocks of sizes 5000, 5400, and 1000 are presented. Total requests add to 11,400; the total available is 11,900. Only first fit will be able to honor the third request. The results of honoring the first two requests are shown in Fig. 2.16. The third request, for a block of size 1000, cannot be honored under best fit, because the largest block now available is of size only 800. Under first fit, however, the block of size 1100 permits the request to be honored.

Request	List of available blocks after honoring request	
	best fit	first fit
	6100,5800	6100,5800
5000	6100, 800	1100,5800
5400	700, 800	1100, 400

Figure 2.16 Comparison of Best-Fit and First-Fit Allocation

When a reservation is made, the difference between the amount required and the total size of the available block used must be returned to the pool. In the foregoing example, the remainder simply replaced its parent block in the same position in the chain, but this is not mandatory. An alternative is to treat the remainder like a liberated block and follow whatever discipline has been adopted for managing the chain.

Two simple chain management disciplines are to maintain the list as a stack, and to maintain it as a queue. For these organizations, no search is required when a block is liberated. This is false economy, however, because major advantages are forgone. Ordering the list by address permits adjacent blocks to be easily coalesced after a liberation search, which averages half of the list length. If the pool is maintained instead in order of size, the average length of the best-fit allocation search is half the list. If the list is doubly linked to permit search in either direction, the average search length can be reduced further. Upon liberation, a search is needed to return the block to the right place in the list. Unfortunately, a size-ordered list is of no help in coalescing adjacent blocks. An explicit search for adjacent blocks can be undertaken whenever the space manager is unable to satisfy a request from a size-ordered pool. On balance, first fit with an address-ordered pool is often a satisfactory solution.

Marked Pool. The reservation of n storage locations from a marked pool is accomplished by scanning storage until n consecutive marked locations are encountered. This accomplishes a first fit reservation with a very simple process that is very slow. A block is liberated merely by marking its every word. No search is required. The amount of searching for marked locations can be reduced by using a marked pool together with a chained pool. Storage is allocated from an address-ordered list, and is liberated by marking. When there is no more available storage in the chained pool, the space manager scans storage once and reorganizes its free blocks (the marked pool) into a new address-ordered list. This is practical if storage is small, which keeps down the cost of unmarking.

It must be remembered that use of a marked pool removes from possible use anywhere as an instruction or data word some one combination of bits. If this restriction cannot be tolerated, marking must be forgone. Some computers provide different representations of positive and negative zero, but generate only one of these by arithmetic. The other zero may provide a convenient marker value. If the storage is large, another disadvantage is the cost of marking and unmarking. That cost is not present for chaining or for the next technique to be discussed.

Buddy System.   Searching a long list for blocks of the appropriate size and for neighbors with which to coalesce liberated blocks is averted in the buddy system by the use of two devices. One is to restrict block sizes to powers of two, and to use their binary addresses to aid in splitting and recombining blocks. The other is to use a separate list for each size of block. The buddy system is practical only on a computer with binary addressing. Each address that ends in k zeros is considered as the starting address of a block of length 2^k. For each value of k in $(0, n)$, where 2^n is the length of the entire storage, a list is maintained of available blocks of size 2^k.

If a block of size 2^k is requested, and none is available, list $k+1$ is checked for a block of size 2^{k+1}. If one is found, it is split into two *buddies,* each of size 2^k, and one of the buddies is allocated. If no block of size 2^{k+1} is found, the next larger size block is sought, and so on, until some block is found, and repeated splitting provides a block of the desired size. When a block is liberated, a test is made to see whether its buddy is also available. If so, they are recombined into one block of the next larger size, which in turn is recombined with its buddy if available, and so on as far as possible.

The splitting method guarantees that the starting addresses of two buddy blocks of size 2^k differ only in the $(k+1)$st digit from the right. This simplifies both splitting into buddies and testing a buddy for availability. Each block includes a 1-bit tag in its first word to indicate whether it is available or in use. Available blocks of size 2^k also include the value of k and two pointers in a doubly linked list of blocks of their size. The reservation and liberation algorithms are straightforward. Their execution can be faster than those of first fit, but storage is wasted because requests must be padded to the next higher power of 2.

2.4.2   Housekeeping

What can be done if the space manager is unable to honor a storage request? The most common response is to deny the request until more storage becomes available to the manager. Another possibility is for the manager to preempt storage that has been allocated to another job. Less drastic, perhaps, than either refusal or preemption, is the invocation of housekeeping routines designed to make more storage available to the space manager. Where can this storage come from? It may be space known to be available, but fragmented. Such fragments can be coalesced by storage compaction. It may be that another type of storage space was once reserved, but has since become inaccessible to the requesting job and is therefore unneeded, but has not been explicitly liberated. Such storage is called *garbage,* and returning it to the pool of available storage is *garbage collection.*

Compaction.   If the storage is nearly full, as it may well become under first fit with random requested block sizes, compaction has little to offer. If storage requests are large relative to the total storage size, the amount of storage still available may be large enough to satisfy a few more requests. In such a situation compaction may prove worthwhile. One reserved block at a time is moved forward against the end of the preceding reserved block, starting at the front of the storage. If the block being moved is a segment in unpaged segmented storage, the corresponding entry in each segment table that refers to it must be adjusted. If the block is a job in a system with relocation hardware, only the origin address needs to be changed. In the absence of relocation hardware, compacting arbitrary regions is infeasible. If the blocks are nodes of a list data structure, algorithms exist for compacting them.

Garbage Collection.   When users of storage do not obey a discipline of liberating storage that they no longer need, garbage collection can be invoked to pick up the pieces. It is predicated on the requirement that all storage in use be reachable via chaining from a fixed number of known locations. Because garbage collection is most commonly used in conjunction with list processing, we shall refer to the storage areas in question as *nodes.* Garbage collection generally proceeds in two steps. The first is to mark all reachable nodes, usually in a field that has been reserved for the purpose. The second is to scan storage for unmarked nodes and return them to the pool of available storage. The marking step is the more complex one, and many marking algorithms have been devised. Unfortunately, garbage collection is by its very nature least efficient when most needed (i.e., when storage is nearly full) and usually consumes more time than does explicit liberation. Although a user manipulating tree structures may be loth to force himself to return nodes before they become unreachable, such discipline is more easily demanded of the operating system designer. Consequently, garbage collection is normally not embodied in the space manager.

FOR FURTHER STUDY

Good general treatments of main storage management are presented in Tsichritzis and Bernstein [1974, Chaps. 4 and 5], Lister [1975, Chap. 5], and a more extensive one in Madnick and Donovan [1974, Chap. 3]. The reader who is insufficiently familiar with the underlying processor hardware can consult almost any hardware-oriented textbook, or study the chapter by Fuller [1975].

Further insights into virtual storage systems are to be found in the article by Doran [1976], the brief Sec. 5.2 of Shaw [1974], and the longer Chap. 7 of Habermann [1976]. The tutorial by Denning [1970] is highly recommended. Watson [1970, Secs. 2.4 and 2.5] offers a careful treatment, emphasizing details of the XDS 940 and Multics systems.

The first paging system is described by Kilburn et al. [1962]. The working-set concept was enunciated and further expounded by Denning [1968, 1980]. Paging behavior is further discussed by Belady [1966] and by Belady, Nelson, and Shedler [1969]. Techniques for sharing segments and pages are presented by Shaw [1974, Chap. 6].

Static and dynamic loading are particularly well presented in the brief Sec. 8.4 of Brooks and Iverson [1969] and Sec. 2.2 of Shaw [1974], the tutorial by Presser and White [1972], and in the following book chapters: Barron [1972, Chap. 5]; Graham [1975, Chap. 6]; Arms, Baker, and Pengelly [1976, Chap. 13]; and Ullman [1976, Chap. 5].

A classic reference on dynamic storage allocation is Knuth [1973, Sec. 2.5], and Habermann [1976, Sec. 8.1] is also helpful. The first-fit and best-fit strategies are more fully compared in the articles by Shore [1975] and Bays [1977].

EXERCISES

2.1 Give an example of an absolute address field in an instruction.

2.2 The program fragment in Fig. 2.4 is to be translated for a machine with direct addressing. Assume that the machine has 16-bit words, addressed by consecutive integers. An instruction word consists of a 4-bit operation code followed by a 12-bit address. The operation code for LOAD is 0110. A data word consists of a 16-bit signed integer in two's-complement representation. Show in hexadecimal (a) the object code generated by the assembler and (b) the machine code as placed in storage by a relocating loader that uses 1AC as the segment origin address. The displacements shown are to be considered hexadecimal.

2.3 A friend maintains that a serially reusable program can be relocated any time during execution, provided that the relocation bits have been saved. State and justify your response.

2.4 For the example described in Fig. 2.5, can the unoverlaid portion of segment 4 be preserved for later use?

2.5 Describe hardware assistance to indicate whether a segment to which an inter-segment reference is made has already been linked.

2.6 How can all copies of the address of a shared segment be updated when the segment is relocated?

2.7 One implementation of segment sharing uses a shared segment table to hold entries for all segments that are shared. In each job's segment table, the entry for a shared segment points not to the segment itself but to its unique entry in the shared segment table. Describe the advantages and disadvantages of this implementation with respect to the one described in Section 2.3.2.

2.8 Show that the cost of prepaging one page that is not referenced exceeds the gain due to prepaging one page that is referenced.

2.9 Can the page table hold track and sector addresses of a page that is not in main storage?

2.10 Under demand paging, when is there a vacant frame?

2.11 [Belady, Nelson, and Shedler, 1969] Consider a demand paging system that uses the FIFO policy for page replacement. A certain job has *five* pages, designated by the first five letters of the alphabet. Let the sequence of page references be ABCDABEABCDE. Assume that all five pages are initially in backing storage.
   (a) On a list of the 12 page references, mark those that result in a page fault if *four* frames are available for the job. What is the number of page faults?
   (b) Repeat for *three* frames being available.

2.12 Under certain circumstances a page that is to be replaced need not be written to backing storage. What are these circumstances? How can they be detected through use of software? What hardware feature could aid in the detection? Assume demand paging.

2.13 How can the operating system maintain the origins of the various page tables?

2.14 Describe an implementation of paged segmentation in which page tables may themselves be in backing storage and there is no guarantee that a given page table is necessarily in main storage. Allow for the possibility that a page table might be longer than one page.

2.15 Compare the best-fit and first-fit criteria for the following modifications of the example in Section 2.4.1.

   (a) Reverse the order of the blocks in the pool.
   (b) Reverse the order of the first two requests.
   (c) Reverse both orders.

2.16 Let the difference between a space request and the available block selected to fulfill the request be returned to a chained pool in the place formerly occupied by the original block. Specify an implementation of the pool such that the return is accomplished by resetting one length field but no pointers. What restrictions does your implementation impose on the order or size of blocks?

2.17 Suppose that the difference e between a space request n and the size $n+e$ of the available block selected to fulfill the request is small. Why might it be preferable to allocate the entire block rather than only the amount requested?

What is the cost? This tactic is followed in several systems, including the B7000/B6000 MCP, where e is 15 words.

2.18 Explain precisely why, in the buddy system, the list of available blocks of a given size is linked doubly rather than singly.

2.19 Write reservation and liberation algorithms for the buddy system. Trace the execution of your algorithms for the following sequence of requests, showing for each value of k the changes in the list of blocks of size 2^k. For each request draw a diagram of the resulting status of storage, showing the position and size of each block, numbering the blocks that are in use. Assume a 1024-word storage (i.e., $n=10$).

Reserve Block 1	256 Words
Reserve Block 2	64 Words
Reserve Block 3	128 Words
Reserve Block 4	64 Words
Reserve Block 5	64 Words
Liberate Block 3	
Reserve Block 6	64 Words
Liberate Block 2	
Reserve Block 7	256 Words
Liberate Block 6	
Liberate Block 4	
Reserve Block 8	128 Words

Chapter 3

PROCESSOR MANAGEMENT

Just as a job cannot run if it is not resident in executable storage, neither can it run unless it has been granted access to the instruction counter of a processor. In this chapter we focus on the processor as a resource. The processor is used to execute programs, and a useful intuitive notion is that of an instance of execution of a program. Such an instance we call a *process*. Thus the execution of an editor program on a given text is a process, and the execution of the same editor on another text is a different process, even if both executions share one copy of the program. In Chapter 4 we give further definitions of process, but for now we follow Parnas's [1974] definition of a process as the unit to which a processor may be allocated. We distinguish henceforth between a process and a batch job in that the latter causes one or more processes (e.g., compilation, linking, loading, and execution) to occur. A batch job entering the system can be thought of as requesting the creation of processes to carry out the job. Each session of a user logged in to an interactive system is also a process. We call such a process an *interactive process*, to distinguish it from a *batch process* associated with a batch job. There are, of course, operating system processes as well as user processes. In this chapter we restrict our attention to computer systems that incorporate a single processor. Multiple-processor systems are discussed in Chapter 8.

3.1   REAL AND VIRTUAL PROCESSORS

A virtual storage system maintains the illusion that each process occupies space independently of other processes and their space requirements, and perhaps even in excess of the storage physically provided. Viewed alternatively, different processes can appear to occupy the same storage locations at the same time. In a similar manner, the multiprogramming of a single *real processor* maintains the illusion that each process uses instruction cycles independently of other processes and their processor requirements. The complementary view is that the different processes appear to be executing instructions concurrently, thus associating with each process its own *virtual processor*.

In both space sharing and processor sharing, a price is paid in reduced speed of operation. The speed of access to paged virtual storage is less than that to the real storage it is intended to represent. The speed of each virtual processor is less than that of the real processor that implements it. Yet there is a qualitative difference, at least psychologically. The capacity of storage is usually reckoned in terms of bit volume, and that of virtual storage is usually not reduced from that of real storage; in fact, it is often greater. The capacity of a processor is generally felt to be synonymous with its speed, and multiprogramming definitely reduces the processor capacity available to each user.

3.2   A MODEL OF PROCESSOR ALLOCATION

In a simple multiprogramming system each process can be thought of as being in one of three conditions or *states*, illustrated in the central portion of Fig. 3.1. With one processor available, at most one process can be executing instructions. That process is in the *run* state. A process that is ready to run whenever the processor becomes free is in the *ready* state. Such a process has necessarily already received an allocation of executable storage, as well as any other resources it requires for execution. It is waiting for only one more resource, the instruction counter of the processor. If a process cannot

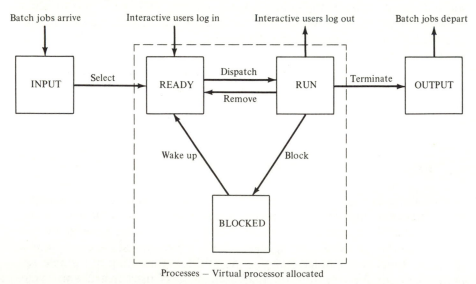

Figure 3.1 Job and Process States

continue to execute because some expected event has been requested, but not yet completed, it is in the *blocked* state. It is not ready to run because it is blocked by the noncompletion of the event. Examples of such events are requests for additional resources, segment and page faults, and I/O operations initiated by the process, including receipt of an end-of-transmission signal from a terminal. It may be decided to swap a blocked process out to backing storage to avoid holding valuable executable storage for a process that cannot run. This is often done to an interactive user process that is waiting while the user thinks. Some systems will swap a ready process out, thereby blocking it. The run state is limited to one process; the ready and blocked states are not.

A process, whether in the run, ready, or blocked state, has at one time received every allocation it needs, except perhaps that of a real processor. It has thus been allocated a virtual processor. We shall refer to the initial allocation of a virtual processor as *creation* of the process. An interactive process is created each time a user is permitted to log in. The process enters the ready state directly. If sufficient resources are not available, permission to log in is simply denied. An arriving batch job is normally placed on the job queue, where it waits in the *input* state, also shown in Fig. 3.1, for the allocation of a virtual processor to each of the processes it requires. We assume for the present that each batch job requests the creation of a single process. Later we shall remove that restriction. Eventually the batch job is *selected* by being granted the necessary resources. The corresponding process is created and admitted to the ready state. When a batch process has finished executing, its virtual processor is released and the process deleted. Output to be printed has usually been accumulated for the associated batch job, which then enters the *output* state to await completion of printing before leaving the system. An interactive process, on the other hand, releases its virtual processor by logging out and leaving the run state directly.

A process can leave the run state for one of three reasons.

1. The process *terminates*. It then leaves the virtual processor.

2. The process *blocks* itself, perhaps by issuing a request for input or output that must be completed before it can proceed. The process passes from the run state to the blocked state, where it lies dormant until the anticipated action is completed.

3. The process is *removed* from the run state by a control program, typically because a time limit has expired. The process passes from the run state back to the ready state.

Removal of a process is an instance of preemption of a resource. Preemption occurs also in other contexts; an example is the preemption of page frames in demand paging. Some resources are more readily preempted than others. Printers and card readers are, practically speaking, not preempt-able. Main storage is rather preemptable, and the instruction counter is highly preemptable. Nevertheless, not all operating systems preempt the processor.

When the event occurs for which a blocked process is waiting in execut-able storage, a control program *wakes up* the dormant process, which passes from the blocked state to the ready state. If the blocked process had been rolled out, wakeup is not complete until the process has been rolled back in. From the ready state, a process passes to the run state when the control pro-gram *dispatches* it by transferring control to it. If a job just waked up has suf-ficiently high priority, it may be desirable to dispatch it immediately, by removing the running process, which enters the ready state.

To manage the flow of processes among the several states, the operating system maintains for each process a *process descriptor*, a record of informa-tion about the process. The records for the processes in each state can be structured in a variety of ways. A commonly used structure is the queue, and the descriptive records associated with one state are therefore often called a queue, even when the organization is not a queue in the strict FIFO sense. The persistence of the term "queue" is probably due to its use in "job queue", which originally designated a genuine queue.

The allocation and preemption of the real processor, and the allocation of virtual processors (which are usually not preempted) constitute the management of the processor resource. Although it is customary to distin-guish management of virtual processors from that of the real processor, there is some disagreement on what to call either. Our terminology is the following.

Selection of jobs is called *scheduling* and performed by the *scheduler*. For each job selected, this control program creates a batch process and enters it into the ready state, allocating executable storage, backing storage, files, and other resources. The scheduler also performs functions associated with ter-minating a batch process. Dispatching, the allocation of the instruction counter to a ready process, is performed by the *dispatcher*. Alternative names are "initiator" for scheduler, and "supervisor" or "monitor" for dispatcher. If "initiator" is used, then the "terminator" performs the func-tions associated with releasing a virtual processor. Another variant is "high-level scheduler" for virtual processor allocation and "low-level scheduler" for real processor allocation. A major difference between scheduling and dispatching is that a job is scheduled but once, whereas its process may be dispatched many times.

The scheduler and dispatcher can be viewed as managing queues of jobs or processes each awaiting acceptance by a processor, real or virtual, or the occurrence of some event. Consequently, the performance of different management algorithms can be compared quantitatively by the use of queu-ing theory. In this book we only cite some of the results, but take this oppor-tunity to advise the reader that a knowledge of elementary queuing theory is essential to a deeper understanding of processor management, and indeed of much of resource management. In the remainder of this chapter we study dispatching and scheduling in turn, then interrupts. We close by examining the implementation of dispatching and scheduling mechanisms.

3.3   PROCESS DISPATCHING

The dispatcher selects for running the particular ready process that has the highest *priority*. The concept of priority often connotes intrinsic importance, due sometimes to having been paid for. Many other factors can be used to determine priority, however, provided that they are maintained in the process descriptor. Among them are the process's creation time, its requesting job's arrival time, service time requested, time spent receiving service, time spent not receiving service, and the extent or nature of nontime resources requested or used. These factors can be applied in many different ways, and there is consequently a large variety of dispatching mechanisms possible.

In choosing among mechanisms, we are particularly interested in their effect on the *wait* of a process, the time it spends waiting in the ready state. A batch user is vitally concerned, of course, with the total time his process spends in the system, and this includes time not only in the ready but also in the blocked state, not to mention time in the input state awaiting scheduling. Because a blocked process is not eligible for dispatching, the choice of mechanism does not affect time in the blocked state, which is therefore excluded from the definition of wait used to compare dispatching mechanisms. An interactive user is normally concerned not with the time used by the entire process, but rather with the time needed to service the most recent request. Generally, the user has neither the knowledge needed to estimate the service time required, nor a means of expressing such an estimate.

A very large variety of dispatching mechanisms have been proposed. A few of the more interesting or more common ones are described here, together with the policies they are intended to implement.

3.3.1   Single-Queue Mechanisms

An apparently admirable policy is to give all users the same service. What does that mean? One reasonable interpretation is that no process should wait, on the average, longer than any other. A more precise formulation of that notion depends upon the concept of *mean wait*.

Consider a system that has been running some mix of processes long enough that the transient effects of getting the system started have died out. Assume that the response properties of the system do not change with time, that is, the system is in *steady-state* operation. An experiment could be performed in which a particular process was entered into the ready state and its wait measured. Repetition of that experiment at many randomly selected points in time would yield several values of the wait. The mean of these values over an indefinitely large number of repetitions of the experiment is the *mean wait* for *that process.* Of course, the indefinitely repeated experiment is not practical, but only conceptual. Nevertheless, queuing theory can be used to calculate a mean waiting time from sufficient information about the process and a precise description of the dispatching algorithm. If the conceptual experiment is broadened to include repeated measurements not on one particular process, but on all processes in the process mix, the *over-all mean wait* is obtained. It, too, can be computed by the use of queuing theory.

The policy of equal service can now be restated simply as providing to each process the same *mean wait.* This can be accomplished by servicing processes in order of their arrival, and allowing each one to run to completion, except of course if it enters the blocked state. This nonpreemptive mechanism is sometimes called "FIFO" because it can be implemented by a true queue as long as no process is ever blocked. Because processes do become blocked, a somewhat better name is *first-come-first-served* (FCFS). Implementation cost is low because the ready queue need merely be kept in order of increasing process creation time, and there is no overhead for preemption. A major disadvantage of FCFS is that many users consider it *un*fair to make short processes wait as long as long processes. They reject equal mean wait as an interpretation of equal service. Queuing theory reveals two further disadvantages. One is that the mean wait increases without limit as the system becomes more and more nearly fully loaded. The second is that as variance in process durations increases, so does the mean wait. For interactive service the FCFS mechanism is unattractive for yet another reason. Under any nonpreemptive mechanism a process that computes extensively without blocking causes intolerable delay to other processes.

A policy that meets the objections to FCFS is that of minimizing *over-all* mean wait. If dispatching priority is based on process duration instead of on creation time, the scheduling mechanism is called *shortest job next* (SJN). This is customarily implemented as a nonpreemptive mechanism. It can be shown that SJN reduces over-all mean wait from that under FCFS, and provides lower mean wait to short processes than to long ones, but at a twofold expense. Mean wait for long processes is increased over FCFS and the variance of wait for long processes is also increased, making it difficult to predict when a process will receive service. For many users, predictability of service is nearly as important as speed of service. By getting rid of short processes quickly, SJN tends to decrease the number of processes waiting in the ready queue. Preemption can be applied to SJN by removing the running process whenever a shorter process appears in the ready state either as the result of unblocking or as a new arrival. This further favors short processes at the expense of long. On the other hand, it appears foolish to remove a nearly completed process in favor of another whose total time request is smaller but whose current need exceeds that of the removed process.

Preemption is more reasonably applied by keeping track of service time received. The system can then implement the *shortest remaining time* (SRT) mechanism. The remaining time is the difference between time required, which is estimated by the user, and time received, which is measured by the system with the aid of a clock in the hardware. Although SRT could be nonpreemptive, this would forgo the advantage of always running the process that is most nearly finished. Consequently, SRT is normally implemented to be preemptive, and can be thought of as the preemptive counterpart of SJN. Short processes are favored even more under SRT than under SJN, at the expense of long processes. It can be shown that SRT achieves the minimum possible over-all mean wait. Because a service time estimate is required for SJN and SRT, they are not appropriate mechanisms for dispatching interactive processes.

Under SJN or SRT the user who requests a short time enjoys higher priority than one who requests a long time. There is therefore an incentive to deflate time estimates to improve one's priority artificially. Counterincentives may need to be applied. A common measure is to expel the process from the system unterminated once its service time has attained its requested time. An alternative is to increase at that point the rate that the user must pay. For all mechanisms there is the problem of the process that has become stuck in an endless loop, and for that reason there is almost invariably an ultimate time limit imposed on each process.

Another mechanism for reducing mean waiting time is to grant higher dispatching priority to processes that are likely, on a basis other than requested time, to require little processor time. Favoring processes with high I/O activity is an example. The greater the I/O activity of a process, the sooner it is likely to become blocked. Maintaining the queue in increasing order of length of time since the last I/O command will usually favor processes whose I/O activity is currently high. It will consequently tend to maximize utilization of the I/O subsystem. The use of a single queue ordered according to I/O activity makes it impossible to take other factors into account. Favoring I/O-bound processes is therefore more often approached by the use of a multiqueue mechanism.

The foregoing mechanisms for reducing over-all wait suffer from the defect of postponing long processes, sometimes interminably. Processes have, in fact, become lost indefinitely in some systems. If we add to the policy of minimizing wait the constraint of ensuring completion of all processes, we are led to other scheduling mechanisms. A favorite is *round-robin*, a preemptive mechanism with extremely simple queue management. Each process in turn is allocated a "time slice" or fixed *quantum q* of time, at the end of which it is removed in favor of the next process in the ready queue, unless it has previously terminated or become blocked. A process that is removed, becomes unblocked, or enters the system afresh goes to the end of the queue. The priority of a process under round-robin is in increasing order of length of wait since the last quantum was received (or, for a new process, since its creation). If there are *n runnable* (ready or running) processes, each appears to receive $1/n$ of the processor time. This is a form of equal service that gives implicit priority to short processes, because they will finish sooner than long ones, but without excessively penalizing long processes. Because of the process-switching time, the over-all mean wait can be even higher than for FCFS. If there is large variance in the process durations, however, the over-all mean wait under round-robin can be less than that under FCFS. Round-robin is widely used in interactive systems.

An important consideration is the size of the time quantum q. For large q, a process can be substantially delayed by the arrival or unblocking of other processes, or speeded up by the blocking of other processes. This unevenness causes a departure from equality of service to all processes, a departure that is more pronounced for greater q. Moreover, the wait between successive attentions to any one process increases with q, a disadvantage in an interactive system. On the other hand, a small q can result in longer over-all mean wait than a larger q, as shown in Exercise 3.4. Moreover, small q increases the frequency of process switching, and the time devoted to that activity can actually exceed the time that remains for the several processes. As a result, it is necessary to choose for q an intermediate value, which is typically in the range 200 to 2000 milliseconds. On the Prime 500 under PRIMOS V, for example, $q = \frac{1}{3}$ second.

A number of variations of round-robin exist. One is used in interactive systems that attempt to guarantee a specific maximum response time t. At the beginning of each cycle through the ready queue, q is set equal to t/n, where n is the number of processes in the queue at that moment. Processes to be inserted are formed into an alternate queue, which is then processed in the same manner when the first queue is exhausted. To allow for the process-switching time s it is actually necessary to set $q = (t/n) - s$. For n large, s will represent a high switching overhead. This can be curbed by holding q to at least some minimum value, at the cost of potentially increasing the response time beyond the guaranteed value t.

Another variation, used in the XDS 940 system, is possible if means exist for predicting when an I/O operation will be completed. If a process issues an I/O request that is expected to complete before expiration of the current quantum, the process is not blocked.

A different means of ensuring that long processes will eventually be run is to increase their priority with the passage of time. This practice is known as *ageing* and essentially involves subtraction of the creation time from the otherwise computed priority (assuming higher numerical values for higher priorities). The older a process is, the less will be subtracted, and eventually its priority will exceed that of every other process.

3.3.2 Multiple Queues

The simple model of process flow in Fig. 3.1 envisions only one ready queue and three states for processes. Information provided by the user or determined in the course of execution can be used to classify ready processes according to one or more criteria. Such information can include service time estimates, the amount of time actually used, and the number of I/O requests issued. It is often worth while to give different treatment to processes in different classes. Separate ready states can be identified with the different classes. One choice in a batch multiprogramming system would be to give higher dispatching priority to I/O-bound than to processor-bound processes. This is reflected in the five-state nonpreemptive model of Fig. 3.2. It would be equally satisfactory to consider *all* the blocked processes to be in a single blocked state. In a paging system, it may be helpful to provide different queues to distinguish between processes waiting for paging I/O and those waiting for user-requested I/O.

    Unrelated to the foregoing classification is the common tripartite classification into *real-time*, *interactive*, and *batch* processes, for which three ready queues can be provided. A real-time process must receive service before a real moment in time, which is imposed on the system, often by an external device. An interactive process must receive service within what a human user considers to be reasonable response time. A batch process (in this view, at least) has no service deadline.

    The provision of more than one ready queue can facilitate the implementation of some of the policies already described. Multiple queues permit

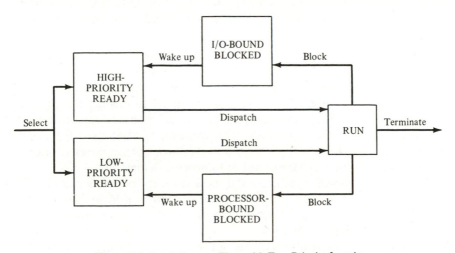

Figure 3.2 Batch Process Flow with Two Priority Levels

the use of more than one dispatching mechanism, one for each queue. Multiple queues also permit the use of more than one value of a parameter (e.g., quantum duration) controlling a mechanism. Under some implementations, the association between process and queue is permanent, or *static*; the process always returns to the same ready queue. Under other mechanisms, the association between process and queue may change as execution progresses; it is *dynamic* and the process may return on different occasions to different ready queues.

Static Association.   Let us consider static association first. In implementing a "favored user" policy, a simple mechanism is to maintain a ready queue for each of several *classes* of processes, to each of which is assigned a different dispatching priority. Whenever the run state becomes empty, the dispatcher selects a process from the nonempty queue of highest priority, typically managing each queue under either FCFS or round-robin. If round-robin is used, different quanta can be associated with different queues. An important multiqueue organization is the three-queue system for concurrent execution of batch, interactive, and real-time processes. Batch processes are assigned to a low-priority queue and both interactive and real-time processes to high-priority queues. The low-priority processes are frequently said to be executing in the *background*, behind the high-priority processes in the *foreground*.

Many other criteria can be used for assigning processes to classes. An elementary one is paid priority; give improved service to a user who is willing to pay a higher price. Others are size of main storage region required, whether the process uses a popular compiler that is always kept resident, and whether the process requires *setup* (mounting of backing storage volumes). Various combinations of these criteria can be used to define a number of classes.

Dynamic Association.   For minimizing mean wait, most of the single-queue mechanisms we have examined rely upon user-supplied information such as estimated service time. Information about each process can also be developed in the course of executing it and used to change the process's priority in the light of that information. The association between process and queue therefore becomes dynamic. The multiple queues used for the different priority levels are sometimes called *feedback* queues because information is fed back from process execution to process dispatching.

The basic feedback mechanism uses a number of ready queues. The process at the head of the nonempty queue of highest priority is dispatched. A process on any queue is allocated a quantum of processor time. If it does not terminate during the quantum, it is placed at the tail of the next-lower-priority queue, perhaps after having waited a while in the blocked state. Once a process reaches the lowest-priority queue, it remains there and is served round-robin. All other queues receive true FIFO service with preemption based on time. A new process is placed at the tail of the highest-priority queue. Although several queues exist, they do not all require service simultaneously. A process is dispatched from only one queue at a time, and a process is appended to only one queue at a time.

The rationale behind this mechanism is the frequent, albeit not invariable, observation that the longer a process has run, the less likely it is to terminate soon. If this is true, the process most likely to finish is the one that has run least. The multilevel feedback mechanism is effective to the extent that process termination rate does indeed decrease with the amount of service received. It tends to give better service to short processes than does round-robin but, unlike SJN and SRT, does not require prior information about time required. Feedback queues are therefore particularly attractive for interactive processes, whether or not batch processes are also present.

One variation is aimed at reducing the overhead in queue maintenance. Fewer queues are used, and each process is permitted to remain a number of times in any one queue before falling to the next lower queue. All queues are serviced round-robin. Another variation is to assign progressively longer quanta to lower priority queues, culminating perhaps in an unlimited quantum (FCFS, see Exercise 3.3) for the lowest queue. This is aimed at reducing the frequency of process switching among the longer processes. The two variations can be applied either singly or in combination.

Feedback can be used to raise as well as to lower a process's priority. One example is a two-queue system in which each process's history of recent I/O activity is used to assign it to a processor-bound or to an I/O-bound queue.

Feedback queues are used in a number of operating systems. In M.I.T. Multics the quantum length is doubled with each transition to the next-lower-priority queue. Each request by an interactive user is treated as a new start. This provides very good service to interactive users, particularly if their requests are modest. On the other hand, the presence of enough interactive users can virtually prevent batch processes from proceeding.

To remedy that problem, TENEX bases a process's priority on a long-term average of processor use rather than only on its immediate past history. A process's priority is decreased at a constant rate c while running and increased at rate c/n while blocked, where n is the number of runnable processes. Of course, the recomputation of priority is not performed continuously, but only when a state transition must be made. To avoid penalizing an interactive process that makes a trivial request after having received a large burst of service, such a process is nevertheless given one quantum at high priority. TENEX keeps in main storage not all processes that would be runnable, but only a subset called the "balance set". These are the runnable processes with highest priority whose total working sets will fit in main storage. After a page fault, another member of the balance set is dispatched. The entire set of ready processes is monitored periodically for changes in priorities and in working set sizes. This permits adjustment of balance-set membership. Storage management and processor management are thus strongly interrelated in that system.

The DEC operating system for the PDP-10 maintains three ready queues, with quanta of 0.02, 0.25, and 2 seconds. A process is allowed one FIFO access to each of the first two queues before dropping to round-robin on the third queue. As under Multics, each new request by an interactive process starts in the highest-priority queue.

3.3.3 Service Guarantees

A more burdensome requirement than ensuring eventual completion is en-suring completion by a specified time or within a specified delay. This policy of meeting *deadlines* is one aspect of a policy of giving preferential service to favored users. What processes have deadlines? In a system that is running both batch and interactive processes, the interactive processes may be given delay deadlines to provide adequate response time to their users. In a proc-ess control application, a computer process communicating with devices external to the computer system might require the instruction counter either with a specified frequency or at specific clock times. A payroll program has such an important deadline that a common practice is to ensure meeting it by starting a day or two in advance. Mechanisms for deadline scheduling ex-ist, but no mechanism can ensure meeting a set of deadlines that demand more processor time than the total available.

A simple way to perform deadline scheduling is to maintain the ready queue in increasing order of deadline. The chief drawback of merely order-ing processes by deadline is that a deadline process may receive better service than it requires, at the expense of other processes. For example, a 5-minute batch process with a deadline 20 minutes away needs only one-fourth of the service available over the next 20 minutes. If deadline processes have priority over others and if this process has the closest dead-line, it may receive all of its service at once. This will delay all other processes, even very short ones, by fully 5 minutes.

Another approach to assuring adequate response is to guarantee levels of service over an interval of time, as opposed to guaranteeing completion of service by a single deadline in time. Three types of service guarantees are the following.

1. Allocating a minimum fraction of the processor time to a class of processes, if at least one of the processes is ready.

2. Allocating a minimum fraction of the processor time to a particular process, if it is ready.

3. Allocating enough processor time to a particular process to permit its meeting a deadline.

Under the first type of guarantee, different classes of processes usually have requirements expressed over different time periods. Thus it might be decided to guarantee 10% of each 10 milliseconds to real-time processes, 45% of each 2 seconds to interactive processes, and 25% of each 10 minutes to batch processes. Of course, the sum of the guarantees cannot exceed 100%. The second type of guarantee may result from paid priority or from the need to run a demonstration program under conditions of heavy system load. The third type of guarantee applies to batch processes such as producing patient medication lists for a hospital.

TENEX provides guarantees of type 2, and Univac's EXEC 8 provides guarantees of type 3. Both systems impose maximum as well as minimum service limits. An implementation of type 1 guarantees can be used to provide the other two types as well. Type 2 can be considered as the sole representative of a type 1 class. A type 3 process can be converted to a type 2 process by using as the guaranteed percentage the ratio of estimated running time to time between submission and deadline, adjusted perhaps for delays in the blocked state. An implementation of type 1 service guarantees is described in Section 3.6.

3.4 JOB SCHEDULING

The basic function of scheduling is to manage virtual processors, allocating and reclaiming resources other than the real processor. For interactive users, the chief question is whether to admit a new user or not. Sometimes the number is limited by a physical resource requirement, such as the amount of storage provided to hold information about each user and his terminal. Of course, if the physical limitation is the number of communication connections, or *ports*, the operating system never even becomes aware of an unsuccessful postulant for service. Sometimes the number of interactive users is limited arbitrarily to prevent service degradation due to excessive contention for resources. If different priorities of users are distinguished, it may be decided to terminate the process of a user already logged in, to make room for a new arrival. The victim may be chosen on the basis of fixed priority or of resource use. In at least one system the interactive process is culled that has consumed the most processor time.

Although the foregoing activities are conceptually related to the allocation of virtual processors to batch processes, in most operating systems they are performed by a control program distinct from the job scheduler. Designations such as "interactive service manager" and "time-sharing supervisor" are common.

Before a new batch process is placed on a ready queue, perhaps even before it is loaded into executable storage, the resources it has requested prior to execution must be allocated. Other than storage, these resources are typically files and devices, and may include mountable volumes. Among the resources requested may be the use of particular programs, such as a compiler or its run-time library, or of a data base shared with other processes. File and device allocation are thus intimately bound with storage and processor allocation. We discuss device allocation in Chapter 5 together with other aspects of device management, and file allocation in Chapter 6 together with other aspects of file management. In Chapter 4 we show the importance of the sequence in which a process's resource requests are honored.

When a process terminates, the resources it held must be freed. The job scheduler is invoked whenever a resource other than the real processor is released. The purpose is to permit the scheduler to determine whether enough total resources have become available to permit another job to be selected for allocation of a virtual processor. The scheduler's objective is to make it possible for the dispatcher's goals to be met. The same policies that guide the choice of dispatching mechanisms can be applied to the selection of scheduling mechanisms.

In allocating storage, devices, and files to jobs waiting for a virtual processor, the scheduler can simply employ the FCFS or SJN mechanism. It can make use of an externally supplied scheduling priority, distinct from the dispatching priority to be used subsequently. The scheduling priority can be based on payment, or on factors such as the demand for unusual amounts of storage or for a resident compiler. Unless a mechanism such as FCFS is used, means must be provided to ensure that each job will eventually be selected. One approach is to increase a job's priority each time it is skipped over for scheduling (i.e., considered but not selected). Another is to impose a maximum on the number of times it may be skipped over. When the maximum is reached, that job is selected next, regardless of what other jobs are present. A third approach is to apply ageing, increasing the priority with the passage of time. The Lancaster University system [Colin, 1968] calculated scheduling priority as $(a/64)^2 - (16t + l)$, where a is the age in seconds, t the requested service time in seconds, and l the number of lines to be printed. Adjustments were then made to account for requests for and availability of main storage and magnetic tape drives. My local computer center calculates scheduling priority (in minutes) as $F(p) + a + b - G(t)$, where p is paid priority, a is age, b is a bonus for express jobs, and t is the requested service time. The functions F and G are shown in Fig. 3.3. The number by each segment of the line for $G(t)$ is the slope of that line segment. The parameters are chosen to make paid priority predominant. The amount charged, incidentally, is equal to the basic charge multiplied by p, except that the multiplier is $\frac{1}{2}$ if $p = 0$.

No matter how complex the calculation of scheduling priority, any scheduling mechanism that focuses only on the requesting jobs can cause substantial inefficiencies. There may be a low-priority job that needs a normally off-line storage volume that happens to be mounted, or that desires to share a reenterable program already loaded and in use. Clearly, optimization of use of that storage volume or program would call for the job to be selected earlier than its normal scheduling priority would otherwise dictate. Such optimization might or might not require the dispatcher to favor the process created for the job. Here we see a benefit of distinguishing scheduling and dispatching priorities.

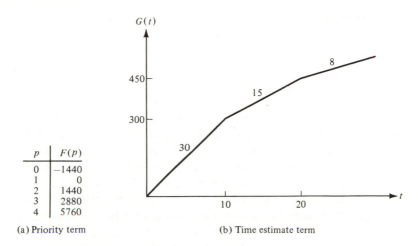

p	F(p)
0	−1440
1	0
2	1440
3	2880
4	5760

(a) Priority term (b) Time estimate term

Figure 3.3 Functions Used in Determining Scheduling Priority

Interactions between scheduler and dispatcher increase as we consider departures from the simple allocation model of Fig. 3.1. If the dispatcher maintains multiple ready queues that correspond to different classes of jobs, the scheduler assigns jobs to classes on the basis of user-supplied information. This function dates at least to the Atlas system. The scheduler and dispatcher may need to coordinate their actions if processes are to be swapped out. Because the scheduler allocates executable storage, it must either take cognizance of swapped-out processes or turn over a portion of its storage resources to the dispatcher for suballocation.

Substantial interaction is necessary if a batch job requests more than one process. Two major approaches are common. One is for the job to comprise a number of subjobs, each of which requests the creation of one process. The scheduler must keep track of the relation among the subjobs, and refrain from selecting one until it has been notified by the dispatcher that the predecessor subjob's process has terminated. The other approach is more general. It permits the original batch process, once in execution, to create child processes. Either the child process uses a suballocation of its parent's resources, or the scheduler must be invoked to obtain additional resources. In many systems, a running process can request new resources. In so doing, it blocks itself and waits for the scheduler to allocate them.

Schedulers can be made more and more complicated, to account for more and more of the many possible interrelations among resource requests and availabilities. This raises an important issue: whether to optimize the service to individual jobs or the utilization of individual resources. The underlying policy question is fundamental not only to processor management, but to the entire operating system.

3.5   INTERRUPTS

Operation of the dispatching mechanism requires communication among the running process, the I/O subsystem, and the dispatcher. Notification to the dispatcher that a time quantum has expired, or that an I/O action has been completed, is typically the result of an *interrupt.* Many other events cause interrupts, too, and the handling of interrupts is an important facet of instruction counter management. Consider a processor that is executing instructions in sequence within a program, except for conditional and unconditional branches in that program. An interrupt can be defined as a transfer of control that is *imposed* on the program, to an instruction in a program other than the one being executed at the time of the interrupt. Note that the definition excludes such transfers as subroutine calls issued by the program. It is fruitful to think of the interrupt as causing the interrupted process to jump to an interrupt process not known to the interrupted process.

Interrupts fall into two major classes. *External* interrupts are those caused by asynchronous events that occur externally to the interrupted processor. Interrupts caused by an interval timer and those generated by the I/O subsystem are examples. *Internal* interrupts are those caused by events internal to the processor and synchronous with its operation. Examples include the following. Arithmetic overflow during fixed-point addition or subtraction is ignored on some computers, but on others it generates an interrupt. Other arithmetic operations that can generate interrupts are attempted division by zero, and floating-point operations that cause overflow or underflow. Other instruction errors include attempts to access protected or nonexistent storage locations. Closely related are the segment fault and page fault interrupts mentioned in Chapter 2. The attempt to use an undefined operation code may cause an interrupt, as may operating on invalid data. An example of the latter is performing decimal arithmetic on a 4-bit subfield that does not represent a decimal digit.

In some systems, certain instructions are not intended for use by user programs, but only by the operating system. Different modes of operation are embodied in the hardware, and user programs are run in a mode in which certain instructions do not work. The mode-switching instruction is always one of them. An attempt to use an instruction prohibited in the mode then in effect causes an internal interrupt. Some systems provide a "prohibited" instruction whose purpose is to permit a user process to communicate with the operating system. Examples are the supervisor call (*SVC*) of the IBM 360-370 and the executive request (*ER*) of the Univac 1100. The detection of certain machine malfunctions, such as parity errors, can also lead to interrupts.

3.5.1 Basic Processing

The first question to be answered in the processing of interrupts is when to make the initial response. By responding immediately, without waiting for completion of the current instruction, a potentially long* wait for critical timing inputs can be avoided. The cost of immediate response is potential loss of the current operation. A more convenient time to respond is after completion of the current instruction, whose execution may be abridged if it is itself the source of the interrupt. The frequency of checking whether an interrupt has been generated can be reduced by responding only at fixed times. The timing of initial response to interrupts is determined by the design of the hardware's interrupt system; it is an external constraint on the design of the control programs that process interrupts.

Although there are some variations in the type of response made to interrupts, the following sequence is typical of many computers.

1. A description of the interrupt is stored, usually at a fixed location.

2. The state of the interrupted process is saved. This state includes at the very least the value of the instruction counter, and may include mode specification (e.g., user mode vs. privileged), register contents, or other information.

3. The instruction counter is set to a fixed address, which is often unique to the particular type of interrupt that has occurred.

4. The interrupt is processed.

5. Normal operation is resumed.

Steps 1 through 3 are usually implemented by the machine hardware and steps 4 and 5 by the operating system software.

The control program that processes interrupts is known as the *interrupt handler*. Its first task is usually to save whatever portion of the process state has not already been saved by the hardware. Some computers automatically save a considerable amount of information in a reserved area of main storage; others do not. It is possible, for example, that the hardware will save the instruction counter but depend upon the interrupt handler to save register contents. Next, the interrupt handler must identify the particular interrupt. Part of the information required is given by the identity of that portion of the interrupt handler to which the hardware transferred control in step 3. This may identify the interrupt, for example, as an I/O interrupt or as

---

*A storage-to-storage copy operation on a long character string can take more than a millisecond on some computers.

a supervisor call. In the former event the interrupt handler must interrogate I/O status bits set by the hardware during or before step 1; in the latter event it must examine the code that specifies which service is requested of the supervisor.

The interrupt handler must next take whatever actions are appropriate to the particular interrupt that has been identified. This may be as simple as setting a testable flag in the event of fixed-point overflow or as complex as initiating the repositioning and rereading of magnetic tape following a read error. It is true that error recovery functions such as tape rereading can be performed in some systems in the hardware of the device or its control unit, perhaps by microprocessor, but enough different activities remain for control program attention that interrupt handlers have not yet gone out of style. If the interrupt processing is not urgent, the interrupt handler may merely enqueue the appropriate processing program for eventual selection by the dispatcher.

Finally, the interrupt handler must provide for resumption of normal execution. Depending on the nature of the interrupt, and on the process dispatching mechanism in use, it may be desired either to return control to the interrupted process or to place that process on a blocked or ready queue and let the dispatcher select the next process. Return of control is accomplished by restoring the process state (including the instruction counter value), whether saved entirely by hardware or with software assistance.

Some aspects of interrupt handling must be performed immediately. These include saving the process state, at least partial identification of the type of interrupt, and such processing as recovery from program errors or initiating service to devices with critical timing needs. To avoid the delay due to loading the required portions of the interrupt handler from backing storage, they must be resident in executable storage as part of the operating system nucleus. If the total size of the interrupt handler makes it impractical to have all of it resident in executable storage, it can be separated into two components, a resident *first-level* interrupt handler and a nonresident *second-level* interrupt handler [to use IBM terminology]. It may be convenient for purposes of program organization to subdivide either component into separate interrupt handlers for different types of interrupts.

Many of the interrupts that pertain to processor management, such as timer signals or requests for and completions of I/O operations, result in control being transferred almost immediately to the dispatcher. Among the processes that the dispatcher may select for execution are not only the user processes in terms of which the earlier sections of this chapter are couched, but also various components of the operating system. These latter include second-level interrupt handlers, accounting routines, the scheduler, and other components, also the loader that brings these components in and relocates them, and in a sense even the dispatcher itself. With only one instruction counter available, the operating system too must often wait for service.

3.5.2 Multiple Interrupts

The foregoing description of interrupt processing has been considerably simplified by ignoring the possibility that an interrupt need not occur in isolation. Interrupts may occur simultaneously, or at least be discovered simultaneously by the hardware. Interrupts may also occur during the handling of other interrupts. How can the system cope with such multiple interrupts?

Of two or more simultaneously occurring interrupts, one must be chosen for response on the basis of priority assigned to the type of interrupt. Priority may be either built into the hardware, as in the IBM 360-370, or determined by software, as for the DEC PDP-10 and PDP-11. Thus a supervisor call might be given higher response priority than an I/O interrupt. Interrupts whose class has lower priority may be either *enabled* or *masked*. If an interrupt is enabled, it is capable of interrupting the processor and will typically do so immediately after the hardware's response to the first interrupt. In this event, lower response priority is translated into higher handling priority, as would be given to the I/O interrupt over the supervisor call in the example just cited. The effective stacking of interrupts causes a reversal of relative priorities. As a consequence it is important in considering interrupt priorities to know which type of priority is meant. A masked interrupt is not capable of interrupting the processor. It can either be kept *pending*, meaning that it is still known to the hardware, or else lost. If a masked interrupt is pending, a later unmasking or enabling action will permit it to be processed at a more convenient time.

If a new interrupt occurs while an old one is being processed, the new one will have been either enabled or masked by the interrupt handler, depending on the types of the two interrupts. If the new interrupt is enabled, it supersedes the old one, whose interrupt handler then assumes the role of interrupted process. If the new interrupt is masked, it may be either lost or kept pending. If pending, it may hang in abeyance until the control program is ready to attend to it. Alternatively, a timer interrupt, which for this purpose must be enabled, can signal the interrupt handler at a fixed time to look for pending interrupts that must be serviced before a critical interval has lapsed.

Whether interrupts of a particular type are to be enabled or masked during processing of other interrupts is a decision that may be effected by hardware, or it may be left to the interrupt handler. Either the hardware or the interrupt handler should mask further occurrences of interrupts of the *same* type. This is to avoid losing the interrupt description and process state of the first interrupt when the fixed locations are overwritten with the corresponding information for the second interrupt. Although the first-level interrupt handler must mask appropriate interrupt types if the hardware does not, the unmasking before resumption of normal operation can be left to the second-level handler.

The processing of multiple interrupts, if different priorities are distinguished, is facilitated by having the hardware associate with each priority different fixed locations for the interrupt description and process state. For a given priority, the control program will have to maintain information about multiple interrupts to avoid forcing each to wait until its predecessor has been processed. For example, I/O interrupts can often be processed in two stages, of which the second is the relatively unhurried execution of I/O instructions, such as disk seeks. Once the request to the I/O control portion of the operating system has been prepared, further I/O interrupts can usually be enabled, and several requests accumulated in the same manner. Such pending requests for interrupt handling are typically maintained in queues.

3.6   IMPLEMENTATION TECHNIQUES

The various mundane activities that must be performed in implementing scheduling and dispatching mechanisms threaten to increase system overhead markedly if they are not themselves performed in a disciplined manner. Process switching may occur even more frequently than every millisecond and if, at each switch, time is spent in extensive queue maintenance, priority calculation, and quantum revision, no time will be left to execute the users' processes.

A general principle used in implementing control programs is that frequently performed activities must take less time than infrequently performed activities. Viewed alternatively, time-consuming activities must be performed infrequently. Application of this principle to processor management leads to what is often known as *multilevel scheduling*, which should not be confused with the use of multiple queues. Multilevel scheduling is typically a separation of processor management functions into two or three levels. The lowest level, invoked the most frequently, includes at least dispatching, which can be as simple as giving control to the process at the head of the one ready queue. The highest level, invoked the least frequently, includes such activities as recomputation of quantum size or recalculation of priorities from I/O activity information. Intermediate between dispatching and these long-term activities is maintenance of the ready queues, into which a process is inserted perhaps every few milliseconds. A process's priority and other status may be recomputed upon insertion, but the implementation principle decrees that they not be recomputed while the process waits in a queue.

We have referred thus far to the job queue and ready queue as though they were really composed of jobs and processes. The cost of manipulating a data structure actually composed of jobs or of a physical embodiment of processes would of course be prohibitive. The queues in question are really lists of descriptors, which can be moved much more easily than the objects they describe. Moreover, it is possible to retain the lists in main storage for jobs or processes that are held in backing storage.

In round-robin dispatching, insertion is always at the tail of the ready queue, but under most other mechanisms the ready "queue" is not really a queue. In SJN and SRT, with or without ageing, and in deadline scheduling, the ready queue must be maintained in sequence on some priority. If the priority queue is maintained as a linear list of n entries, insertion of a new entry requires $O(n)$ operations. If the queue is maintained instead as the data structure known as a *heap*, insertion requires only $O(\log n)$ operations. The particular variety of heap that is most applicable is the so-called *tree of losers*. A reader unfamiliar with heaps or with the order notation need merely remember that there is a better way to organize a long priority queue than as a linear list.

If processor management is to depend on timing, some kind of timing device is required. Many computers provide a single *interval timer* that can be loaded with an arbitrary value and counts down to zero, whereupon it issues an interrupt. To make of one such timer a set of virtual timers for different purposes, a priority queue can be used. Each entry identifies the process that requires a signal and the time at which the signal is required. The queue is in increasing order of time. After each timer interrupt, the timer interval is set to the difference between the time specified for the interrupt that has just occurred and the time for the next one. Only one insertion requires special action. If the requested time to be inserted is earlier than that for which the timer is set, the timer must be reset.

Lists are used in managing not only the timer and the processes in the ready and blocked states, but also the jobs in the hands of the scheduler. The job queue to which we have referred is not necessarily unique. Multiple job queues can be maintained for different classes of jobs. This is particularly convenient if the dispatcher distinguishes among the same classes. Before selecting a job, the scheduler must have first placed all candidate jobs in the proper queue positions. If the scheduler is invoked only when a resource is freed, it must defer job selection until after it has enqueued those jobs that arrived since it was last invoked. An alternative to invoking the scheduler only when a resource is freed is to invoke it also when a job arrives. That job can then be enqueued and perhaps even selected if the needed resources are already available. Selecting a job involves straightforward actions. A process is created by entering its descriptor on the appropriate ready queue, and marking that descriptor as having certain storage, files, and devices allocated to it. In a virtual storage system, segment and/or page tables are initialized at this time.

As an example of list and timer techniques, we present here an implementation of type 1 service guarantees adapted from Habermann [1976]. The scheduler maintains two lists of classes of processes, those that have already received the service guaranteed during the current period on the *satis-*

fied list, and those that have not on the *unsatisfied* list. An entry on either list contains five fields: an identification of the class (perhaps in the form of a pointer to the head of the associated ready queue), the duration of each period, the amount of time guaranteed to the class during each period, the amount of time remaining to be provided to the class during the current period, and the current deadline (i.e., end of the current period). Figure 3.4 shows the pair of lists and the timer queue for a system that offers different guarantees, totaling 85%, to five classes of processes. Real-time processes are in the satellite and wind tunnel classes, interactive processes are in the graphics and APL classes, and batch jobs are in the remaining class. To simplify the illustration, the class lists and timer queue are shown as linear structures, although a heap implementation might well be chosen for the latter. Time intervals are in milliseconds, and all times are in milliseconds since a fixed origin. For ease of exposition, we shall omit the first few digits when referring to times.

Each list is in increasing order of deadline. Thus the unsatisfied class with the closest deadline is at the head of the unsatisfied list. The processor is allocated to processes in that class until either of two types of timer interrupt occurs. One type signals that the class's guarantee in the current period has been met, at which point the class becomes satisfied. The class is then removed from the unsatisfied list and inserted into the satisfied list. The other type of timer interrupt occurs when the class at the head of the satisfied list reaches its deadline, at which point the class becomes unsatisfied.

class	period	guarantee	remaining	deadline
satellite	20	1	0	79254500
wind tunnel	20	1	0	79254510

(a) Satisfied list

class	period	guarantee	remaining	deadline
graphics	100	15	5	79254510
APL	1000	400	80	79254600
batch	60000	12000	5318	79298430

(b) Unsatisfied list

time	class	event
79254498	graphics	guarantee
79254500	satellite	deadline
79254510	wind tunnel	deadline
79254510	graphics	deadline
79254600	APL	deadline
79298430	batch	deadline

(c) Timer queue

Figure 3.4 Implementation of Service Guarantees

The class is then removed from the satisfied list and inserted into the unsatisfied list with its deadline incremented by the length of its period. After either type of interrupt, execution resumes with the class standing at the head of the unsatisfied list after the interrupt.

In the example of Fig. 3.4, the current time is 495, and processes in the graphics class are running. They have been running since 493 and will receive their service guarantee at 498. At time 498 a timer interrupt signals fulfillment of that guarantee. The graphics class entry has its remaining time field changed from 5 to 0 milliseconds. It is removed from the unsatisfied list and inserted at the bottom of the satisfied list. The next class to receive service will be APL, which requires 80 more milliseconds this period. An entry is therefore inserted in the timer queue to request an interrupt at 578 to indicate completion of the APL service guarantee. The APL class receives only 2 milliseconds of service, however, before the next timer interrupt signals expiration of the deadline for the satellite class. The APL remaining time field is reduced from 80 to 78. The satellite class deadline is incremented from 500 to 520 and its service requirement is reset to 1. The satellite class entry is removed from the satisfied list and inserted at the top of the unsatisfied list. A timer queue entry is inserted to signal reaching the satellite deadline at 520. Because the highest-priority class is now satellite, another timer queue entry is inserted to signal attainment of the satellite service guarantee at 501. The timer queue entry for 578 is no longer applicable, and is deleted. Of course, each timer queue entry for which an interrupt occurs is deleted. Figure 3.5 summarizes both the changes described here and those that will take place at the next few timer interrupts.

| Running class | Interrupt | | | (1) | (2) | (3) | (4) | (5) | (6) |
	time	class	reason						
graphics	498	graphics	guarantee	0		S		578	
APL	500	satellite	deadline	78	1	U	520	501	578
satellite	501	satellite	guarantee	0		S		579	501
APL	510	wind tunnel	deadline	69	1	U	530	511	579
	510	graphics	deadline		15	U	610		
wind tunnel	511	wind tunnel	guarantee	0		S		580	511
APL	520	satellite	deadline	60	1	U	540	521	580

(1) New time remaining for class that was running
(2) New time remaining for nonrunning class that caused interrupt
(3) New list for class that caused interrupt
(4) New deadline, inserted into timer queue
(5) New guarantee time inserted into timer queue
(6) Old guarantee time deleted from timer queue

Figure 3.5 Trace of Service Guarantee Implementation

The unsatisfied list may become empty because the sum of the guaranteed fractions is less than unity or because all the processes in at least one class are blocked. In this event, the class at the head of the satisfied list can be moved immediately to the unsatisfied list, where it will begin to receive service in excess of the guaranteed minimum. It is also possible instead to run processes to which no guarantee has been given. Because of the occurrence of blocking, it may be possible to meet the guarantees most of the time even for guaranteed fractions whose sum exceeds unity. If such "guarantees" are used, however, it will be necessary to accept the possibility of failure to meet them during periods when few process classes are blocked.

How much of the processor management apparatus should itself be resident in executable storage? Those parts that are concerned only with the initiation and termination of processes certainly can be brought in when required. Those others that are used in managing the various stacks and queues are invoked so often that they must be resident in executable, and preferably in main, storage.

FOR FURTHER STUDY

Bull and Packham [1971, Chap. 2] present a good nonmathematical discussion of the issues in scheduling and dispatching. So does the article by Bunt [1976], which describes the mechanisms used in OS/360, M.I.T. Multics, and UNIX. The development by Habermann [1976, Chap. 6] makes moderate use of queuing theory and that by Muntz [1975], extensive use. An excellent theoretical treatment of operating systems, not limited to matters discussed in this chapter, is the book by Coffman and Denning [1973].

Scheduling is well covered by Colin [1971, Chap. 15] and by Lister [1975, Sec. 8.4]. Madnick and Donovan [1974, Sec. 4.1] present some interesting analyses. Among the more readable treatments of dispatching are a brief one by Shaw [1974, Sec. 7.5], a more extensive one by Tsichritzis and Bernstein [1974, Sec. 3.3], and a more mathematical one by Brinch Hansen [1973a, Chap. 6].

Interrupts are discussed by Watson [1970, Sec. 4.2], and the first-level interrupt handler by Lister [1975, Sec. 4.4].

Implementation issues are discussed in general by Tsichritzis and Bernstein [1974, Sec. 3.4] and by Habermann [1976, Sec. 6.5], who explains the use of a heap for implementing a priority queue. Brinch Hansen [1973a, Sec. 4.2] offers a detailed view of dispatcher implementation, and Bull and Packham [1971, Sec. 4.1] examine swapping and time slicing.

EXERCISES

3.1 [Tsichritzis and Bernstein, 1974] A page replacement algorithm maintains a list of pages of each of the five following types, stated in order of increasing priority.

(1) Accessed-only page from an inactive task.
(2) Written-into page from an inactive task.
(3) Control program page not accessed in previous half-second.
(4) Page from an active task in the blocked state.
(5) Page from an active task in the ready state.

The page to be replaced is selected from the nonempty list of lowest priority. Explain (**a**) the reasons that might underlie the foregoing policy and (**b**) how the policy could be implemented.

3.2 Is it possible for the run state to have no process in it? Explain.

3.3 Show that as the round-robin quantum q is increased without limit, the round-robin mechanism approaches FCFS.

3.4 Five processes, each requiring 10 time units, are placed on a ready queue at the same time. Calculate the wait for each process and the mean wait for the set of five processes under round-robin with quantum (**a**) 10 units and (**b**) 1 unit.

3.5 A variant of round-robin is to return a process that has received its full quantum to the tail of the queue, one that has received half its quantum to the middle of the queue, and so forth. What is the objective of such a mechanism?

3.6 Devise a single-queue variant of the round-robin mechanism that gives more service to processes of higher priority.

3.7 Under the class of single-queue dispatching mechanisms known as *linearly increasing priority*, the priority of each job is increased at the constant rate a while in the ready state and at the constant rate b while in the run state.

(**a**) Show that $a > 0$, $b \geqslant a$ yields FCFS.
(**b**) Show that $a > 0$, $b = 0$ with preemption yields round-robin.
(**c**) *Selfish round-robin* is defined by $a > b$ and $b > 0$, with preemption. Describe what happens to a process under this mechanism. What advantage is offered over FCFS, or over round-robin?

3.8 How can multiple priorities be provided without multiple queues?

3.9 What is the correspondence between process completion deadline and process start deadline?

3.10 What information about a job needs to be kept in the job descriptor?

3.11 What information about a process needs to be kept in the process descriptor?

3.12 What queue management is required for blocked processes?

3.13 Describe (in terms of the set of run, ready, and blocked states, and of transitions into and out of the set and among its states) the implementation and properties of a *non*preemptive SRT (shortest remaining time) dispatching mechanism. Cite its advantages and disadvantages as compared with more commonly used mechanisms.

3.14 Consider the job priority calculation in TENEX, described in the penultimate paragraph of Section 3.3.2. Specify what variable(s) are needed in the process descriptor and what other variable(s) must be maintained by the operating system. Write the algorithm associated with each of the following six transitions: select, dispatch, terminate, remove, block, and wakeup. State any required initializations. It is not necessary to show details of queue management.

3.15 A request to be inserted into a timer queue specifies an earlier time than that at which the timer is set to interrupt. Explain what information is used, and how, in resetting the timer.

3.16 Extend Fig. 3.5 to show actions through time 604.

Chapter 4

PROCESS MANAGEMENT

Chapters 2 and 3 have emphasized the management of resources for which both user jobs and control programs contend, particularly under multiprogramming. This chapter devotes less emphasis to those resources and more to the contending processes. Their interactions, whether planned by the programmers or not, need to be carefully managed both to avoid certain pitfalls and to simplify the users' programming burden. Section 4.1 sets forth the problems and requirements of interacting concurrent processes. Sections 4.2 to 4.4 are devoted to ways of ensuring the correct behavior of such processes, and present the chief primitive operations used therefor. Section 4.5 discusses higher-level constructs for the management of concurrency. Section 4.6 treats the important problem of deadlock, and Section 4.7 is concerned with mechanisms of process invocation.

4.1 CONCURRENCY

The literature on operating systems offers many explanations of *process*, from a formal definition couched in terms of the set of states of a computation to the informal notion of a process as an instance of execution of a program. Perhaps the most useful for our purposes is due to Shaw [1974], who defines a *sequential process* as "the activity resulting from the execution of a program with its data on a sequential processor". Thus the compilation of a source program on a conventional computer processor is a sequential process. If a reenterable compiler is being used to compile three source programs, working on a portion of each in turn before switching to another, then each compilation is a distinct process, although only one copy of the compiler program is being executed. An IBM "task" or Univac "activity" is a process.

Sequential processes whose executions are overlapped even in part are *concurrent*. Two concurrent processes may be either *disjoint* or *interacting* (not to be confused with "interactive"). Disjoint processes are those that operate on disjoint sets of variables. The result of execution of a process is independent of the progress of a process from which it is disjoint. There is no way the latter process can change the values of the variables that affect the outcome of the former. Interacting processes, on the other hand, share variables and it is easy to show that the progress of one can affect the result of another. "Variable", in this context, needs to be interpreted rather broadly, and may include data files in backing storage as well as the main storage location associated with a variable in a source-language program.

The interaction between two processes may be due either to sharing by *competing* processes or communication by *cooperating* processes. An example of the former might be an operating system's page fault handler and I/O supervisor. To a linked list of outstanding I/O requests, each appends a request for a particular disk read operation. An example of the latter is the familiar producer–consumer pair of programs. One such pair in an operating system is the resource use recorder and the billing program. The producer and consumer can, of course, be user processes. The producer might be validating transactions generated by an automatic banking terminal and the consumer performing bookkeeping for validated transactions. The producer writes records, which are read at approximately the same rate by the consumer. To accommodate fluctuations in the rates of production and consumption, the producer and consumer share a buffer that holds records after writing, but before reading.

The effect that one program has on another with which it is interacting is not always predictable or even reproducible. This is because the relative speeds of execution of two concurrent processes are not under the control of either process. Moreover, the rates of two interacting processes may be influenced by scheduling decisions concerning yet other processes with which neither interacts. Furthermore, the rate of one process is usually not even known to the other. All sorts of time-dependent errors can occur. Because it is often impossible to reproduce the exact conditions that prevailed when an error occurred, it can be extraordinarily difficult to correct it. Possibly even worse is the potential for apparently correct, but actually erroneous, operation.

Let us look at the effect of time dependency on each of two examples of interacting processes. Consider first the processes *PFH* and *IOS*, which are appending disk requests to a queue called *diskreq*. The queue, shown in Fig. 4.1(a), has both a head pointer to facilitate removal of requests and a tail pointer to facilitate insertions. The relevant portions of the programs for *PFH* and *IOS* are listed in Fig. 4.2. If the invocations and processing rates of *PFH* and *IOS* are such that their attentions to the pointer tail do not overlap in time, both insertions will be performed correctly. If they do overlap in time, they may still be performed correctly. Suppose, however, that after process *PFH* has executed its first assignment statement, process *IOS* executes its two assignment statements before *PFH* continues. The result,

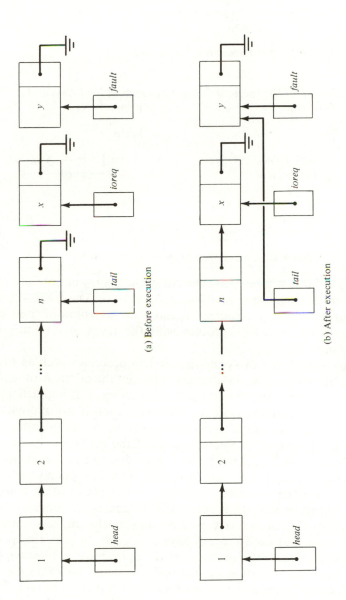

(a) Before execution

(b) After execution

Figure 4.1 Queue of I/O Requests

```
pointer tail
record (.. pointer link)
cobegin
      repeat  PFH(..,f,..)
      repeat  IOS(..,i,..)
coend
```

(a) Execution of processes

```
procedure PFH(..,fault,..)            procedure IOS(..,ioreq,..)
   pointer fault                         pointer ioreq
   ..                                    ..
begin                                 begin
   ..                                    ..
   tail↑.link ← A(fault)                 tail↑.link ← A(ioreq)
   tail ← fault                          tail ← ioreq
   ..                                    ..
end                                   end
```

(b) Definition of processes

Figure 4.2 Uncontrolled Access to Shared Variable

shown in Fig. 4.1(b), will be to append the request *ioreq* but not the request *fault*, and to set *tail* to point to *fault* instead of to *ioreq*. The foregoing pair of processes illustrates a *race condition*, because the outcome of their executions is determined by which process wins the races to set the pointers *tail↑.link* and *tail*.

It may be argued that two operating system processes such as *PFH* and *IOS* should be so written that neither can interrupt the other. Although such an approach may be feasible for one pair of processes, it is impractical to apply it to an entire operating system. Moreover, even if the approach were practical, high priority control programs would be forced to wait for low priority control programs, and performance of the operating system would be slowed down markedly. Furthermore, attention to the operating system alone ignores the possibility of race conditions in user programs.

A second example of a race is given by two processes that update different fields of payroll records. Process *ADDR* updates the address and process *SAL* updates the salary, each by first copying the entire record into a private work area. Let each process have an update to perform on record *Calingaert*. Suppose that after process *ADDR* copies record *Calingaert* into its work area, but before *ADDR* writes the updated record back into *Calingaert*, process *SAL* copies the original record *Calingaert* into its work area. The updating action performed by whichever of the two processes is the first to write the updated record back into *Calingaert* will be lost, and perhaps no one will be the wiser.

Both the queue management and the record updating suffered from race conditions due to undisciplined access to shared variables, the pointers in the first example and the payroll record in the second. To prevent incorrect execution of competing processes, what is required is a means of *mutual exclusion*, whereby it is guaranteed that not both processes access the shared variable simultaneously.

In the producer–consumer example mentioned earlier, a different problem arises. One danger is that the consumer will attempt to read from an empty buffer. If the buffer is considered empty because the consumer has already read all records produced, the consumer will reread a previously read record and overbill a user. If the buffer is really empty, the read operation will fail, and the consumer may need to be terminated. The complementary danger is that the producer will attempt to write into a full buffer. If the buffer is considered full because the producer has written more records than the consumer could read, the producer will overwrite an unread record and the consumer will underbill a user. If the buffer is really full, the write operation will fail, and the producer may need to be terminated.

The difficulty with producer–consumer pairs is not that both processes can access the buffer simultaneously (as long as they do not access the same record within the buffer). It is rather that their accesses proceed asynchronously, permitting excessive local variations in the rates of production and consumption. What is required is a means of interprocess *synchronization*.

Although an exchange of signals is sufficient to ensure synchronization, processes often need to exchange much more extensive data than merely timing signals. A compiler used interactively carries on a running dialog with each user process. Requests for I/O operations are often passed as messages from one process to another. Even the mail facility of UNIX [Ritchie and Thompson, 1974] and other interactive systems can be viewed as a form of data exchange among processes. For the foregoing activities, what is needed is interprocess *communication*.

Provision of mechanisms for mutual exclusion, synchronization, and communication make it possible for interacting concurrent processes to yield correct results independent of their execution speeds. To the extent that the mechanisms adopted can be embodied in the programming language, it is possible to provide compile-time checks for many of the errors we wish to avoid. Among the languages that have been designed for programming concurrent processes are Concurrent Pascal, Modula, and CSP/k.

Interrupts can serve as a mechanism for process cooperation, and are often so used, especially in controlling I/O. In many situations, however, it is not necessary that one process interrupt execution of the other. Instead, shared variables are more often used for cooperation, especially by the set of control programs in an operating system.

4.2 MUTUAL EXCLUSION

The reason why the queue management programs of Fig. 4.2 work incorrectly is that they may make interleaved accesses both to the pointer *tail* and to the element *tail* points to, both of which are shared between the two processes. In particular, the first or second assignment statement of either program must not be executed between the executions of the other program's first and second assignment statements. Clearly, something is special about the region of each program that comprises the two assignment statements. For correct operation the two processes must be mutually excluded from executing those regions concurrently. Dijkstra [1965] first proposed the concept of such *critical regions* (also "critical sections"). A critical region bears the requirement of mutual exclusion with respect to a particular variable.

Language constructs that associate critical regions with a shared variable can be used to simplify the writing of interacting concurrent programs. We declare such a variable with the attribute **shared**. In programming the critical region we refer to the shared variable explicitly. Our notation is adapted from Brinch Hansen [1972].

shared *variable*
region *variable* **do** statement

In Fig. 4.3 we rewrite the queue management programs with their critical regions identified. Technically, a critical region is not a sequence of pro-

```
shared pointer tail
record (.. pointer link)
cobegin
      repeat PFH(..,f,..)
      repeat IOS(..,i,..)
coend
```

(a) Execution of processes

```
procedure PFH(..,fault,..)          procedure IOS(..,ioreq,..)
   pointer fault                        pointer ioreq
   ..                                    ..
   begin                                begin
      ..                                    ..
      region tail do                      region tail do
         tail↑.link ← A(fault)              tail↑.link ← A(ioreq)
         tail ← fault                       tail ← ioreq
      ..                                    ..
   end                                  end
```

(b) Definition of processes

Figure 4.3 Critical Regions Implementing Mutual Exclusion

gram statements, but rather the sequence of actions that result from executing statements. Hence several processes that are instances of execution of the same program can all execute critical regions based on a single program region. The single program of Fig. 4.4 suffices for several processes to write into a data base with mutual exclusion. When a process has advanced to the statements that define a critical region, it is said to be *inside* the critical region, whether or not the process is currently running.

Three requirements are imposed on the critical regions associated with a given variable shared by several processes.

1. At most one process can be inside its critical region at one time.

2. No process can remain inside its critical region indefinitely.

3. No process can be compelled to wait indefinitely to enter its critical region. In particular, no process stopped indefinitely outside its critical region (a state that is permitted) can impede the progress of other processes waiting to enter.

It is possible for critical regions to be nested, as in

region *x* **do begin** .. **region** *y* **do** .. **end**

but careless nesting can lead to possible violation of requirement 2. If another process executes

region *y* **do begin** .. **region** *x* **do** .. **end**

each process can enter its outer critical region at about the same time and find itself excluded from ever entering its inner critical region. This problem is explored in Section 4.6.

Now that we have discussed the use of critical regions and noted the requirements they must meet, it is appropriate to consider how they can be implemented. Any implementation must ultimately rely on mutual exclusion provided by hardware. All computers offer a basic form of mutual exclusion called *storage interlock*. This prohibits the concurrent execution of two instructions that access the same main storage location. If that storage location holds the value of a shared variable, only one sharing process can

shared *database*

procedure *WRITER*
   begin
      ..
      region *database* **do write** into *database*
      ..
   end

Figure 4.4 Mutual Exclusion of Competing Writers

access that variable during a given instruction cycle. Storage interlock prevents simultaneous access but not *interleaved* access. Thus if the critical regions are short enough to be implemented using at most one instruction that requires main storage access, storage interlock can be used to implement critical regions directly.

If the critical regions require more than one storage access, they can still be implemented by the use of storage interlock. Flags, whose integrity is guaranteed by storage interlock, indicate which process is free to enter a critical region. As we shall see, the proper way to set and test these flags is far from evident.

The program of Fig. 4.5 shows a first attempt. Associated with each of processes *P1* and *P2* is a flag that has the value **true** when that process is in its critical region, and **false** otherwise. Before entering its critical region, process *P1* tests *inside2* to ensure that access is permitted, and then sets *inside1* to **true** to lock out process *P2*. The reason the program fails is that between the test of *inside2* by process *P1* and its subsequent setting of *inside1*, the concurrently executing process *P2*, finding *inside1* to have value **false**, can set *inside2* to **true** and enter the critical region simultaneously with process *P1*.

We can enforce mutual exclusion by postponing *P1*'s test of *inside2* until after it has locked out *P2* by setting *inside1* to **true**. The resulting program is shown in Fig. 4.6. Unfortunately, it too is deficient. It is possible for each process to set its flag to **true** and to enter an endless loop while the other's flag is **true**. This violates the requirement that no process wait indefinitely to enter a critical region.

```
boolean inside1, inside2
inside1 ← false  /* P1 is not in its critical region */
inside2 ← false  /* P2 is not in its critical region */
cobegin
    P1: begin
            ..
            while inside2 do begin end
            inside1 ← true
            critical region
            inside1 ← false
            ..
        end
    P2: begin
            ..
            while inside1 do begin end
            inside2 ← true
            critical region
            inside2 ← false
            ..
        end
coend
```

Figure 4.5 First Incorrect Implementation of Mutual Exclusion

```
boolean inside1, inside2
inside1 ⟵ false  /* P1 is not in its critical region */
inside2 ⟵ false  /* P2 is not in its critical region */
cobegin
    P1: begin
            ..
            inside1 ⟵ true
            while inside2 do begin end
            critical region
            inside1 ⟵ false
            ..
        end
    P2: begin
            ..
            inside2 ⟵ true
            while inside1 do begin end
            critical region
            inside2 ⟵ false
            ..
        end
coend
```

Figure 4.6 Second Incorrect Implementation of Mutual Exclusion

A correct implementation of critical regions, using only storage inter-lock, is surprisingly difficult to write. The earliest solution was proposed by Th. J. Dekker. His and more recent solutions are complex and inefficient enough, especially when generalized from two to n processes, that other approaches are advisable.

An alternative to associating a flag with each process is to associate a single flag with the set of critical regions. This flag can be thought of as a key. Initially, access to the critical regions is unlocked. Before entering, however, a process picks up the key and locks other processes out. Upon leaving its critical region, the process unlocks the access by replacing the key. If a process that desires to enter its critical region finds the key missing, it waits until the process that holds the key returns it. Thus each entering process must first test whether the key is available and, if so, then make it unavailable to other processes. The two actions cannot be separated, lest two or more processes find the key available before any of them can pick it up. The hardware mechanism of storage interlock guarantees the integrity of each individual storage access, but not that of a pair of distinct accesses.

The second hardware mechanism for mutual exclusion plugs the gap between the testing of a flag (or key) and the setting of a flag. It is the indivisible instruction *test-and-set* (*TS*), introduced by IBM for multiprocessing System/360 computers. In a single read–write storage cycle, it copies a bit from storage to the condition code and writes a fixed value into the byte of storage that includes the copied bit. For our purposes, we can think of *TS* as a function procedure that has one boolean parameter (the storage bit) and returns a boolean value (to the condition code). Thus $TS(x)$ delivers the value of x and sets x to **false**. No activity, such as testing x by another process, can intervene between the two halves of the TS instruction. To use TS we associate with the critical region a boolean flag s, which is **true** if no process is in the critical region. Each of n competing processes Pi has a local variable *permission* which is **true** if Pi has permission to enter its critical region.

A concurrent program for the n processes is given in Fig. 4.7. Before entering its critical region, process Pi tests the flag s by executing the TS instruction. If no other process is in its critical region, s is **true** and *permission* becomes **true**, allowing Pi to proceed. After Pi leaves its critical region it resets s to **true**, enabling another process (or even a subsequent iteration of Pi) to enter. If, on the other hand, some process Pk is in its critical region, s is **false**, and process Pi waits in a testing loop until Pk resets s to **true**. Whether s was **false** or not before the test, the value **false** set into s indicates that the corresponding critical region is no longer enterable, either because it was originally not enterable or because Pi has just entered it.

The hardware mechanisms of storage interlock and test-and-set can be used to satisfy the requirements on critical regions, albeit not without difficulty. For example, if one of the processes using the program of Fig. 4.7 is particularly sluggish, it may never get around to testing the flag s before some faster process has entered its critical region, setting s to **false**. This "starvation" can be avoided by the use of multiple flags. If there are more than two processes, the solution is rather complex.

Even if the processes are reasonably well behaved, there are serious drawbacks in using either of the two mechanisms. The implementation of critical regions by proper reliance on storage interlock or by use of test-and-set provides mutual exclusion at the cost of forcing excluded processes to remain in resource-consuming, but unproductive, wait loops. This is known

```
boolean s
s ←— true  /* no process is in its critical region */
cobegin
    ..
    Pi: boolean permission
        ..
        begin
            ..
            repeat permission ←— TS(s)  /* makes s false */
            until permission = true     /* after Pk made s true */
            critical region
            s ←— true
            ..
        end
    ..
coend
```

Figure 4.7 Mutual Exclusion Using Test-and-Set

as the *busy* form of waiting. Not only does busy waiting consume the processor resource unproductively, but it may in fact tie up the very resource needed by the process that is being waited for. Moreover, the responsibility for testing whether a critical region can be entered is abandoned to the competing processes, whereas it is more safely assigned to the operating system.

To overcome the difficulties of storage-based control of concurrency, Dijkstra invented two operations, called *P* and *V* for reasons to be revealed later. These operations access a variable shared by the concurrent processes and known as a *semaphore*, the name given to the device used to control occupancy of sections of railroad track by competing trains. In the simplest formulation the semaphore can assume two values. Representation of its value by a binary 1 or 0, rather than **true** or **false**, makes it more natural to associate the higher value 1 with a *raised* semaphore, which permits a train to pass, and the lower value 0 with a *lowered* semaphore, which blocks a train from passing. The association leads to the customary designation of this type of semaphore as *binary*.

With each semaphore *s* is associated a *list* (not necessarily a queue) of processes waiting to pass the semaphore. The operating system can perform three operations on processes. It can dispatch a ready process. It can block a running process, and place it in the list associated with a particular semaphore. It can wake up a blocked process, thus placing it in the ready state and permitting it eventually to resume execution. We have already seen these operations depicted in Fig. 3.1. While in a blocked list, a waiting process does not continually inspect the semaphore, as in the busy form of waiting. Instead, another process can perform useful work on the processor that has been released by blocking the waiting process.

The operations *P* and *V* are executed by the operating system in response to calls issued by some process and naming a semaphore as parameter. The effect of executing *P* and *V* is the following.

$P(s)$: **if** $s=1$
        then $s \leftarrow 0$ /* lower semaphore */
        else *BLOCK* calling process on *s*
             DISPATCH a ready process

$V(s)$: **if** the list of processes waiting on *s* is nonempty
        then *WAKE UP* a process waiting on *s*
        else $s \leftarrow 1$ /* raise semaphore */

It is not specified which of several waiting processes will be selected for wakeup. In proving the correctness of programs that use the *P* and *V* operations, it is necessary to demonstrate that the programs work correctly under arbitrary choice of process waked up. Once this is done, the details of the selection process no longer affect the programming of concurrent processes.

Figure 4.8 shows a sequence of 14 states of 6 processes invoking *P* and *V* operations on semaphore *s*. Initially, none of the processes is in its critical

	Action		Resulting Status		
	invoking process	operation invoked	running in c. r.	blocked on s	value of s
1					1
2	A	$P(s)$	A		0
3	A	$V(s)$			1
4	B	$P(s)$	B		0
5	C	$P(s)$	B	C	0
6	D	$P(s)$	B	C,D	0
7	E	$P(s)$	B	C,D,E	0
8	B	$V(s)$	D	C,E	0
9	F	$P(s)$	D	C,E,F	0
10	D	$V(s)$		C,F	0
11	none of $A,..,F$		E	C,F	0
12	E	$V(s)$	F	C	0
13	F	$V(s)$	C		0
14	C	$V(s)$			1

Figure 4.8 Effect of P and V Operations

region (abbreviated c. r. in the figure) and the semaphore is raised. The second state results from process A invoking $P(s)$. It lowers the semaphore and passes into its critical region. Although the sequence of states is straightforward, two of them deserve especial notice. State 8 is introduced by a V operation when processes C, D, and E, in that order, have been blocked waiting on s. The process selected for wakeup need not be the one that has waited longest; here D is waked up and immediately dispatched. The V operation that introduces state 10 wakes up process E, but E is not immediately dispatched. Instead, it remains in the ready state until some event not connected with processes A through F allows it to be dispatched. It is also possible for a V operation to wake up process X, then a second V operation to wake up process Y, but for process Y to be dispatched before X.

The queue management processes and the competing writer processes can be implemented using P and V as shown in Figs. 4.9 and 4.10. Each pair of processes enforces mutual exclusion of the critical regions bu use of a binary semaphore called *mutex*. Although the choice of *mutex* as the identifier is traditional in this application, its use is not mandatory. The semaphore *mutex* is initialized to 1. In the first pair of processes, assume that *PFH* is the first to invoke P. Then the operating system lowers the semaphore *mutex* and *PFH* proceeds into its critical region. If *IOS* invokes P while *PFH* is in its critical region, the operating system blocks *IOS* and causes it to wait on *mutex*. When *PFH* leaves its critical region, it invokes V and the operating system wakes up a process waiting on *mutex*. If *IOS* is the only such process, it then becomes ready to run. A similar analysis applies to the second pair of processes.

```
semaphore mutex
record (.. pointer link)
mutex ⟵ 1
cobegin
    repeat PFH(..,f,..)
    repeat IOS(..,i,..)
coend
```

(a) Execution of processes

```
procedure PFH(..,fault,..)          procedure IOS(..,ioreq,..)
    pointer fault                       pointer ioreq
..                                  ..
begin                               begin
    ..                                  ..
    P(mutex)                            P(mutex)
    tail↑.link ⟵ A(fault)              tail↑.link ⟵ A(ioreq)
    tail ⟵ fault                       tail ⟵ ioreq
    V(mutex)                            V(mutex)
    ..                                  ..
end                                 end
```

(b) Definition of processes

Figure 4.9 Queue Management with Semaphore

```
global database
semaphore mutex
mutex ⟵ 1

procedure WRITER
    begin
        ..
        P(mutex)
        write into database
        V(mutex)
        ..
    end
```

Figure 4.10 Competing Writers with Semaphore

```
semaphore s
s ← 1
cobegin
    ..
    Pi: begin
            ..
            P(s)
            critical region
            V(s)
            ..
        end
    ..
coend
```

Figure 4.11 Generalized Mutual Exclusion Using *P* and *V*

Mutual exclusion among *n* arbitrary processes is illustrated in Fig. 4.11. Comparison of that program with the one of Fig. 4.7 shows that the flag that is tested by the *TS* instruction can be viewed as a binary semaphore, with **true** equated to 1. Test-and-set, because of the busy wait, is clearly inferior to *P* and *V* as a mechanism for using the semaphore.

4.3 SYNCHRONIZATION

For processes to cooperate it is not sufficient that they mutually exclude each other from shared variables; information must be transmitted. The least unit of information that it is helpful to transmit is a simple timing signal. The basic requirement is that one process be enabled to wait until another process signals the occurrence of a particular event. The first process awaits the occurrence of the desired event by invoking *AWAIT(event)*; the second signals the occurrence by invoking *SIGNAL(event)*. Before considering implementations of *AWAIT* and *SIGNAL*, let us see how they can be used to synchronize two processes.

As a first example, consider a simple pair of processes, a producer and a consumer. The former produces records one at a time and the latter consumes them one at a time. A one-record buffer is available to hold records that have been produced but not consumed. The processes must therefore be synchronized in such a manner that between each pair of productions of a record there is interleaved exactly one consumption, and vice versa. The synchronization primitives *AWAIT* and *SIGNAL* are used by the programs of Fig. 4.12 to guarantee the interleaving. The producer writes the first record and signals the event *start* before the consumer is free to proceed beyond its wait for that event. Similarly, the consumer reads the *i*th record and signals the event *finish* before the producer is free to proceed beyond its wait for finish and write the $(i + 1)$st record. Mutual exclusion of the accesses to the buffer does not need to be stated explicitly, because in this case the synchronization guarantees mutual exclusion.

```
global buffer
event start, finish
cobegin
    repeat PRODUCER
    repeat CONSUMER
coend
```

(a) Execution of processes

```
procedure PRODUCER                          procedure CONSUMER
    local record                                local record
    begin                                       begin
        write record into buffer                    AWAIT (start)
        SIGNAL(start)                               read record from buffer
        AWAIT (finish)                              SIGNAL(finish)
    end                                         end
```

(b) Definition of processes

Figure 4.12 Single-Buffer Producer–Consumer
with Event Synchronization

The foregoing synchronization can be implemented by using a binary semaphore for each event, a P operation for $AWAIT$, and a V operation for $SIGNAL$. The programs are given in Fig. 4.13. A somewhat different version is presented in Fig. 4.14. There the distinction between producing and writing a record is shown explicitly, as is that between reading and consuming. The synchronization is restricted to the reading and writing proper. Note that in this version the required initialization of *finish* is 1 rather than 0.

```
global buffer
semaphore start, finish
start   ←  0
finish  ←  0
cobegin
    repeat PRODUCER
    repeat CONSUMER
coend
```

(a) Execution of processes

```
procedure PRODUCER                          procedure CONSUMER
    local record                                local record
    begin                                       begin
        write record into buffer                    P (start)
        V (start)                                   read record from buffer
        P (finish)                                  V (finish)
    end                                         end
```

(b) Definition of processes

Figure 4.13 Single-Buffer Producer–Consumer
with Binary Semaphores

```
global buffer
semaphore start, finish
start   ⟵ 0
finish  ⟵ 1
cobegin
    repeat PRODUCER
    repeat CONSUMER
coend
```

(a) Execution of processes

```
procedure PRODUCER              procedure CONSUMER
    local record                    local record
begin                           begin
    produce record                  P(start)
    P(finish)                       read record from buffer
    write record into buffer        V(finish)
    V(start)                        consume record
end                             end
```

(b) Definition of processes

Figure 4.14 Alternative Single-Buffer Producer–Consumer

In our second example, the producer and consumer share a larger buffer, which is managed as an unbounded queue. Whenever the producer has prepared a record, it appends it to the tail of the queue. Whenever the consumer is ready to use a record, it severs the first one from the head of the queue. The synchronization problem is to ensure that the consumer never attempts to remove a record from an empty queue. It is clearly advisable to keep track of the number of records in the queue. A first attempt is shown in the program of Fig. 4.15, where *number* (initially 0) is the instantaneous

```
queue buffer
event number
number ⟵ 0
cobegin
    repeat PRODUCER
    repeat CONSUMER
coend
```

(a) Execution of processes

```
procedure PRODUCER              procedure CONSUMER
    local record                    local record
begin                           begin
    produce record                  AWAIT(0 < number)
    APPEND(record, buffer)          number ⟵ number − 1
    number ⟵ number + 1             DETACH(record, buffer)
    SIGNAL(number)                  consume record
end                             end
```

(b) Definition of processes

Figure 4.15 Incomplete Queue-Buffer Producer–Consumer

number of records enqueued in the buffer. Only one event is used rather than two, because there is no need to restrain the producer from appending a record to the unbounded queue. This first attempt fails, unfortunately, for two reasons. A fairly evident defect is that the shared variable *number* must be protected against simultaneous access. Another is that the lack of restraint on the producer now permits both processes to access the queue pointers simultaneously, with potentially disastrous results (see Exercise 4.8). The necessary mutual exclusions are embodied in the revised program of Fig. 4.16, where it is assumed that *AWAIT* and *SIGNAL* are critical regions with respect to *number*. All manipulation of *number* is performed in these critical regions.

These more complex forms of *AWAIT* and *SIGNAL* can be implemented by the use of *P* and *V* operations generalized to operate on a *counting* semaphore, which can assume any nonnegative integer value. Definitions of the generalized *P* and *V* follow.*

$$P(s): \textbf{ if } s > 0$$
$$\textbf{then } s \leftarrow s - 1$$
$$\textbf{else } BLOCK \text{ calling process on } s$$
$$DISPATCH \text{ a ready process}$$
$$V(s): \textbf{ if } \text{ the list of processes waiting on } s \text{ is nonempty}$$
$$\textbf{then } WAKE\ UP \text{ a process waiting on } s$$
$$\textbf{else } s \leftarrow s + 1$$

With counting semaphores and the *P* and *V* operations defined in this manner, the initial value of a semaphore is the number of times an attempting process can pass the semaphore (in the absence of *V* operations on it) before the semaphore is lowered to 0, blocking further processes from passing. By using *number* as a counting semaphore, we can write the program of Fig. 4.17 as an implementation of the queue-buffer producer–consumer. The semaphore *mutex* can equally well be considered a binary semaphore or a counting semaphore; the definitions are consistent.

Closely related to the queue-buffer version is our third example, the bounded-buffer version of the producer–consumer pair. The total buffer space, whether implemented as a queue or otherwise, is now limited to *n* records. It becomes necessary to prevent not only reading from an empty buffer but also writing into a full buffer. Two counting semaphores are used, *empty* to indicate the number of empty record positions in the buffer and *full* to indicate the number of full positions. The program is given in Fig. 4.18.

Consider now an alternative pair of definitions of *P* and *V*.

$$P(s): \ s \leftarrow s - 1$$
$$\textbf{if } s < 0 \textbf{ then } BLOCK \text{ calling process on } s$$
$$DISPATCH \text{ a ready process}$$
$$V(s): \ s \leftarrow s + 1$$
$$\textbf{if } s \leqslant 0 \textbf{ then } WAKE\ UP \text{ a process waiting on } s$$

*This form of *P* and *V* helps to explain the source of the names of the two operations, the Dutch *proberen* (to test) and *verhogen* (to increment).

```
queue  buffer
event  number
semaphore  mutex
number ← 0
mutex  ← 1
cobegin
    repeat PRODUCER
    repeat CONSUMER
coend
```

(a) Execution of processes

```
procedure PRODUCER              procedure CONSUMER
    local record                    local record
begin                           begin
    produce record                  AWAIT(0 < number ← number − 1)
    P (mutex)                       P (mutex)
    APPEND(record, buffer)          DETACH(record, buffer)
    V (mutex)                       V (mutex)
    SIGNAL(number ← number + 1)     consume record
end                             end
```

(b) Definition of processes

Figure 4.16 Queue-Buffer Producer–Consumer
with Event Synchronization

```
queue  buffer
semaphore  mutex, number
mutex  ← 1
number ← 0
cobegin
    repeat PRODUCER
    repeat CONSUMER
coend
```

(a) Execution of processes

```
procedure PRODUCER              procedure CONSUMER
    local record                    local record
begin                           begin
    produce record                  P (number)
    P (mutex)                       P (mutex)
    APPEND(record, buffer)          DETACH(record, buffer)
    V (mutex)                       V (mutex)
    V (number)                      consume record
end                             end
```

(b) Definition of processes

Figure 4.17 Queue-Buffer Producer–Consumer
with Counting Semaphores

```
            global  buffer
            semaphore  empty, full, mutex
            empty  ←  n
            full   ←  0
            mutex  ←  1
            cobegin
                  repeat  PRODUCER
                  repeat  CONSUMER
            coend
```

(a) Execution of processes

```
procedure PRODUCER                procedure CONSUMER
    local record                      local record
    begin                             begin
        produce record                   P (full)
        P (empty)                        P (mutex)
        P (mutex)                        read record from buffer
        write record into buffer         V (mutex)
        V (mutex)                        V (empty)
        V (full)                         consume record
    end                               end
```

(b) Definition of processes

Figure 4.18 Bounded-Buffer Producer–Consumer with Counting Semaphores

Under this pair of definitions, counting semaphores can now also assume negative values, which have the following useful interpretation. If s is negative, then $-s$ is the number of processes waiting on s. This second formulation of counting semaphores can be shown to be fully equivalent to the first.

An important and interesting synchronization challenge arises in the well-known *readers* and *writers* problem. There are two classes of processes accessing a resource. Processes in the first class must have exclusive access to the resource. Processes in the second class may share access concurrently with any number of other processes in the same class. An example might be an airline reservation system. Processes in the first class write into a flight record, as in booking seats. Processes in the second class read from the flight record, as in determining seat availability, issuing a list of passengers, or checking the schedule. The solution to the readers and writers problem proposed by Courtois, Heymans, and Parnas [1971] is given in Fig. 4.19. The shared resource is accessed by passing semaphore w. If the resource is not in use, the first process to arrive will execute $P(w)$, entering its critical region and lowering the semaphore. If that process is a reader, the variable *readcount* will be incremented, and subsequent readers will access the resource without having to test w. The last reader to leave the critical region is the only one to execute $V(w)$, raising the semaphore. To ensure that only one reader or writer enters at a time, the semaphore *mutex* protects both *readcount* and the readers' invocations of $P(w)$ and $V(w)$.

```
integer readcount
semaphore mutex, w
readcount  ← 0
mutex      ← 1
w ← 1
cobegin
   repeat READER
   ..
   repeat READER
   repeat WRITER
   ..
   repeat WRITER
coend
```

(a) Execution of processes

procedure *READER*   procedure *WRITER*
   begin   begin
     $P(mutex)$
     $readcount \leftarrow readcount + 1$
     if $readcount = 1$ then $P(w)$ $P(w)$
     $V(mutex)$
     read   write
     $P(mutex)$
     $readcount \leftarrow readcount - 1$
     if $readcount = 0$ then $V(w)$ $V(w)$
     $V(mutex)$
  end   end

(b) Definition of processes

Figure 4.19 Readers and Writers

If a writer is inside its critical region, at most one reader can be blocked on w, but any number of other readers can be blocked on *mutex*. Other writers are blocked on w. When the writer invokes $V(w)$, it is not specified whether it is the waiting reader or a waiting writer that will pass the semaphore w. To guarantee that readers obtain the latest information, it might be desired to give priority to a waiting writer over a waiting reader. This could be accomplished by specifying a particular discipline for managing the list of waiting processes. Because a discipline useful for one synchronization problem may be inappropriate to another problem, this approach would require the provision of many different forms of P and V. Two disadvantages would result. One is the increase in complexity of the operating system. The other is the increased burden on the programmer, who would be required to understand a large number of synchronizing primitives, select the appropriate ones, and verify that they have been used correctly. A preferable approach is to make fuller use of the P and V primitives, using such techniques as requiring a process to pass one semaphore before being permitted to test a second semaphore. Arbitrary synchronization problems can, in fact, be solved by the use of P and V with counting semaphores.

The executions of $P(s)$ and $V(s)$, which both access the same semaphore, must themselves be implemented as critical regions, lest a V operation intervene between the test of the semaphore and the blocking of a process. Each must be executed indivisibly and only one concurrent process can cause either to be executed at one time. Thus the arbitrary critical region of the users is implemented by means of a pair of simpler, system-provided critical regions. The two members of the pair are coded only once, and are incorporated in the nucleus of the operating system, where they make use of critical regions at progressively lower levels, terminating at the indivisibility of storage operations.

If, as we have assumed, there is only one processor, each of P and V is implemented as a critical region by the simple expedient of disabling interrupts. The semaphore s can be implemented as a two-field record. One field is the integer value of s. The other is a pointer to the list of processes blocked on s. Figure 4.20 shows an implementation of P and V for counting semaphores that may assume negative values.

The T.H.E. system [Dijkstra, 1968] includes implementations of P and V at the lowest level of a hierarchical structure. The Venus system implements P and V in a specially modified microprogram and manages each blocked list as a priority queue. PRIMOS V provides semaphores to signal such events as end of time slice, completion of disk read, and receipt of character from terminal. For each semaphore it uses one word in main storage for the count and one to point to the head of an associated wait list. Each wait list, like the ready list, is a linked list of descriptors in priority order with FIFO used to break ties.

```
procedure P (s)
    record s (integer count; pointer ptr)
    process p
    begin
        disable interrupts
        s.count ← s.count − 1
        if s.count < 0 then insert calling process on s.ptr↑
                            p ← some ready process
                            DISPATCH p with interrupts enabled
                       else enable interrupts
    end
procedure V (s)
    record s (integer count; pointer ptr)
    process p
    begin
        disable interrupts
        s.count ← s.count + 1
        if s.count ⩽ 0 then p ← remove some process from s.ptr ↑
                            WAKE UP p
        enable interrupts
    end
```

Figure 4.20 Uniprocessor Implementation of P and V

Several operating systems, among them OS/360 and TOPS-20, provide mutually exclusive access to resources through the use of the operations *ENQ* (enqueue) to request a resource, and *DEQ* (dequeue) to release it. In its simplest form *ENQ* results in allocation of the resource if it is free, and in blocking the requesting process on a queue for that resource otherwise. *DEQ* causes the resource to be granted to the process at the head of the list, or to be freed if the list is empty. Variations allow for requesting multiple resources simultaneously, for requesting shared access, and for withdrawing the request if the resources are not immediately available.

Some operating systems provide synchronization on events by means of *AWAIT* and *SIGNAL* operations. Those of OS/360 and Honeywell's GCOS6 are called *WAIT* and *POST*. In their simplest form they use one bit as an event variable and permit only one process to wait for a given event.

Many operating systems provide shared access control specifically for files. TOPS-20, for example, offers four choices: *n* readers but no writer; one writer but no reader; one writer and *n* readers; and *n* readers and *n* writers.

4.4 COMMUNICATION

Our discussion of interprocess cooperation has concentrated thus far on the exchange of timing signals. Closer cooperation requires a mechanism for *communication*, the sending and receiving of arbitrary data. Examples include output data directed to a line printer, commands (e.g., roll process out, seek on disk), requests for status (particularly of I/O devices), and even mail from one interactive user to another. In the context of interprocess communication, all of these are referred to as *messages*. On a uniprocessor system, the sending and receiving processes cannot be running simultaneously. On a multiprocessor system there is usually no guarantee that they will be. Consequently, a place is needed to hold a message after it has been sent, but before it has been received. That place is known formally as a *message buffer* or informally as a *mailbox*. If the data to be communicated are extensive, it is more efficient not to transmit them directly, but rather to put in the mailbox a message informing the receiving process where they can be found.

A mailbox may be dedicated to a pair of processes, or to the sender alone or receiver alone. Alternatively, it may be acquired from a pool of mailboxes that serve many or all processes. If the mailbox is not dedicated, the message must include identification of both the sending and receiving processes. A mailbox dedicated to a receiving process facilitates the sending of messages from many different processes to a fixed destination, usually a busy control program such as the I/O controller. A two-way mailbox permits messages to be acknowledged. If a mailbox pool is used, each mailbox holds either a message or an acknowledgement. To prevent the blockage of acknowledgements by all mailboxes being full, the protocol can be imposed whereby the acknowledgement of a message is placed in the mailbox used for that message, and the mailbox is not used for another message until its acknowledgement is received. Communication can still be halted by processes that fail to retrieve their messages. If messages are time stamped, a control program can periodically delete old messages. Processes can also be stopped by the failure of other processes to send the messages being awaited. If the time of each stopped process's entry to its blocked queue is recorded, a control program can periodically send dummy messages to those that have been waiting too long.

For bilateral transmission of streams of messages that are independent of each other, rather than one containing only acknowledgements or replies, two separate one-way mailboxes can be used. Facilities can be provided for delivery of messages to destinations whose identity is unknown to the sending process. Such a destination might be the process that has issued a seek command to a disk drive, whose response is independent of the identity of the seeking process.

For one-way communication between two processes, the producer–consumer pair already studied suffices. By and large, arbitrary communication can be viewed as requiring the combination of a shared variable (the mailbox) with synchronization of senders and receivers. The techniques for mutual exclusion and for synchronization can be applied in a straightforward manner to arbitrary communication.

Implementation of mailboxes requires the use of low-level primitives such as P and V, but these can be concealed from the user in favor of higher-level mechanisms, much as a programming language shields the programmer from concern about machine-language instructions. The RC 4000 system [Brinch Hansen, 1969, 1970] controls concurrency by means of a pool of 8-word message buffers, a true FIFO message queue for each process, and the following set of four primitive operations, which are executed in uninterruptable mode.

1. *SEND MESSAGE* (*receiver,message,buffer*)

2. *WAIT MESSAGE* (*sender,message,buffer*)

3. *SEND ANSWER* (*result,answer,buffer*)

4. *WAIT ANSWER* (*result,answer,buffer*)

SEND MESSAGE copies *message* into a pool buffer, returns its address in *buffer*, and appends the buffer to the queue of *receiver*. The calling process continues.

WAIT MESSAGE blocks the calling process until a message arrives in its queue. When the process is dispatched, it receives the name *sender*, the contents *message*, and the address *buffer*. The buffer is then removed from the queue and made available to hold the caller's answer.

SEND ANSWER copies *answer* into a *buffer* in which a message has been received and appends the buffer to the queue of the original sender. That sender is waked up if it is waiting for the answer. The calling process continues.

WAIT ANSWER blocks the calling process until an answer arrives in *buffer*. After arrival, and dispatch of the caller, it copies *answer* into the process and releases the buffer. The *result* indicates whether the answer is a dummy provided by the system because the original message was addressed to a nonexistent process.

The foregoing operations require a process to serve its queue in FIFO order and to block itself while other processes are handling its own requests. To remove these restrictions, two further operations are provided.

  5. *WAIT EVENT* (*last buffer,next buffer,result*)

  6. *GET EVENT* (*buffer*)

WAIT EVENT blocks the calling process until an event (either a message or an answer) arrives in its queue after *last buffer*. After the process is dispatched, the address of the buffer in which it arrived is returned in *next buffer*, and *result* reports whether the event is a message or an answer.

GET EVENT removes *buffer* from the queue of the calling process. If it contained a message, it is made ready for the answer. If it contained an answer, it is released to the pool. The calling process must explicitly copy the message or answer before the call.

The RC 4000 system uses the foregoing operations for all interprocess communication, including the special cases of synchronization and mutual exclusion. The chief advantages claimed for message buffers include the following.

  1. A process need not be aware of the existence of other processes until it receives messages from them.

  2. Two processes can exchange more than one message at a time.

  3. The operating system can ensure that no process can interfere with a conversation between other processes.

  4. The queuing of buffers permits a sending process to continue without waiting for the receiver.

The chief disadvantage of message buffering is the introduction of yet another resource to be managed, the pool of buffers.

A very attractive form of one-way mailbox is the *pipe* provided by UNIX. This is a nameless buffer for data produced by one process and consumed by another. The user needs to specify only the processes and their sequence. For example, the command ls invokes a process to list on the terminal the names of all files in the user's directory. The command grep acpt invokes a process that selects from its input those lines that contain the string "acpt". The command wc −l invokes a process that yields the number of lines in its input. The use of a pipe is indicated by "|", as in

ls | grep acpt | wc −l

which displays the number of files, in the user's directory, whose names include the string "acpt". The user need have no concern for synchronization and buffering, which are provided by the system.

4.5 CONVENIENCE

The various mechanisms we have described thus far are adequate to ensure the correct execution of concurrent processes. Using them, however, is rather like writing assembler language code with load, add, and conditional jump instructions. How much more convenient it is to write in a programming language with assignment statements, expressions, and program structuring mechanisms. Higher-level operations for process concurrency are also more convenient for the user, and are expected to play an increasingly important role in programming systems. Implementations of these operations require the use of lower-level primitives, such as P and V. Although the definition and use of such operations is properly a matter of programming language design, a brief look here at two of them is nevertheless appropriate.

The mechanisms presented thus far are designed to delay a process until a *particular* condition has been satisfied. Critical regions cause delay until a shared resource is released; semaphores, until a timing signal is received; mailboxes, until a message is available. The *conditional critical region* is a program construct that provides to the programmer a means for synchronizing a process with the attainment of an *arbitrary* condition.

This condition is associated with the shared variable of the critical region. Upon entering the conditional critical region, a process first tests the shared variable to see whether the associated condition is satisfied. If so, it proceeds. If not, it waits in an *event queue* associated with the critical region. Whenever a process leaves the critical region it is possible that it has changed the shared variable associated with the condition. At that time, therefore, all the processes in the event queue are returned to the normal ready queue from which they may reenter the critical region and once again test the condition. Thus the ability to use arbitrary conditions for synchronization is obtained at the cost of a controlled amount of testing by the interacting processes. The busy form of wait is still avoided.

Condition variables are often more powerful than semaphores, because a semaphore can only count occurrences of a specific event. For each event (e.g., record written, record received) that contributes to a synchronizing condition, a separate semaphore is required, although a single variable may suffice if conditional critical regions are used. Moreover, to a reader of the program, that variable can be much more perspicuous than the relations inherent among several semaphores.

Alternative to the conditional critical region is another higher-level construct, the *monitor* (or "secretary"). This use of the word "monitor" is highly specific, and should not be confused with its more general use in expressions such as "job monitor". In concurrent programming, the monitor is a dormant collection of shared variables and of reenterable procedures for accessing them. A process that desires access to the shared variables must call the monitor, which either grants or refuses access. To grant access, the monitor executes the procedure appropriate to the call, which may have parameters. In refusing access, the monitor blocks the calling process and specifies the condition upon which the process is waiting. The test of the condition, which is internal to the monitor, is not performed by the calling process itself, as for conditional critical regions. Instead, the monitor performs the test and executes *WAKE UP* to unblock a waiting process.

A simple example adapted from Hoare [1974] is presented in Fig. 4.21. A single resource is dynamically acquired and released by processes that call the procedures *ACQUIRE* and *RELEASE*. If a process calls *ACQUIRE* while the resource is in use, the value of *busy* will be **true** and *ACQUIRE* will perform the monitor operation *WAIT(nonbusy)*. That operation blocks not the monitor procedure *ACQUIRE*, but rather the calling process. That process is then appended to the end of a queue of processes waiting for the condition *nonbusy* to be signaled. When a process that is using the resource calls *RELEASE*, the monitor operation *SIGNAL* wakes up the process at the head

```
monitor resource
condition nonbusy
boolean busy
begin
    busy ← false
    procedure ACQUIRE
        begin
            if busy then WAIT(nonbusy)
            busy ← true
        end
    procedure RELEASE
        begin
            busy ← false
            SIGNAL(nonbusy)
        end
end
```

Figure 4.21 Monitor for Allocating a Single Resource

of the queue without permitting an intervening call of a procedure within the same monitor. That process then becomes ready to resume execution of *AC-QUIRE* from after the *WAIT* operation. If *SIGNAL* is executed when no process is waiting for the condition, it has no effect.

An important constraint is that at most one process at a time is permitted to execute any of the monitor's procedures. The shared resource is accessible only through the monitor. Consequently, the monitor replaces the critical region as an implementation of mutual exclusion. The monitor is dormant in the sense that it is not a process; its procedures are executed only upon the demand of a process. The monitor can also be viewed as having a protective shell that encloses a critical resource and the means of accessing it. If several procedures share a variable in the same manner by the use of semaphores, each requires its own copy of the same critical region. If a monitor is used instead, a single copy, enclosed within the monitor, suffices.

4.6 DEADLOCK

An important consequence of concurrency is the possibility of situations arising in which two or more processes are permanently blocked. The simplest case is that in which each of two processes is waiting for a resource held by the other. Because it is waiting, neither process can progress to where it can release the resource claimed by the other. This impasse has been colorfully described by the term "deadly embrace", and is more conventionally known as *deadlock*. Although deadlock can be the result of a programming error, more often it is not. Usually the deadlocked processes are intended to be disjoint, but are in fact competing for operating system resources.

Whether deadlock will in fact occur depends upon the generally irreproducible relative speeds of the processes. Consider, for example, three processes contending for a resource that is available in discrete interchangeable units, such as tape drives, page frames, or buffers from a pool. Let there be 10 such units in all, of which 8 have been allocated as follows. Process A has 2 units, and will need a total of 9 to finish. Process B has 2, and will need 7. Process C has 4, and will need 6. Processes B and C have reached the point where each requests two more units. If C's request is honored first, the process can proceed to completion, eventually releasing all 6 units held. This will permit B and then A to obtain their total allocations and finish. If, on the other hand, B's request is honored first, none of the processes will be able to terminate, and deadlock will ensue. The cause of this deadlock is the undisciplined attempts of the processes to access the critical region associated with the allocation of units of the resource.

To examine the causes of deadlock more thoroughly, we present in detail an example adapted from Coffman, Elphick, and Shoshani [1971]. For simplicity, we focus our attention on only two processes, *PROC1* and

PROC2. They share two resources, *r1* and *r2*. Mutual exclusion of accesses to the resources is enforced by the semaphores *s1* for resource *r1* and *s2* for *r2*. The two processes access the two resources as in the programs of Fig. 4.22. Other detail has been suppressed, and statement numbers have been supplied. Both semaphores have been initialized to 1. Instead of $P(s1)$ and $V(s2)$ one might write *ACQUIRE r1* and *RELEASE r2*. A planar representation of the space of possible computations is given in Fig. 4.23. The horizontal axis represents progress in the execution of *PROC1*; the vertical axis, of *PROC2*. The vertical lines numbered 1 through 4 correspond to statements 1 through 4 in the program executed by process *PROC1*. A position on the horizontal axis between lines 1 and 2 represents progress in the execution of *PROC1* beyond statement 1 but before statement 2. Similarly, the horizontal lines numbered 5 through 8 correspond to statements 5 through 8 in the program executed by process *PROC2*.

The instantaneous status of a computation is represented by a point in the plane. Thus point *W* corresponds to a situation in which process *PROC1* has begun but not yet reached statement 1, and process *PROC2* has passed statement 6 but not reached statement 7. As execution progresses, the point moves horizontally to the right while *PROC1* is executing and vertically upward while *PROC2* is executing, and stands still while neither is executing. Thus the course of each possible computation (with respect to *PROC1* and *PROC2* only) is represented by a piecewise linear *trajectory* of horizontal and vertical line segments. Trajectory *A* represents a computation in which the time sequence of resource requests and releases is defined by statements 5, 6, 7, 8, 1, 2, 3, 4.

Execution intervals during which resources *r1* and *r2* are in use are shown for each process by means of brackets. Thus resource *r1* is in use by process *PROC2* after the process has passed the semaphore at statement 6 (not merely executed the statement) and remains in use until after *PROC2* has executed statement 7, calling *V* to release *r1*. The lines 1 through 8, which demarcate the execution intervals, also subdivide the plane of the computation into 25 rectangles, each of which represents a *state* of the computation. The shaded states are inaccessible because of mutual exclusion.

*PROC*1: ..	*PROC*2: ..
1. $P(s1)$	5. $P(s2)$
..	..
2. $P(s2)$	6. $P(s1)$
..	..
3. $V(s1)$	7. $V(s1)$
..	..
4. $V(s2)$	8. $V(s2)$
..	..

Figure 4.22 Programs Leading to Deadlock

Two states are inaccessible because *PROC1* and *PROC2* are mutually excluded from accessing resource *r1*. Six states, including one of those two, are inaccessible because of mutual exclusion in accessing resource *r2*.

The time sequence of statement executions 1, 2, 5, 3, 4, 6, 7, 8 leads to a trajectory such as *B*. When *PROC2* requests *r2* (statement 5), the resource is unavailable. Although statement 5 is executed, the semaphore is down. Process *PROC2* is therefore blocked at the point *X* in Fig. 4.23, from which *PROC1* continues to execute. Once *PROC1* reaches statement 4, *PROC2* is waked up. If, however, the sequence 5, 1, 6, 2 is executed, process *PROC2* becomes blocked at point *Y* on trajectory *C* when statement 6 is executed, and *PROC1* becomes blocked on executing statement 2 at point *Z*. Both processes are now deadlocked, *PROC1* waiting for *PROC2* to reach statement 8 and *PROC2* waiting for *PROC1* to reach statement 3. Indeed, deadlock was inevitable once the computation entered rectangle *U*, an *unsafe* state.

The cost of deadlock is great. Neither *PROC1* nor *PROC2* can finish execution. Moreover, *all* resources held by either, including at least *r1* and *r2*, are permanently unavailable, thus reducing the capacity of the system to serve other processes.

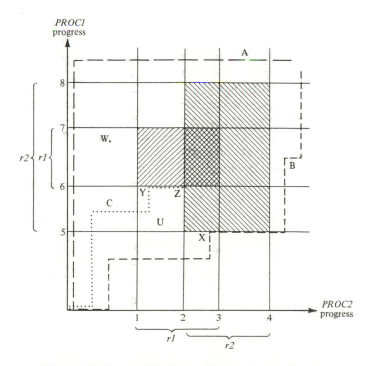

Figure 4.23 Computation States, Trajectories, and Deadlock

4.6.1 Conditions

For deadlock to occur, four conditions must hold simultaneously. One is the *mutual exclusion* condition, under which processes exercise exclusive access to resources. A second is the *wait for* condition. A process that has requested a resource will wait for the request to be met, continuing to hold all the other resources it has acquired. A third condition is that of *no preemption*. No resource can be preempted from a process that has acquired it but not released it. The fourth is the *circular wait* condition. There exists a circular chain of processes each of which is waiting for a resource held by its predecessor in the chain. For the simple example of trajectory C it is easily verified that the four conditions hold when point Z is reached.

One of three fundamental policies can be selected to cope with the problem of deadlock. The policy of *prevention* is based upon a judgement that deadlock is so costly that it is best to spend extra system resources to preclude the possibility of deadlock arising under any circumstances. The policy of *avoidance* is to ensure that deadlock, although it is in principle not impossible, will not occur for the particular set of processes and requests being run at the moment. The policy of *detection* and subsequent recovery is based on the judgement that deadlock occurs infrequently enough that it would cost more to prevent or avoid it than to test for its occurrence and effect recovery when it is found. Prevention can be thought of as prohibiting the existence of unsafe states, avoidance as prohibiting entry into unsafe states, and recovery as prohibiting permanent residence in unsafe states. We review in turn mechanisms for implementing each of the three policies.

4.6.2 Prevention

A mechanism to enforce prevention need merely ensure that some one of the four conditions necessary for deadlock cannot arise. The *mutual exclusion* condition is suppressed by permitting unrestricted sharing of resources. Although this is quite convenient for such resources as reenterable code segments or the use of a disk drive to access different data sets, it is wholly untenable for shared variables in critical regions or for a reel of magnetic tape.

The *wait for* condition can be suppressed by *preallocation*. A process must request all of its resources initially and cannot proceed until all resources have been allocated. Consequently, the total resources required by the concurrent processes cannot exceed the capacity of the system. Although preallocation is often used (as in OS/360), it entails a substantial cost in the inefficiency of resource utilization. Each process must wait until all of its resources are available, even one not needed until late in its execution. The resources allocated may not all even be used by the process if it requests resources needed only in exceptional circumstances. The resources that are not used until late in execution are denied to other processes, causing them to wait. Another disadvantage is the difficulty of formulating resource requests for a process whose requirements cannot be predicted before execution starts.

The *no preemption* condition is suppressed by allowing the operating system to take resources away from a process. This is practical if the state of the process can be easily saved for later restoration. Preemption of a processor is relatively easy, and commonly performed for the purposes discussed in Chapter 3. Preemption of a true I/O device or a magnetic tape drive can be extraordinarily unpleasant. For readily preemptable resources, the cost of preemption is chiefly the time required. Two different disciplines may be applied. One is to require a job that requests more of a resource to divest itself first of whatever amount of that resource it already holds. Although this may often help, it is not a total suppression of the no preemption condition. To see this, just consider $r1$ and $r2$ in the example to be unrelated resources. The other discipline, total suppression, takes away *all* resources from a job that becomes blocked by requesting any further resource.

The *circular wait* condition can be suppressed by preventing the formation of a circle. This is accomplished by *hierarchic* allocation. Resources are grouped into a hierarchy of levels. Once a process has acquired resources at one level, it can request further resources only at a higher level. It can release resources at a given level only after releasing all resources acquired at every higher level. After a process has acquired and subsequently released resources at a given level, it can again request resources at that same level. Preallocation can be viewed as a special case of hierarchic allocation that has but one level. Hierarchic allocation is a bit more costly to perform than preallocation, but it can reduce the waste associated with full preallocation. The reduction may not materialize, however, if the order in which a process needs resources is different from that in which the levels are ordered. If a plotter is needed early in execution and a tape drive only toward the end, but the tape drive is at a lower level than the plotter, the tape drive will have to be allocated early and remain idle until needed.

4.6.3 Avoidance

If none of the four conditions is suppressed, entry to an unsafe state can still be forbidden if the system has knowledge of the sequence of requests associated with each of the concurrent processes. It can be proved that if the computation is in any safe state, there exists at least one sequence of states that a trajectory can follow therefrom without ever entering an unsafe state. Consequently, it is sufficient to test whether a requested resource allocation will immediately admit a computation to an unsafe state. If so, the request is denied. If not, it can be granted. The test whether a state is safe or not requires a search over sequences of future process actions. Methods have been devised to perform these searches rather efficiently. The foregoing approach is an example of *controlled* allocation.

It is often the case that the sequence of requests associated with each process is not known in advance. If, however, the total demand for resources of each type is known in advance, it is still possible to control the allocation to avoid unsafe states. What is done is to determine for each request whether there exists, within the total demands of all processes, any subsequent sequence of requests that can lead to an unsafe state given the total amount of resource available.

The classical solution to this problem is known as the *banker's algorithm*. In brief, it works as follows. A banker lends funds, all in one currency, to a number of clients, each of whom has told the banker in advance the maximum amount he will need to borrow. A client may choose to borrow this amount a portion at a time, and there is no guarantee that he will make any repayment before having taken out the maximum loan. The banker's total reserve is usually smaller than the sum of the clients' demands, because the banker does not expect all the clients to request maximum loans simultaneously. If, at a given moment, some client requests funds, can the banker lend them without incurring the risk of not having enough left to make the further loans that will permit the clients eventually to repay?

To answer this question, the banker assumes that he has honored the request and asks: "Is there a way out?" The banker identifies the client whose current loan is closest to his limit. If the banker cannot lend the difference to that client, the banker denies the original request. If, on the other hand, the banker can indeed lend the difference to that client, the banker assumes eventual full repayment and turns his attention to the client, among those now remaining, whose loan is closest to his limit. Continuing in this manner through all the customers, the banker discovers whether at every stage he will have enough funds to permit the least demanding client to finish. Only if this is so does the banker honor the original request. For "banker", "client", and "funds" read "operating system", "process", and "resource" and we have the application to computer systems.

If, as is usually the case, more than one resource type is involved, our analogy must be to an international banker who lends in several different currencies. It is insufficient to apply the one-currency algorithm to each currency separately. It is necessary instead to test the different currency reserves jointly. The required algorithm is more complex. For p processes and r resource types a straightforward approach requires computation time proportional to rp^2. Solutions in linear time (i.e., proportional to rp) have also been developed, but they require the storage of more information than does the slower algorithm. A major cost of deadlock avoidance by controlled allocation is nevertheless the time required to execute the avoidance algorithm, because it must be invoked for every request. Moreover, the avoidance algorithm runs particularly slowly when the system is near deadlock. Despite the calculations, poor use of resources can result because the analysis assumes the worst case at each step. The effect of a deadlock avoidance policy on scheduling can be substantial. A stream of small-resource jobs can postpone indefinitely the selection of a large-resource job. Avoidance is not even applicable, of course, in the absence of information concerning the processes' resource requests.

4.6.4 Detection

At the price of a different computation, but again a costly one, it can be ascertained whether there exists a set of deadlocked processes. To perform this computation, the operating system must maintain a list of what resource each blocked process is waiting for and a list of what process holds each unavailable resource. An algorithm to detect circular chains can be executed with whatever frequency is deemed appropriate. This may be as often as each time a resource request is denied, or as infrequently as once an hour. The complexities of requiring the control program to prevent, avoid, or detect deadlock can all be obviated by relying on the system operator to detect deadlock. If the occurrence of deadlock is as rare as a few times per year, this may well be the wisest choice. It is true, of course, that deadlock may escape the operator's notice for some time, especially if some processes continue to execute. The cost in process delay and reduced system capacity may nevertheless be worth the price. Many operating systems rely on a policy of detection, and count on the operator to do the detecting.

Once deadlock has been detected, *recovery* must be effected. This will necessarily involve restarting one or more processes. A deadlocked process is blocked at some point in its execution. It must be restored to a condition from which it can resume execution. For most processes this is possible only from the beginning, and some hurdles may need to be surmounted even then. If the process has made an occasional record of its state, a *snapshot* of its execution, in order to permit resumption from a specific point, a *checkpoint*, it is possible to resume without repeating all of the computation prior to the preemption. Checkpoints are not normally provided for the purpose of assisting in recovery from deadlock. They are often provided, however, to facilitate recovery from error, particularly in long production jobs and in real-time systems.

The simplest recovery method is to terminate all processes, and restart the operating system afresh. A less drastic method is to terminate all deadlocked processes, whose users will eventually reintroduce them. A third method is to terminate deadlocked processes one at a time, invoking the detection algorithm (or operator) after each termination, until the deadlock has been dissolved. A fourth method, applicable if checkpoints have been provided, is to restart the deadlocked processes from checkpoints and hope that the deadlock will not recur.

Whereas the foregoing methods decrease resource demand by the deadlocked processes, a fifth method increases resource availability. It preempts resources from one or more processes, which may or may not be among the deadlocked set. The resources are assigned to one of the remaining deadlocked processes, and it resumes execution. A sixth method is applicable in theory if, when deadlock is detected, there exist some user processes that are not deadlocked. If those processes are allowed to run to completion, with the creation of new processes inhibited, they may release enough resources to break the deadlock. This situation may, in fact, occur unnoticed in some systems.

The cost of the detection policy depends upon how often, if at all, a detection algorithm is executed. The principal cost of recovery from deadlock is the loss of time, which can be substantial.

4.7 INVOCATION OF COOPERATING PROCESSES

Concurrent processes may be either competing or cooperating. Cooperating processes may be either concurrent or sequential. Our attention in this chapter has been focused thus far on problems of concurrency, and it is now appropriate to examine some other aspects of cooperation. A brief survey of the ways in which cooperating processes are invoked will be followed by a closer study of the most mundane of them, but perhaps the most common, the subroutine call. Rather than restrict our attention to the process, which is a unit of processor allocation, we concentrate instead on a smaller unit that can be invoked without risking loss of allocation of the processor. This unit is the program *module*, which can be thought of informally as a segment of program code. An instance of execution of a program module is normally represented at execution time by an *activation record*. This contains, among other information, storage for local variables, a pointer to the program code being executed, and the value of the instruction counter in that code.

4.7.1 Modes of Module Invocation

A program module can be activated in at least six ways, almost each of which is associated with a different type of module. The simplest module is the BEGIN *block* of PL/I. Execution begins when the instructions in the block (after translation) are encountered by normal progression from earlier instructions. Execution terminates when normal progression leads to an instruction outside the block. A major purpose of the BEGIN block is to provide nesting in the static text of the program, thus delimiting the scope of source language names. Even more important is the deferral of storage allocation for AUTOMATIC variables. For these purposes, a separate activation record is required. It is created upon entry to the BEGIN block, stacked above the activation record of the enclosing block, and deleted upon exit from the BEGIN block.

A widely used type of module is the *subroutine*, with which all but the greenest of computer programmers are familiar. Associated with the subroutine, or *called procedure*, is a *calling block* to which it is subordinated in an asymmetric relation of dependence. Execution begins upon specific naming of the called procedure by the calling block and, upon termination, control is returned to the caller. An activation record for the called procedure is created upon invocation, stacked above that for the calling block, and destroyed upon termination. For intermodule communication, parameters can be passed from the calling to the called module. The mechanisms for invoking a subroutine, passing parameters, and returning control are referred to collectively as *subroutine linkage*. Issues in subroutine linkage are treated in Section 4.7.2.

The *interrupt function module* is also invoked asymmetrically, either explicitly or, more commonly, in response to the occurrence of some stated condition during execution of the calling block. The archetypal example is the ON unit of PL/I, activated by the SIGNAL statement or by detection of the status associated with an ON condition. There are no parameters. The principal problem in programming with interrupt function modules is the opacity of programs that incorporate them. There can also arise substantial problems in translating programs that incorporate interrupt function modules.

Unlike the subroutine, which is subordinate to its caller, the *coroutine* is a module coordinate with other modules. Whereas a subroutine *call* creates an activation record for the subroutine, and return of control from the subroutine to its caller destroys the activation record, a coroutine *resume* neither creates nor destroys an activation record. Execution of the coroutine is merely resumed from wherever it last left off, rather than from a fixed entry or reentry point. Its activation record must therefore store the current restart point. Coroutine invocation is thus seen to be symmetric. Figure 4.24 contrasts the coroutine invocation pattern with that of the subroutine.

Creation of a coroutine activation record is caused by an initial invocation distinct from the resume. This initial call may be termed an *allocate* because it allocates an activation record. Deletion of the coroutine activation record may occur either automatically upon the coroutine executing its last instruction or explicitly as the result of a *free* command in another module, typically the one that caused the activation record to be created.

Parameters can be passed to a coroutine, just as they can to a subroutine, but at a choice of times. The values of actual parameters can be passed in the allocate call, or else in the first resume that follows allocation. It may even be possible to pass parameters with each resume.

The original illustration of coroutines [Conway, 1963] is a program for printing characters read from cards, with the substitution of the single character "↑" for each occurrence of the character pair "**", which represents

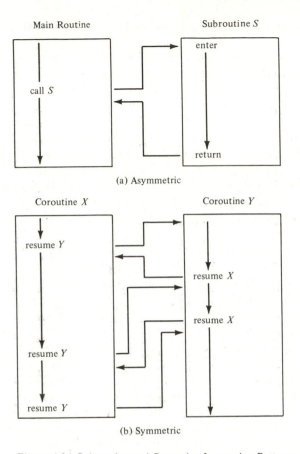

(a) Asymmetric

(b) Symmetric

Figure 4.24 Subroutine and Coroutine Invocation Patterns

exponentiation. An "asterisk squasher" coroutine interacts with a coroutine that provides the next input character. Another application is in searching a tree of unbounded depth. A coroutine can search within one subtree and, if unsuccessful after a certain time, resume a coroutine to search in a disjoint subtree.

Coroutines can sometimes be substituted for a multipass algorithm. UNIX pipes provide a good example. Figure 4.25(a) depicts an algorithm that makes three successive passes over a sequential file. In the coroutine implementation, Fig. 4.25(b), coroutine A resumes coroutine B when pass 1 would have written a record to the first intermediate file; coroutine B resumes A when pass 2 would have read a record and resumes C when pass 2 would have written a record to the second intermediate file; coroutine C resumes B when pass 3 would have read a record. The one-pass coroutine algorithm saves the time needed to pack, write, read, and unpack the intermediate data records. It requires enough space, however, to hold all the programs at once. Some algorithms, of course, are essentially multipass and

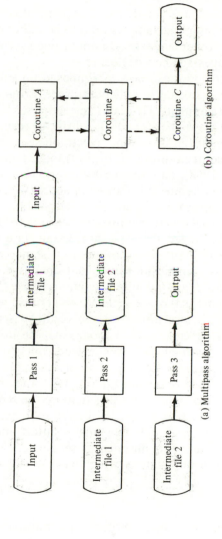

(a) Multipass algorithm

(b) Coroutine algorithm

Figure 4.25 Alternative Algorithms

115

cannot conveniently be replaced by coroutines.

Coroutines provide synchronization among *interleaved* cooperating processes. The processes may appear to be concurrent, but are not, because only one is in execution at a time. Coroutines do provide, however, for the efficient simulation of concurrent processes and are so used in the language SIMULA, where the coroutines are known as *classes* or *activities*. Simple examples in which coroutines are clearly more efficient than subroutines are difficult to produce; meaningful examples tend to be rather complex. This is perhaps one reason why other languages do not provide coroutines, and why the use of coroutines appears to be a neglected art.

A fifth mode of activation can be superimposed on subroutines or coroutines. Each module is treated as a distinct process. Instead of issuing a call, return, or resume command, it issues instead a *scheduling* command. This is a request to the dispatcher for a call, return, or resume to be issued. Use of this control program to determine execution sequence can result in greater efficiency of resource utilization. In this mode, processes have been called *events* [Wegner, 1968], and scheduling information for each process whose execution has been requested is an *event notice*. Whenever execution of one module ceases, control is passed to the dispatcher, which examines the event notices and selects one module for execution. The search over all event notices can be traded for extra processing time earlier to insert each event notice into an *event queue*, ordered on some criterion, such as simulated time, or a dispatching priority. Event queues provide for global supervision of the scheduling of module activation. These "event queues", of course, are not the same as those associated with critical regions.

Events are executed consecutively as the result of scheduled invocations. Unscheduled sequencing, a sixth mode, may be used instead when multiple processors are available to provide true concurrency rather than only interleaving. A module can invoke another module to be executed in parallel with the instruction sequence that follows the invocation, often termed an *attach* or *fork* invocation. In this situation, the sequence of execution of the different modules is unspecified once each has been invoked, whereas for coroutines it is specified by the resumes and for scheduled processes by the dispatcher. This absence of sequence specification raises important problems of synchronization, which have already been discussed.

4.7.2 Subroutine Linkage

When one module calls or resumes another, it communicates information by means of parameters and preserves enough status information to permit its own resumption. This activity is termed *linkage*, and must not be confused with the "linkage" performed by the linker in binding intermodule symbolic references. The linkage with which we are concerned here is performed at execution time, by executing instructions that have been prepared by the translator. Although linkage applies to coroutines as well as to sub-routines, the ensuing description is couched in terms of subroutines. The changes required for coroutines are for the most part straightforward.

The four most common ways to transmit and receive parameters are the following. A *common data area* for parameters can be shared by both calling and called routines. The use of storage that is global to the two routines requires that both use the same names or addresses, which are external references, to access the parameters. The advantage of using such global variables for communication is simplicity. Disadvantages are the need to know external names, the time to translate external references, and, in some systems, particularly those with explicit-base addressing, restrictions on addressability.

Processor *registers*, if available in the machine, provide another locus for parameters. This, too, permits simple communication as long as the registers are not needed for other purposes. Disadvantages are that several registers are likely to be needed for frequently used values such as increments and limits, for the return address, and perhaps for base-register addressing. The consequence may be fewer available registers than parameters to be passed.

All parameters for one call can be grouped into a *parameter area* in storage, and its starting address passed to the called routine. This has the advantages of keeping the registers free and of being easy to implement. The need to pass an address is at worst a minor disadvantage, and the use of a parameter area is often attractive.

A *shared stack* of parameters works as follows. The calling routine transmits the parameters by pushing them onto the stack. The called routine receives the parameters by popping them from the stack. Prior to returning control, it can push them back on if necessary. Subroutines nested dynamically at multiple levels can share a single stack. Advantages of the shared stack are that it can consume less storage space than separate parameter areas and that it is convenient for recursive calls. A major disadvantage is the need to provide either an implicitly addressed stack mechanism in the hardware or else software stack manipulation with a fixed address. A concomitant of the latter is the extra execution time required.

Whatever method is used to communicate parameters, it is usually also necessary, for all but the simplest routines, to save the calling routine's program status when a subroutine is called and to restore it upon return from the subroutine. A program's status information includes (1) its register contents; (2) its instruction counter setting, condition bits, timer request, and interrupt status; (3) its regions of main storage and, if paging or segmentation is used, the associated tables and backing storage; (4) logically associated operating system storage, such as job and process queue entries; and (5) outstanding I/O requests and the positions of noncyclic I/O devices and volumes.

Fortunately, when subroutine calls are issued, the vast majority of this information is not in danger of loss. Usually, only the register contents need be saved and a return address passed. To save the required information, two things are required: an owner of space to hold the information and an agent to perform the storing and restoring. The two possibilities for each are the calling and called routines. If the agent is the caller, the save–restore code for *each call* must be written in the caller. Alternatively, a single copy of that code, which is invoked as needed, can be used. Of course, that one copy then becomes another subroutine, although a very limited one. If the agent is the called routine, the save–restore code must be incorporated there, but often one copy will suffice. The most that will be required is one copy of the save code per entry point and one of the restore code per return point.

If the storage area is owned by the routine that is not the agent for storing and restoring, the agent needs to learn the storage area's location. Suppose first that the called routine owns the space and the caller is the agent. The storage space could be provided by convention at a fixed distance from the beginning of the called routine. More flexible would be to put there a pointer to the storage area. Then if multiple entry points are used, multiple storage areas would be obviated by provision of a pointer at the same fixed offset relative to each entry point. Suppose, on the other hand, that the caller owns the space and the called routine is the agent. The caller can pass the storage area location to the called routine in the same manner as the parameters. Because only one call by a given routine can be outstanding at a time, a separate storage area is not needed for each call in the calling routine. If the routine is recursive, one storage area is needed per activation.

Each programming system has a subroutine linkage convention that is not only adopted for use among components of the operating system, but also imposed on the users, because of the interactions between their programs and the operating system. If the linkage convention is complex, the operating system provides as a service the execution of the required sequence of instructions. A user who prepares both the calling and called routines is free, of course, to adopt his own linkage convention.

FOR FURTHER STUDY

The classical monograph by Dijkstra [1965] introduces concurrent statements, critical regions, semaphores, and the operations P and V. It also presents Dekker's algorithm for mutual exclusion based solely on storage interlock. The algorithm is reproduced in Brinch Hansen [1973a, p. 291], Shaw [1974, p. 64], and Tsichritzis and Bernstein [1974, p. 33]. The use of messages for synchronization was introduced by Brinch Hansen [1969, 1970]. The conditional critical region was proposed by Hoare [1972] and generalized by Brinch Hansen [1972]. The origin of the monitor is not entirely clear; contributions are due to Brinch Hansen, Dahl, Dijkstra, and Hoare. A relevant early description is that of the "secretary" in Dijkstra [1971]. A fuller discussion of monitors is presented by Hoare [1974]. All of these original sources are quite readable, still relevant, and highly recommended.

Tutorial and survey articles on the topics of Secs. 4.1 to 4.5 include those by Brinch Hansen [1973b], Presser [1975], and Atwood [1976]. Elementary textbook treatments are offered by Brinch Hansen [1973a, Chap. 3], Shaw [1974, Chap. 3], and Tsichritzis and Bernstein [1974, Chap. 2], and a more advanced one by Habermann [1976, Chaps. 3 to 5]. The entire textbook by Holt et al. [1978] is devoted to issues of process concurrency and operating systems, and emphasizes the use of monitors.

Deadlock is discussed in all the foregoing books. An excellent tutorial is that by Coffman, Elphick, and Shoshani [1971]. Deadlock avoidance is explored by Havender [1968]. A graph theoretic model of deadlock is presented by Holt [1972]. The banker's algorithm for avoiding deadlock was developed for a single currency by Dijkstra [1965], and extended to multiple currencies by Habermann [1969]. The single-currency version is reproduced in Tsichritzis and Bernstein [1974, Sec. 2.7.1] and the multiple-currency version, with extensive discussion, in Brinch Hansen [1973a, Sec. 2.6].

Modes of module activation are treated by Wegner [1968, Secs. 4.9 and 4.10]. The original description of coroutines appears in Conway [1963]. Brief explanations are to be found in Wegner [1968, Sec. 4.10.3], Stone [1972, Sec. 7.2], and Knuth [1973, Sec. 1.4.2]. A more extensive treatment is offered by Sevcik [1975]. Subroutines and linkage conventions are mentioned in Secs. 7.1 and 7.3 of Stone [1972] and Sec. 1.4.1 of Knuth [1973].

EXERCISES

4.1 Starting with the queue of Fig. 4.1(a), show the result of each different interleaving of executions of the processes defined in Fig. 4.2.

4.2 Describe circumstances under which one of the processes using the program of Fig. 4.7 is prevented from ever entering its critical region.

4.3 [Habermann, 1976] Write programs to implement mutual exclusion by use of the indivisible instruction $EXCH(r,x)$, which interchanges (in a single read–write storage cycle) the content of register r with that of storage location x.

4.4 Consider a set of processes with mutual exclusion implemented using semaphores. If a process A loses control of the processor while executing a critical region, all the other processes with respect to which the region is critical will remain blocked until A regains control. Outline a way that the dispatcher can avoid stopping processes in critical regions.

4.5 In what sense can the dispatcher dispatch itself?

4.6 For each of the following modifications to the procedures of Fig. 4.18, state whether correct operation is preserved. If so, explain why. If not, cite a sequence of executions for which the modified procedures fail.
   (a) Interchange the two *P* operations of *PRODUCER*.
   (b) Interchange the two *V* operations of *CONSUMER*.

4.7 Write an implementation of *P* and *V* on a counting semaphore by using *P* and *V* on a binary semaphore together with a variable to hold the count.

4.8 Let the procedures *APPEND* and *DETACH* of Fig. 4.15 be implemented as follows, where *head* and *tail* are pointers.

```
procedure APPEND(item, list)
    queue list
    record item (.. pointer link)
    begin
        if list.head = null then list.head ⟵ item
                          else list.tail↑.link ⟵ item
        list.tail ⟵ item
    end
procedure DETACH(item, list)
    queue list
    record item (.. pointer link)
    begin
        if list.head ≠ null then item ⟵ list.head
                            list.head ⟵ list.head↑.link
    end
```

Let *PRODUCER* and *CONSUMER* be executing concurrently when the queue *buffer* contains one record. Suppose that the assignment statements of *APPEND* and *DETACH* are executed in the following order: (1) first assignment of *DETACH*; (2) first assignment of *APPEND*; (3) second assignment of *DETACH*; (4) second assignment of *APPEND*. What is wrong with the resulting data structure? Do any other circumstances result in incorrect operation?

4.9 [Courtois, Heymans, and Parnas, 1971] Modify the programs of Fig. 4.19 to give all waiting writers priority over a waiting reader. *Hint*: Introduce a semaphore *r* on which the first writer blocks readers (and other writers), a semaphore *mutex2* to protect a variable *writecount*, and a semaphore *mutex3* to block readers (but not writers) from testing *r*.

4.10 Show how the message primitives of the RC 4000 system can be used to implement (a) mutual exclusion and (b) synchronization.

4.11 A monitor enforces mutual exclusion on the execution of its procedures. Explain why its procedures must nevertheless be reenterable.

4.12 List all ways in which the two four-step sequences *P1* and *P2* of Section 4.6 can be interleaved without deadlock.

4.13 Describe the problems (not their solutions) that may be encountered in resuming the execution of a program from the beginning (which may be necessary after deadlock has been detected).

4.14 Why are programs with interrupt function modules hard to read?

4.15 Exhibit and explain the subroutine linkage convention for the operating system you use.

4.16 Design a coroutine linkage convention for the operating system you use. Exhibit the actual program code.

Chapter 5

DEVICE MANAGEMENT

As computer systems grow in complexity, an increasingly larger role is played by components other than main storage and processors. The orderly utilization of the many *devices* that may be connected to a system, whether routinely or rarely, is a major concern of operating systems. These devices, whether used by the system for true input, true output, or backing storage, are used to transmit information to and from other parts of the system. The manner in which information held by these devices is organized is discussed primarily in Chapter 6. Nevertheless, certain aspects of file organization, such as blocking and buffering, are so closely related to the properties of many devices that they are treated in this chapter. Most of the chapter, however, deals with the management of the I/O subsystem itself. The organization of the underlying hardware is discussed first, followed by an examination of device management with special attention to the problems of error detection and recovery. The chapter closes with a brief view of devices as cooperating processes.

5.1 HARDWARE ORGANIZATION

5.1.1 Devices

Literally hundreds of different devices may be provided by a manufacturer for incorporation in a given computer system. Although only a minority will be attached to any one embodiment of the system, multiple devices of the same type will almost surely be used, and the total number of devices incorporated in one system can be quite large. Computers are generally also equipped for the attachment of arbitrary devices (i.e., those not specifically provided for by the manufacturer). This permits computers to be coupled, with modest engineering effort, to practically any external system, such as

122

an airplane, nuclear reactor, or blast furnace. Even within the computer system, the variety of possible devices is extensive. The difference between two devices may be substantial, as for a magnetic tape drive and a character display screen, or it may be relatively minor, as for two different models of disk storage unit.

Control signals transmitted to the device govern its actual operation. It is undesirable to have a unique signal for every possible function of every conceivable device, including future devices that may be developed during the lifetime of the system. Consequently, a given signal transmitted by the system might mean to skip a line if directed to a printer, but to rewind if directed to a magnetic tape drive. A *control unit* associated with the device interprets the signal and controls the device accordingly. Often, several devices will share one control unit. Sometimes the control unit and device will be integrated into a single physical package; sometimes several devices will be packaged in a single box. Nevertheless, it is convenient to distinguish functionally between the device and its control unit.

Whereas the processor and executable storage are purely electronic, many devices are electromechanical. The mechanical motion confers upon such devices two extremely important properties. Their operation is both *slower* than and *asynchronous* with that of the processor. It is true that some of the faster backing storage devices do indeed have information transfer rates comparable to the transfer rate of executable storage. Moreover, a number of devices are purely electronic and could be synchronized with the processor, although for various reasons they usually are not. Nevertheless, hardware speed imbalance and asynchronism have permeated the design of modern operating systems, because all computers must communicate asynchronously with slow devices. Speed imbalance must be handled in such a manner that the operation of the processor is not retarded by the attachment of slower devices. Asynchronism, having the effect that processor and device are not ready at the same time, imposes a requirement to hold somewhere the information that has been transmitted by the one but not yet accepted by the other.

5.1.2 Intermediaries

To permit slow, asynchronous I/O operations to proceed *overlapped* with processor operation (i.e., concurrently with the processor), a separate intermediary is used between device control units and the processor. The earliest of these (developed for the IBM 709) were called I/O *channels*. Although "channel" now connotes different functions on different systems, we shall use the word in a generic sense. The channel is a programmable machine that executes programs known as *channel programs*. Although the simplest channels are limited to one-instruction programs, many channels can execute sequences of instructions. These instructions specify the operations to be effected by the devices and also control the transmission of data between the control units and main storage, which also serves in part for communication between channels and processor. Channels are relatively costly, hence there are typically many fewer channels than there are devices or control units. Because channels are typically about as fast as the associated processor, provision is sometimes made for the interleaved use of one channel by several slow devices. Each device then has the use of a virtual channel, generally called a *subchannel*. A channel shared in this manner is sometimes termed a *multiplexor* channel. An unshared channel can be thought of as having a single subchannel.

The IBM 360-370 series computers are endowed with rather simple channels. Their only operations are to read and write data, read status information from the control unit, write control information to the control unit, branch unconditionally, and stop conditionally. Private storage is provided for one byte of data, status, or control. To permit access to consecutive storage locations, a counter is provided for adding 01, but arbitrary addition is not possible. Access to nonconsecutive storage locations requires the use of new read or write instructions. The CDC 6000 and CYBER series computers, on the other hand, are provided with much more powerful channels, called peripheral processors (PPs). These have an instruction set comparable to that of many minicomputers, 4K 12-bit words of private storage, and fuller arithmetic processing ability. They can be programmed to perform many operations on data, such as validation, reformatting, and code conversion.

5.1.3 Communication

In the I/O subsystem, data are transmitted from main storage through a channel to a control unit, and finally to a device. Several channels may be physically connected to the storage, several control units to each channel, and perhaps several devices to some of the control units. To accommodate the huge potential variety of devices with a very restricted number of channel types, it is common for the various links to conform to a standard interface, which every control unit must be capable of matching. This permits new devices to be introduced with no hardware redesign of processor, storage, channels, or transmission lines. It also simplifies the operating system's provision of device independence, the ability to specify I/O devices after a program has been translated.

It is not necessary that each control unit have its own private cable to the channel. A single cable may link the channel with several control units that are capable of operating independently but are enjoined from simultaneous communication with the channel. It is usually adequate, however, to think of each control unit as being separately connected to the channel. The basic interconnection pattern is then a tree, as shown in Fig. 5.1, and does provide one-to-one correspondence between device identity and transmission path.

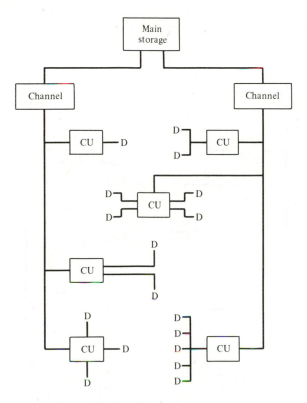

Figure 5.1 Tree-Structured I/O Subsystem

If a control unit is ready to transmit, but its channel is busy, it must be delayed. Such problems can be minimized, and communication flexibility enhanced, by connecting a control unit to more than one channel. Similarly, a device can be connected to more than one control unit. The different control units are themselves typically, but not necessarily, connected to different channels. These multiple interconnections also increase the reliability of the I/O subsystem by providing communication paths around a malfunctioning component. Although the graph that represents the I/O subsystem is still loop-free, as illustrated in Fig. 5.2, it is no longer a tree. An ensuing complication is loss of the one-to-one correspondence between device identity and communication path. Two distinct paths can now represent the same device.

Once a communication path is established, only one channel can access a given control unit and will not interfere with another channel in so doing. The control unit, on the other hand, cannot with impunity initiate communication with its channel because of the risk of interfering with a communication between that channel and another control unit. Similar considerations apply to communication between the processor and its associated channels.

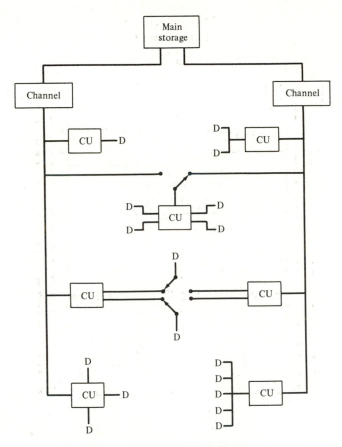

Figure 5.2 Non-Tree I/O Subsystem

How is the component at the lower level in the hierarchy to request service by the one at the higher level? Two techniques are available: interrupt and polling. The channel can generate an interrupt to the processor, which can respond immediately or later, as explained in Chapter 3. The IBM 360-370 uses this technique.

Alternatively, the processor can *poll* the channels by interrogating them periodically to determine which, if any, require attention. Polling has the advantage that it is conducted only when the processor is ready to provide the service that may be requested. The chief disadvantage is the loss of time spent polling to discover that there is no request outstanding. Because most computers have interrupt systems anyway for other purposes than I/O, the use of interrupt for I/O as well is widespread. Some computers, however, do poll their channels. A major example is the CDC 6000 series. In one sense, of course, interrupt and polling are identical in that interrupt recognition at one level is effected by polling at a lower level. For example, a computer that is interruptible between instructions discovers the generation of an interrupt by examining a set of bits in hardware after each instruction execution.

Because the CDC CYBER series PPs can access any communication path, it is necessary to restrict two of them from accessing the same physical equipment. The restriction is performed by requiring the PP to request access rights from the operating system. While waiting for the access right to be granted, the PP enters a busy wait. Because the PP is an *unshared* processor, the busy wait can readily be tolerated.

5.2 REQUEST PROCESSING

Much of device management is concerned with honoring I/O requests issued by the processes in the system. Although a user is likely to think of an I/O request in terms of an elementary machine action, the operating system must in fact consider several aspects of resource management. One is the allocation of storage space on the requested device. Another is the right to use the communication path to the device. A third is the actual control of device operation. We now examine each of these aspects.

5.2.1 Space Allocation

A device requested by the user may be either *dedicated* to serve him alone or *shared* with other users. A paper tape reader or a graphic display cannot readily be shared, and is normally assigned to one user for the duration of a job, or at least for a substantial interval. A line printer is not readily shared either, but it is neither technically practicable nor economically feasible to furnish one to each user. The typical solution to this dilemma is to provide each user with a *virtual* printer, as mentioned briefly in Section 1.2 and discussed more fully in Section 5.5. Dedicated devices can be allocated by the job scheduler prior to allocating executable storage.

Devices such as disk drives can be readily shared by a number of users, whose requests are typically for short bursts of service, such as a seek or a read. For two reasons it is unwise to allow each user to access shared I/O devices directly. One is the potential reduction in efficiency of using the device, particularly a disk, whose seek time can significantly exceed transmission time. If the sharing users alternate accesses to widely separated cylinders, the useful work performed by the disk can be drastically diminished. The other reason is the danger of interference with another user's data. Consequently, the rationing of accesses to shared devices is performed by an operating system component, often known as the *IOCS* (I/O control system) or the *I/O supervisor*. For consistency, this program usually controls accesses to the dedicated devices as well.

Shared devices, which are typically used for backing storage, must be allocated before they are accessed. The use of shared devices generally entails two forms of allocation. The first is an allocation of space in backing storage; the second is an allocation of the right to make an access to that space. Either of these allocations may be static, usually holding for the duration of a process, or dynamic, made in response to each separate request. Static allocation of a resource is less costly than repeated dynamic allocations, but it can have the effect of making a valuable resource unavailable for a long time. Dynamic allocation, when properly performed, increases the operating system's need for processor time in return for more efficient use of the resource being allocated. To maximize efficiency of device use, access allocations are usually made dynamically. Space may be allocated dynamically from a pool or allocated statically, especially if full or partial preallocation is used. Many systems with a large public disk storage allocate space to files dynamically as they are created. Files whose space was first allocated dynamically may then remain resident; for subsequent processes their allocations will appear static.

Sometimes the space, or *extent* of backing storage, is specifically defined by the user, as by naming a file whose location on a mountable disk volume is known to the operating system. If the needed volume is not mounted, a mounting message is sent to the operator. It may then be desirable to swap out the requesting process. If full preallocation is in effect, however, *premounting* is mandatory. Sometimes only certain characteristics of the extent are specified, as when the user needs a temporary work file. In that event the degree of specificity is variable; the user might ask for so many words of scratch file, or of drum storage, or of Model X drum unit. The more general the request, the greater the likelihood that it can be satisfied promptly, but the more the control program must work to determine in which of the several possible ways to make the allocation. If full preallocation is used, device extents can be allocated by the job scheduler; otherwise, an IOCS component often called the *I/O scheduler* must do the work.

Effective allocation of space can be more difficult than may at first sight appear. If space is always allocated on the emptiest disk, for example, lots of time may be lost in making accesses to that disk while disks on another channel remain idle.

5.2.2 Access Allocation

Because of the slowness of I/O operations, as compared with computation, maximizing the productivity of the I/O subsystem is often the key to maximizing that of the system as a whole. Consequently, the most common policy for controlling accesses to available devices is to maximize the total rate of data transmission. Alternative policies are to favor certain operating system or user processes, particularly processor-bound jobs, to favor heavily used channels or devices, or to avoid extremely long I/O delays. The scheduling of outstanding I/O requests is not only dependent on policy choice, but also influenced strongly by the differing properties of specific devices. These are most readily reflected in device-dependent scheduling algorithms that are applied by the *I/O device handlers*, portions of the IOCS responsible for the different devices. Device scheduling algorithms are most important for backing storage devices with mechanical delays. We shall use the disk as an example; similar approaches can be easily developed for other devices.

The two delays in disk access are arm movement time to position the heads over the correct cylinder, and the subsequent rotational delay for the desired track sector to pass under the heads. Minimum rotational delay is zero; maximum is the period for one revolution. Minimum arm movement time is zero; maximum is typically several times the maximum rotational delay. Cylinder-to-cylinder seek time is a function, often nonlinear, of the difference between cylinder numbers. For some disk drives it is not even a monotonic function. No matter how complicated the function, however, it can be made known to the device handler. Given a set of access requests, expressed as cylinder number and sector number, and knowing the current cylinder position, the program can compute approximately in which sequence the requests can be satisfied with the shortest total delay. If rotational position sensing is provided and the corresponding information available to the program, an exact calculation can be made.

Unfortunately, such extensive computation is costly. Less optimal but quite satisfactory results can be obtained by considering cylinder number or sector number alone. In *cylinder ordering*, sector number is ignored on the grounds that it is more important to avoid very long arm movements than to minimize rotational delay. *Rotational ordering*, which ignores cylinder number, is even easier to perform. If the cylinder-to-cylinder distances are short, as will often be the case for a process updating a data set well placed on adjacent cylinders, rotational ordering can be rather close to optimal. Often, however, the sector numbers are not known, and rotational ordering is impossible.

The simplest form of cylinder ordering is to perform local optimization one request at a time. The request is honored next that results in the shortest arm movement time. This can be as low as zero time if there are two requests present for the same cylinder. If no new requests arrive, arm motion will tend to be unidirectional to the innermost or outermost requested cylinder, followed by reversal of direction. This mechanism is sometimes referred to as *SSTF* (shortest seek time first).

While some requests are being taken from the queue and honored, other requests arrive. Efficiency in use of the I/O subsystem can be enhanced by inserting each new request into the queue at the position determined by a new computation. If I/O traffic is high, the frequent computation can actually slow down the performance of I/O operations. Of greater concern is the danger that requests for nearby cylinders will arrive fast enough to delay access indefinitely to some more distant cylinders. As a result, it is often most satisfactory to exhaust the queue before rebuilding it from requests that have arrived meanwhile.

A more attractive solution is simply to forbid reversal of direction as long as an unsatisfied request lies ahead in the current direction. The alternating inward and outward sweeps that result preclude indefinite postponement, and also make it possible to handle newly arrived requests if they lie in the current direction.

Scheduling of device access may or may not require availability of the channel. When information is to be transmitted to or from disk, the channel will be needed for the read or write. It is not needed during the seek, however, and it is possible to schedule the seek to begin before the channel becomes available. This practice is implemented in the EXEC system for the Univac 1100 series.

Section 1.4 mentioned the incompatibility of two resource management policies. One was the policy of holding as few jobs in main storage as possible with at least one of them not waiting for I/O. The other was the policy of minimizing total arm movement. The reason for the incompatibility should now be evident. Arm movement is minimized by having a large number of I/O requests enqueued, so that one can always be found that does not require excessive movement. But a large number of unserviced requests typically means a large number of processes in the system, not as few as possible.

5.2.3 Maintaining Status

Individual accesses to devices can be made only when the devices are indeed accessible, and they should be made in a sequence that uses the hardware efficiently. Determination of accessibility requires the maintenance of device status information. Efficient use of the I/O subsystem leads to algorithms for the dynamic allocation of accesses.

Determining whether a device is available is chiefly a matter of finding whether there exists a communication path to it with the property that the channel (or subchannel), control unit, and device are all free. In a tree-like I/O subsystem only one path exists to each device and only that path must be tested. In a multiply connected subsystem, there may be several paths. The IOCS can test all paths and make a choice among the free paths that depends on the current loading of the I/O subsystem. Alternatively, it can test the paths in a predetermined order of preference until a free one is found. The IOCS component responsible for this activity is often called the *I/O traffic controller*. To perform its job the traffic controller must maintain lists that indicate for each channel, subchannel, control unit, and device what its status is and what is connected to it. A relatively simple search start-ing at the requested device can determine whether any communication paths are available. It is also convenient for the traffic controller to maintain in its lists an identification of the requests that are waiting to use each hardware component. This permits it to find quickly which request can be honored after a component becomes free.

The lists maintained by the traffic controller may appear to be relatively simple, but the status information indicates more than just whether a com-ponent is free. Other states include those in which the component is not operational (switched off, being reloaded, malfunctioning, etc.) and those in which an interrupt is pending. The reason for an interrupt may also be im-portant status information. To determine the reason, it may be necessary to service the interrupt at least in part. In a polling system the status informa-tion is current as of the most recent polling cycle; in an interrupt-based sys-tem it is current except that the status "interrupt pending" often means that the status is really not known.

5.2.4 Device Operation

A major duty of the device handler, other than access scheduling, is to con-trol operation of the device. For each user's I/O request or series of related requests it must build a channel program and, at the appropriate time, ini-tiate its execution. Before building the channel program it must verify that the requested device has been allocated to the requester, and that, for a shared device, the space extent thereon to which access is requested lies within the allocated extent. These checks may have already been performed by another IOCS component. Clearly, a tremendous amount of time can be lost if a channel program is constructed afresh at execution time for each I/O operation. Ideally, the bulk of the construction is performed at translation time by the language translator. This is possible if the device type is known to the translator. The device handler then needs only to generate portions, such as specific addresses. If device independence is provided, more of the channel program construction must be deferred, and the appropriate part built after the corresponding information has been bound.

The device handler also serves as the second-level interrupt handler for its type of device. The precise nature of the interrupt must be determined. If device status has changed, the I/O traffic controller must be notified. If, for example, a seek is complete, reading can be started. If an error has occurred, appropriate action, as described in Section 5.4, can be initiated. The number of possible interrupts varies widely with the type of device. Interrupt han-dling, for errors in particular, accounts for a major portion of the size of the device routines.

Although the functions of status determination and access scheduling have been described separately, they are clearly interrelated. The device

handler and the I/O traffic controller interact considerably. The status information maintained by the latter is in large measure derived from actions of
the former. Reciprocally, the device handler relies on status information in
determining which operation to initiate next. One mechanism is therefore to
enqueue an access request only after the device has been found to be available. An opposite mechanism is to check availability only after the request
has been scheduled. The obvious problems caused by these extremes sug-
gests an intermediate approach in which the two functions are not strictly
separated in time.

The interaction between the I/O supervisor and the device handlers is illustrated by two processes adapted from Lister [1975]. The procedure
DOIO, shown in Fig. 5.3(a), is executed by the I/O supervisor whenever a
process requests I/O. Its fourth parameter is the main storage location at
which reading or writing is to begin, and the fifth identifies an event variable
or semaphore that the requesting process can use for synchronization. The
procedure *HANDLER*, shown in Fig. 5.3(b), is typical of input operation.
For output, the translation of characters and transfer of data would precede,
rather than follow, the I/O operation. By use of a switch the program could
be made to serve for both input and output.

The UNIX system strives for simplicity by the use of two completely
separate I/O subsystems. One provides structured I/O under which every
device is treated as though it consists of randomly addressed 512-byte
blocks. The device handler must make its physical device appear to have that

> **procedure** *DOIO*(*device, operation, quantity, location, flag*)
>   look *device* up in process descriptor
>   check parameters against device characteristics
>   **if** error **then** ..
>   assemble parameters into an I/O request
>   *INSERT* I/O request on request queue for *device*
>   *SIGNAL*(*device.request*)
>
>   (a) Action requester
>
> **procedure** *HANDLER*   /* specific to *device* */
>   *WAIT*(*request*)
>   *DETACH* I/O request from request queue
>   disassemble I/O request into details
>   initiate **read**
>   *WAIT*(*completion*)   /* to be posted by interrupt handler */
>   **if** error **then** ..
>   translate characters
>   **write** characters into destination
>   *SIGNAL*(*serviced*)
>
>   (b) Device handler (input version)

Figure 5.3 Input/Output Control Programs

property. The other subsystem provides unstructured I/O to handle data as streams of characters. This is used both with such character-oriented devices as printers and communication lines, and with other devices when the user does not wish to accept (and to program around) the constraints of 512-byte blocks. The structured I/O is implemented with the aid of a pool of 512-byte buffers, each of which can be allocated to a device. The unstructured I/O is implemented with queues of characters sharing space from another pool.

5.3 INPUT/OUTPUT ACTIONS

Transfer of data between main storage and other devices is characterized by (1) a data transfer rate that is typically slower, and often much slower, than that of main storage; (2) a long time, relative to the data transmission rate, to access the start of the device data area; (3) asynchronism between device and processor operation; and (4) interrecord gaps on magnetic surface recording media. Because of these characteristics, it is necessary to start reading input data well before they can be used, and to finish writing output data well after they have been produced. Often it is advantageous to transfer at one time larger aggregates of data than the program requires. Such coalescing of I/O transfers can reduce the frequency, hence the cost, of the I/O operations needed to support a given computation.

Acquisition of data in advance of computation, and dissemination following computation, are accomplished by setting aside storage areas, called *buffers*, to and from which I/O transfers can take place simultaneously with computation involving other data. In modern computers the buffers are almost always located in main storage. Their use is called *buffering*. If each aggregate of data transferred in an I/O operation consists of not one but several data records *blocked* together, the system is said to be using *blocking*. For each collection of records, known as a *file*, different buffering and blocking disciplines can be specified. Means must be established for implementing the buffering and blocking for each file. This preparation, as well as buffering and blocking, is discussed in the ensuing sections.

5.3.1 Buffering: *READ* and *WRITE*

Records are read into an *input buffer*, processed in a *work area*, and written from an *output buffer*. The work area typically holds one record. Each buffer holds a block of data, which may be one record or several, depending upon whether blocking is in use. The command used to initiate filling an input buffer with data is almost universally known as *READ*; that for emptying an output buffer, as *WRITE*.

In the prototypical form of buffering there is one input buffer and one output buffer. When the processing of a record in the work area is terminated, the record is copied into the output buffer and a *WRITE* issued. Then the next record is copied from the input buffer into the work area and a *READ* is issued to obtain the following record. Access to the input buffer is a critical region with respect to the *READ* command and the copying of a record into the work area. Access to the output buffer is similarly a critical region. The need to enforce mutual exclusion can cause delays due to momentary variations in the relative rates of internal and I/O processing. Mutual exclusion without long delays is much more easily enforced if two input and two output buffers are provided, and this is the form of *double* buffering (also "standby" or "copy" buffering) that is most commonly encountered. While one input buffer is being filled, records are drawn for processing from the other. When no more records are available in that buffer, the roles of the two input buffers are interchanged. A similar alternation is applied to the two output buffers. Figure 5.4 illustrates double buffering.

A tacit assumption thus far has been that the output and input records are of the same size, and that input and output files are associated in pairs. Such is often the case, but it is not a necessary restriction. A program may use several input and several output files, each associated with a pair of buffers of the appropriate size. The work area size depends on how many records from each file are interrelated by the processing algorithm. In

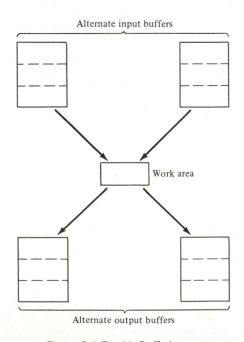

Figure 5.4 Double Buffering

many applications, however, including most file updating, the input buffer, work area, and output buffer do have a common record size.

The continual copying of records from input buffer to work area to output buffer is obviated by the use of indirect addressing. A given area in main storage serves first as an input buffer, then as a work area, and finally as an output buffer before returning to serve again as an input buffer. If the storage requirements for an input buffer, a work area, and an output buffer are not all equal, some storage will be wasted. Each buffer area is identified by a pointer to its start, and instead of copying records the system resets pointers. This approach, called "exchange" buffering by IBM, but perhaps more suitably called *indirect* buffering, is illustrated in Fig. 5.5. Note the availability of one or more spare buffers for use when an input buffer is full or output buffer empty.

A variant of indirect buffering is known as *cyclic* (or "circular") buffering. It is used when input, processing, and output are reasonably well synchronized. Under cyclic buffering the input, work, and output functions are cycled in synchronism around a set of buffers. Figure 5.6 shows three successive stages in the use of a set of circular buffers. The upper buffer serves first for input, then for work, and finally for output, before the cycle repeats from stage $k + 3$. The rotating segmented circle is not a real device, but rather an aid to understanding. The letter in each of its three sectors specifies the function of the adjacent buffer. When the input, processing, and

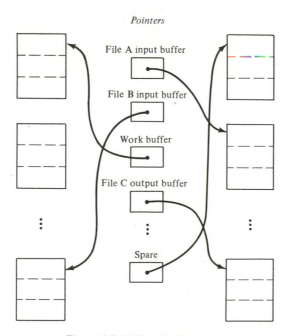

Figure 5.5 Indirect Buffering

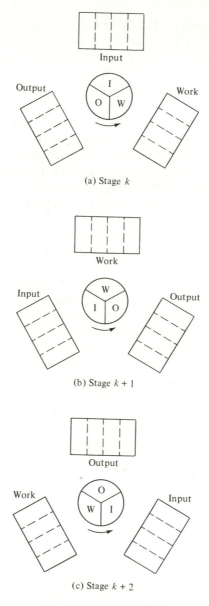

(a) Stage k

(b) Stage $k + 1$

(c) Stage $k + 2$

Figure 5.6 Cyclic Buffering

output for one stage are all complete, the circle is rotated one-third turn counterclockwise. Alternatively, the buffers can be thought of as being rotated among the different duties.

If a process is using several files, with the rates of use varying with time, it may be attractive not to devote to buffer areas the sum of the maximum number of buffers required to handle each one. Instead, a *pool* of buffers can be established and individual buffers assigned to or freed by file handlers as requirements vary. Storage for buffers can also be shared by several processes, each of which obtains space from, and returns it to, a single storage pool.

5.3.2   Blocking: *GET* and *PUT*

The data transferred in an I/O operation are grouped into blocks, or *physical* records, whose size is often constrained, sometimes even dictated, by physical device characteristics such as card width or track length. The data used in a program are grouped into *logical* records according to the needs of the program. There is no inherent reason why the physical records should necessarily have the same length as the logical records. If they do have the same length, programming of I/O operations is simplified, and the logical record length is therefore often chosen to match the physical record length.

The programming savings thus effected can be very costly, however, in terms of other resources, particularly for short logical records in backing storage. One cost is inefficient use of the storage medium. If the storage device uses magnetic surface recording, there is a gap of unused recording surface between successive records. On magnetic tape, where one purpose of the gap is to allow the tape to accelerate before and to decelerate after reading or writing, the gap can easily be as long as the space needed to record 800 characters. If the logical record is an 80-character card image, only one-eleventh of the storage capacity will be used, and the device will transmit information at only one-eleventh of its nominal speed. A second cost is extra time in executing the device handler, which requires about the same amount of time to process an I/O operation, whether it transmits a short record or a long one. For a given number of logical records, it is clearly more costly to transfer only one at a time than to block several together. For these reasons blocking is in widespread use. The number of logical records per physical record is known as the *blocking factor*. For 360-character payroll records stored on magnetic disks, a physical record length of 7200 and blocking factor of 20 would not be uncommon.

Under blocking, the basic operation of the program is very simple, and can be easily understood with reference to the example of Fig. 5.4, for which the blocking factor is 3. Each buffer is as large as a physical record. When the program needs to copy a logical record into its work area, it issues a *GET* command. In executing the *GET* command the blocking routine causes the desired record to be copied. Then it checks whether the copied record was the last one in the buffer. If so, the buffer is empty and the blocking routine issues a *READ* command to refill the buffer with a new physical record. If the blocking factor is n, the execution of every nth *GET* will cause the issuance of a *READ*; the intervening $n-1$ will not access the device. Copying from the work area to an output buffer works similarly. A *PUT* command causes one logical record to be copied. If the record is the one that fills the output buffer, a *WRITE* is then issued to transmit the entire physical record to an output device. Thus the program uses as primitives the *GET* and *PUT* commands, which deal with the logical record as data unit. Executions of *READ* and *WRITE*, which deal with the physical record, are generated automatically and concealed from the programmer.

Blocking has its price, of course. Time is required to unpack the logical records from, and to pack them into, the physical records. Space is needed to hold the blocking routines that do this. Furthermore, the buffers must be *n* times as large for blocking factor *n* as for unblocked operation. Actual copying can be reduced, of course, by the judicious use of pointers to logical records.

The foregoing simple view of buffering ignores many potential complications. A few will be mentioned, to illustrate the richness of buffering, but the reader will be spared a detailed examination.

1. If the number of records is not an integral multiple of the blocking factor, there will be a partially filled block at the end of an input file. Care must be taken to avoid processing the block content beyond the file end. Similarly, special attention must be devoted in writing the last block of an output file.

2. Sometimes it is inconvenient to have an integer blocking factor. Circumstances may dictate, for example, that the logical record length should be 2000 and the physical record length 5000. In this situation every fifth logical record will span the boundary between two blocks. Processing such *spanned* records requires special care.

3. Often the logical record length is not fixed, but variable. This may lead to use of one or more of the following: variable-length blocks, variable blocking factor, unused space in the buffers, and spanned records.

5.3.3 Preparation: *OPEN* and *CLOSE*

The many details of blocking and buffering are quite specific to each file whose records are to be processed. Record lengths, blocking factors, and buffering disciplines must all be reflected in the record handling routines. The method of file organization, a topic explored in Chapter 6, also affects the design of the routines. Some of the requisite information is known at translation time, but the specification of other elements can be deferred until scheduling time or, even later, until execution time. The command used at execution time for this specification is called *OPEN*.

The operating system designer must decide to what extent to specialize various routines to match file characteristics. Among the candidate routines are those for *GET/PUT*, blocking/deblocking, and buffer management. Two ways exist to use information that may not be available until the *OPEN* command is issued. One is to supply interpretive routines that use the file description as parameters to specialize their execution. The other is to use the file descriptions to generate specialized routines at *OPEN* time. The latter choice yields efficient routines at the price of generation time and generator space.

Execution of the *OPEN* command sets up the file and associated routines so that I/O processing can begin. It is a prelude to the use of *READ* and *WRITE, GET* and *PUT*. In many systems each file incorporates not only data records but also identifying information known as the file *label*. Typical actions caused by *OPEN* include (1) reading and checking the label of an input file or writing the label for an output file; (2) allocating buffers and, for input, filling them initially; (3) generating specialized routines, or collecting parameters for interpretive routines; and (4) requesting the loading of the needed standard routines for device and file handling.

Just as *OPEN* precedes the use of a file, so does *CLOSE* follow use. It is less complex than *OPEN*. Execution of *CLOSE* is generally limited to (1) writing from partially filled output buffers; (2) freeing buffers; (3) writing end-of-file markers and perhaps trailer labels on output files; and, in some instances, (4) repositioning files (e.g., rewinding magnetic tapes). Some further actions of *OPEN* and *CLOSE* are discussed in Chapter 6.

The pairs *OPEN/CLOSE, READ/WRITE,* and *GET/PUT* provide for the specification of I/O operation at three different levels: file, block, and logical record, respectively. Their proper function is a responsibility of the I/O supervisor, which is concerned also with the enqueuing of multiple I/O requests and the selection of paths to each requested device. To prevent one process from accessing a device that belongs to another process, all requests for device access are funneled through the I/O supervisor, which also handles both normal interrupt processing and error recovery. Because much of the I/O supervisor's operation is characterized by the pedestrian details of potentially hundreds of device types, it is at once the least glamorous and the most extensive of the major components of the operating system.

5.4 ERROR RECOVERY

Any part of a computer system can occasionally fail to function correctly. This is true not only of hardware, but also of software, even carefully written and tested control programs. No part of the system, however, is more subject to malfunction than is the hardware of the I/O subsystem. The reason is simple. Mechanical operations are involved in addition to electronic. Unike electronic operations, mechanical operations involve physical wear, do not enjoy the benefit of reliance on quantization of analog values, and are subject to interference by foreign substances. A secondary reason for the prevalence of I/O errors is human interaction with the recording medium.

The fundamental policy most widely adopted for coping with error is that the system, rather than the user, is responsible for detecting error. Because of the many possibilities for error, checks are widely incorporated into both software and hardware, including numerous checking circuits in device hardware. Checking circuits are designed to test for readily manifest symptoms, the underlying causes of which may be more or less difficult to ascertain. Widely varying errors can cause identical symptoms, such as reading the bit value 0 from a magnetic surface when a 1 was supposed to have been recorded. One potential cause might be a defective spot on the recording medium. Another might be electromagnetic induction by an external signal (lightning, static discharge from operator's clothing). A third might be the presence of a particle of cigarette smoke between the medium and the read head. In one sense it is important to know only which error has been detected, to prevent its being propagated into subsequent computation. In another sense it is important to determine the cause of the error, to permit corrective action to reduce the chances of the error recurring.

Several different techniques are used to detect errors in the data recorded on magnetic media. Standard magnetic tape is treated differently from other media. The individual information bits of a 6- or 8-bit byte are usually recorded simultaneously across the width of a tape (i.e., in tracks parallel to the edges of the tape). A redundant bit can be recorded along with each byte of information bits. This *VRC* (vertical redundancy check) bit is customarily chosen to impart a specified *parity* to the total number of ones recorded for the byte. If the total number of ones must be odd, the bit configuration is said to have odd parity. A relatively simple circuit can test the parity of each byte as it is read and identify any byte in which exactly one bit (or any odd number of bits) is in error. The use of a parity bit restricts the acceptable bit configurations to what is termed a single-error-detecting code. Also common is a redundant byte at the end of the record. This *LRC* (longitudinal redundancy check) byte has each bit so chosen as to impart a specific parity for all the bits in its track. The use of VRC and LRC together permits the detection of *any* pattern of three or fewer errors in the record, as well as many patterns of more than three errors.

The checking of redundant bits is performed when the recorded data are read. Other actions can be taken at the time of writing, when it is usually easier to recover from an error than during the later reading. One is the *echo* check, which verifies that at least one of the writing circuits emitted a 1 signal. It is necessary, of course, that each acceptable bit configuration include at least one 1. This condition is guaranteed by odd parity. A more thorough action is the *read-after-write* check, in which an extra set of heads, just beyond the write heads, reads each byte. This check verifies that a valid byte is read. It is not practical to compare the byte as read with the one intended to be written, because of the need to store copies of the very many bytes, possibly several hundred, on the portion of tape between the two sets of heads. Such a comparison becomes practical, however, for disk and drum recording. An extra revolution can be used to read each track immediately after writing, and a programmed check for agreement can be made while the data are still available in main storage.

In recording on disks, drums, and cassette tapes, the bits of each byte are commonly recorded serially by a single head. An attempt to record VRC bits would require a second head, which is normally not available. It would also halve the information storage capacity of the device, because one VRC bit would be needed for each information bit. The detection of multiple errors uses instead a redundant character of bits chosen according to the requirements of what is called a *polynomial* code, *group* code, or *cyclic* code. This code, whose mathematical description is based upon an encoding polynomial, permits the easy generation of the redundant bits by a cyclic process performed (with the aid of a shift register) during writing and again during reading. The *CRC* (cyclic redundancy check) character is recorded after the information bits. The CRC character computed from the information bits received during reading is compared with the one actually read.

Not only are cyclic codes easily generated and verified, but they have the ability to detect a very large fraction of all possible error patterns. In particular, these patterns include *burst* errors, in which the erroneous bits are concentrated in bursts. Because many sources of error (e.g., dust particle, electromagnetic interference) affect several successive bit positions, burst errors are particularly likely. The length of a burst is the number of bits between the first and last incorrect bits in the burst, inclusive of those end bits. The IBM 2841 drum controller, for example, uses a 16-bit CRC character that is capable of detecting all patterns with an odd number of errors, all burst errors of length 15 or less, and in fact all but 0.00152% of all error patterns in a record of any length. The powerful detection capability of CRC codes has led to the use of CRC characters on magnetic tape as well as on disks and drums.

The types of error are legion. A misaligned keypunch can cause a card reader to be unable to read a punched card. A careless keypunch user can create an illegal combination of punches that may be unreadable by a particular card reader or unacceptable to the associated device handler. A line printer may attempt to print but find no paper, or the ribbon may be broken, or the line control tape may be out of synchronism with the feed mechanism. Shop grease may cause short circuits in electrical reading of mark sense cards, resulting in erroneous data. What is not often appreciated is the number of possible error conditions that can be associated with even a single device. A magnetic tape drive can suffer from vacuum pump failure, reel brake failure, door unsecured, dust on the heads, tape breaking, or simply not being plugged in. For one model alone the list extends to dozens of different error conditions.

What can be done when an error occurs in device operation? One policy of error management is to provide extra resources to *correct* the result of error. For failure of redundancy checks in reading it is sometimes possible to determine which bit or bits are in error, and to transmit corrected data. This requires the use of error-correcting codes (such as the Hamming codes), the availability of extra storage to hold redundant information, the investment of time to transmit the redundant information, and the provision of either special hardware or extra processing to perform the correction. The benefits of being able to continue without delay are often well worth these costs, and error-correcting codes are used in the backing storage of many systems.

Most errors, however, cannot be corrected and a policy of *repetition* is applied instead. It may be possible to repeat the operation without propagating the original error. A card reader might stop on the card that it fails to read, giving the operator the opportunity to reinsert the offending card or to keypunch a replacement. If a magnetic tape drive is encountering difficulty in reading a record, the operation may be reattempted several times, in both directions (if possible) and with different levels of bias current. Parity errors encountered during reading from magnetic disk can also be handled by the repetition policy. Repeated reading of a given record is more easily performed from disk than from tape because no change in physical motion is required. The B7000/B6000 MCP rereads a disk automatically as many as ten times, without indicating to the requesting program that any trouble has occurred. If trouble is encountered in communicating with a device that is accessible by multiple paths, an alternate path may be requested. Sometimes it may be necessary not merely to repeat the operation during whose performance the error was detected, but rather to return to an earlier point in the computation and restart. If, for example, a scratch file is unreadable, it is usually necessary to repeat the computations whose results were recorded on that file.

For more drastic errors, the only suitable policy for containing its effect is to quit (i.e., to *abort* execution of the job). If the master file is on a magnetic tape drive whose fuse blows, there may well be no other solution. The most unwelcome error in disk operation is the *head crash*, which occurs when the failure of an air bearing or other component allows a recording head, in what is supposed to be noncontact recording, to touch the recording medium. When this is detected, the device must be removed from service. All jobs that had requested the use of that device will be affected.

Recovery from device error is often a complicated process, closely tied to device characteristics. The device handler, which must in any event post error status information, is the natural choice of program to implement any retry or to initiate abnormal termination. It is by no means essential, however, that error handling be performed only under control of the processor.

Any site from the processor to the device can be given responsibility for some error recovery. Device-specific control can be built into the device itself, and is becoming more and more common as the cost of embedding microprocessors in devices and control units decreases.

5.5   DEVICES AND PROCESSES

In this chapter the I/O device has thus far been treated rather literally, as a piece of hardware to which are sent data and control information and from which are received data and status information. A computer program, together with its data area, really works in similar fashion, receiving data and control information and returning data and status information. Such a process can be used to simulate the operation of a device; conversely, a device can be considered to be a process. Computer programs have indeed been used to simulate devices, as for example in providing a simulated load of terminal responses for a time-sharing system under development.

The concept of the device as a process has been used in the design of control programs. These device processes operate concurrently, of course, and the synchronization techniques discussed in Chapter 4 can be applied. Rather than consider the device alone to constitute a process, it is often more convenient to consider the process to incorporate also the programs for communicating with the device. Organizing the I/O supervisor in this manner enhances the ability to offer the feature of device independence. Substitution of one device for another, even at scheduling time, can be accomplished with a minimum of disruption to related portions of the operating system.

Perhaps the greatest benefit of viewing devices as processes is the creation of *virtual devices*. A real device together with associated programs can be made to appear to external programs as a (possibly different) real device directly accessible by the user. We have already seen an example in the structured I/O subsystem of UNIX, in which one type of virtual device is simulated by every real device. Virtual devices find two other major applications. One is the simulation of direct device control. Testing of devices that are as yet unavailable, simulation of dedicated systems in which devices will be controlled directly, and the development of new I/O supervisors all embody instances of such simulation.

The second major application of virtual devices is in *spooling*. (The word is derived from the acronym for Simultaneous Peripheral Operation On-Line.) The chief purpose of spooling is to permit the apparently concurrent sharing of sequentially sharable I/O devices. If a line printer is shared by several concurrently executing processes, whether cooperating or independent, the result of permitting each process to print a line on demand would be a stream of output of no value to any of the processes. What is done, therefore, is to provide each process with a virtual printer. The printer characteristics (character set, paper stock, line width, etc.) can be different for the different processes. Each process directs print lines to its own virtual printer; eventually, each user receives output that is not interleaved or, worse yet, interlined with that from another process.

The implementation of spooling, which is widely used not only for printers but also for card readers and punches, is straightforward. With each process and its virtual device is associated an image area, which holds the data to be transmitted. For input, the image area is filled, often before process initiation, by reading from the real device and emptied as the process subsequently issues reading commands. For output, the image area is filled as the process initially issues writing commands and emptied after process termination by writing to the real device. The image areas are commonly enqueued in backing storage. The priority order in which the queues are maintained is an important determinant of a system's response time to the user. A common organization for a print queue is to maintain it in increasing order of length of files to be printed.

FOR FURTHER STUDY

A particularly attractive overview of device management appears in Chap. 5 of Freeman [1975]. Other good treatments are those of Colin [1971, Chaps. 7 to 9] and Lister [1975, Chap. 6]. That of Watson [1970, Sec. 6.2] is particularly oriented toward terminals. A brief explanation of the underlying hardware subsystem is given in Sec. 2.4.4 of Fuller [1975].

Lister [1975] gives readable examples of I/O supervisor routines in Secs. 6.2 and 6.3. Detailed attention to *OPEN* and *CLOSE* is paid by Shaw [1974, Sec. 9.4.4] and Lister [1975, Sec. 7.6]. Madnick and Donovan [1974, Sec. 5 and 6] present a good discussion of virtual devices, including the design of a spooling system. Another implementation of spooling is described by Holt et al. [1978, Chap. 6].

EXERCISES

5.1 A leading computer designer has stated: "There is no point in interrupting a CPU to handle I/O because the CPU won't service the interrupt until it's ready. It's better for the CPU, when ready, to poll for I/O". Do you agree? If so, why? If not, why not?

5.2 What problems arise from giving the user the option of specifying scratch storage vs. drum storage, or drum storage vs. a particular drum?

5.3 Describe the advantages and disadvantages of FIFO as a mechanism for scheduling disk accesses.

5.4 What mechanism is appropriate for scheduling a paging drum having page-size sectors?

5.5 Let disk access requests be serviced in alternating inward and outward sweeps with no reversal of direction as long as an unsatisfied request lies ahead. Why should a newly arrived request for the current cylinder *not* be honored during the current sweep?

5.6 Should job priority be applied before or after seek ordering?

5.7 State the advantages and disadvantages of the various buffering disciplines described.

5.8 Why is it not necessary to specialize error-handling routines at *OPEN* time?

5.9 In some systems, execution of *CLOSE* does not free buffers. Why might this be?

5.10 What can be done to mitigate the effect of those errors that might be classified as *blunders* (e.g., mounting the wrong tape)?

5.11 A line-drawing graphics subsystem is more expensive than a line printer. Why is the printer spooled, but not the graphics subsystem?

Chapter 6

FILE MANAGEMENT

The principal commodity of a computer system is, of course, information. Although we intuitively think of a computer as providing information, it can be shown that, in the sense of information theory, the operation of a computer actually decreases information content. For example, a set of numbers implicitly contains information about their sum. Once they have been added and discarded, however, the computer holds no information about the individual values. Despite this seeming paradox of information loss, the information in the output of a useful computer program is more valuable than that in its input. In deriving and producing output, the user community may rely on vast amounts of information. The system programs, be they translators, utilities, or controllers, and the user programs, ranging from undebugged source to tested object code, as well as all the collections of data to be processed by those programs, constitute a large library of information. This collection of information constitutes a resource whose management by the operating system can facilitate the tasks of the many users.

Information is represented by sequences of bits often grouped into *files* and stored by the physical devices of main storage or, more commonly, backing storage. Files are normally composed of *records,* one for each entity represented by the file. The records are usually further subdivided into *fields.* Each field usually contains the value of a single quantity, and the fields of one record together contain a set of related values, all associated with the same entity. Thus a payroll master file would have one record for each employee, and that record would have fields for name, address, hourly wage, and so on. A program file record might hold a source-language program line or a group of machine-language instructions.

A given sequence of bits might represent the name of an employee in character form, the atmospheric pressure in millibars as a floating point number, or an instruction to decrement the content of an index register. In fact, solely from examination of the bit sequence, it is not possible to tell which of the potential interpretations is intended. Moreover, a user may employ any of several representations for a variable known to him, for example, as *atpress* and holding the value of the atmospheric pressure in millibars. One representation is as characters for the digits of the decimal encoding of the value, punched in a card in the hopper of the card reader. A second is as a floating-point binary number in some field of a record in a scratch file on a backing storage device. A third is as a fixed-point binary number in an input buffer area in main storage.

In most systems it is possible for the user to know, often even to specify, precisely how and where the values associated with symbolic names are to be represented. More often than not, however, some of the details of representation and most of the details of location are immaterial to the user. Various transformations can be applied to progress in steps from the symbolic name used in the program to the bit sequence stored by the hardware. Some of these transformations, such as those effected by blocking and buffering, are due in large measure to the properties of storage devices. Others are influenced more by the nature of the intended use of the information items and by the desire to strike a balance between flexibility and efficiency in mapping symbolic names to bit sequences. Operating systems can assist both in the manipulation of each individual file and in the supervision of the information resource represented by the collection of files. The extent of such assistance varies considerably from one operating system to another.

6.1 FILE SYSTEMS

There are two principal reasons for incorporating file management in an operating system. One reason is to relieve the user of the burden of storing files separately from the computer system. If the user's files are extensive, the required cards or tapes (whether reels or cassettes) can be both numerous and voluminous, creating problems of cataloguing and retrieval. The user also shoulders the burden of ensuring that the appropriate volumes are brought to the computer for mounting before use and are taken away afterward. How much easier for the user it is if the system relieves him of that burden. For interactive use, in particular, on-line file storage is a tremendous convenience.

The second reason for providing file management is to permit two or more users to share a file. Ten programmers developing an application system can inspect the project documentation, and contribute to it. A hundred students can share the use of a symbol table manager program prepared by an instructor. A thousand airline sales agents can examine availability of seats on any of the company's flights. Two researchers can combine their experimental data for a single analysis.

Regardless of what particular detailed file management functions are chosen for implementation, several general policies usually influence the design. A fundamental policy is that the file management system should provide a high degree of independence from processor and device details, even from choice of device. A corollary is that it must be possible to access a file by using a symbolic name.

A second policy is to provide protection against information loss due to hardware or software malfunction, or to interference by other users. In some systems there is a concern not only for this *integrity* of the data, but also for its *security* against unauthorized use.

A third policy is dictated by economic considerations. Efficiency is required both in the allocation of backing storage to hold the files and in the implementation of commands to manipulate the files. Counter to this policy runs that of making file access as flexible and versatile as possible. Different systems end up at different points on the resulting spectrum.

A fourth policy is to provide mechanisms that are, to the extent possible, invisible to the user. If the file management system is justifiable in part on grounds of user convenience, the provision of a simple user interface is particularly important.

6.1.1　Function

The functions performed by a file management system fall into two classes: functions explicitly invoked by the user, and functions performed automatically. Among those invoked, the most obvious perhaps are to *READ* and *WRITE* a file. A special case of writing is to *MODIFY* a file, by appending or inserting new information, by deleting old information, or by rewriting, which can be viewed as a combination of deletion and insertion. Before any function can be performed on a file, it is necessary to *CREATE* it, an action distinct from the *OPEN* discussed in Section 5.3.3. The complementary operation is to destroy or *DELETE* the file, not to be confused with *CLOSE*. Creation and deletion of a file occur in the context of a file system, and are concerned with the system's knowledge of a file. On the other hand, *OPEN* and *CLOSE* occur in the context of executing a process, and are concerned with the availability of a file to that process.

The many files managed by the system are generally identified by a number of different names. Each program that accesses the file uses a name local to the program, often a source-language identifier. Different programs may refer to the same file by different names. Any of these names may coincide with the name used by another program to refer to a different file. For the control program that manages access to the library, such freedom of naming would lead to unresolvable conflicts. An important function, therefore, is to *RENAME* a file.

Some form of communication between files is often provided. At the very least, it is normally possible to *COPY* into one file the content of another. If the information is deleted from the source file, the operation is a *MOVE* rather than a copy. Particularly useful is the ability to copy or to move a portion of a file, perhaps even a single record.

If the user is given a measure of control over file placement in backing storage, he may be allowed to move a file from one device to another. The user may also be able to move a file into and out of main storage, usually in pieces if the file is long. Much movement, however, is automatic rather than user-invoked.

An example of automatic movement is the *migration* of files, typically between different levels of backing storage. An infrequently accessed file is migrated by being moved to a lower, hence cheaper, level of storage. A common implementation is to migrate files from disk to tape. When access to a migrated file is requested, the file is moved back at least to on-line storage.

Migration is one facet of a fairly broad function, that of managing the resources used by files. The dynamic allocation of backing storage space is an important component of this management. A related component is the allocation of backing storage accesses, discussed in Section 5.2.2.

A particularly important automatic function is to *organize* the file system, and to keep track of what files are present in the system and where they are located. The primary data structure used for organization is called the *catalog*.

In carrying out functions invoked by users, the file management system automatically controls user access to a file, ensuring that the user has the right to access the file in the manner specified. The specification of user access rights is performed explicitly by users. Of course, the right to make such specifications is not granted to every user. In permitting access to files, the system may need to enforce mutual exclusion, particularly for writing.

The performance of backup and recovery procedures to protect against irrecoverable loss of data is another automatic function. Even though it may be explicitly invoked by the operator on consulting the clock or the calendar, it is automatic from the point of view of the user.

The duration of the system's knowledge of a file depends both on the physical medium and on the file owner's desires. During execution, a process's files must be known to the system, but prior and subsequent knowledge may be limited. A file of cards just punched by the computer will normally not be known after termination of the process. A file on a permanently mounted magnetic disk will usually be known from the time of creation to the time of deletion. A file on a mountable volume that is removed, particularly a reel of magnetic tape, is to some systems unknowable but to others known or not as specified by its owner. This specification is typically made in the commands for the process that uses the file. Requests for allocation of known but unmounted files result in volume mounting messages to the operator.

6.1.2 Organization

Access to information in the library usually requires two steps. The first is to locate the file given its name. The second, which is often unnecessary if the file is a program to be executed, is to find a particular physical record by position in the file, or a logical record either by key or by the content of one or more data fields. File organizations that facilitate this second step are discussed in Section 6.2.

Each file known to the operating system must have a global name that is unique within the entire system. This uniqueness can be achieved by requesting the system to assign a unique name, by combining the user identification with a name unique for that user, or by automatically qualifying the user-assigned name by the time of file creation on a uniprocessor system.

Finding the file requires a translation from the process's nonunique local name to a physical location. The unique global name that corresponds to the local name is often identified at scheduling time from information in the process commands, but sometimes not until *OPEN* time, if part of the information is not available until then. The global name is then used to access the catalog, which associates with each global file name the file's physical location.

A purely linear organization of the catalog is rarely suitable, because entries are often subject to frequent change. Moreover, the set of file names used to access it is far from dense. Hashing may therefore be used to good effect in implementing a catalog of modest size.

An alternative organization, suitable for large catalogs, is as a tree, with choices at each level used both to ensure uniqueness of names and to facilitate lookup. Multilevel names are used with a system-wide discipline enforcing uniqueness at higher levels and the user guaranteeing uniqueness at lower levels. Each level of the name specifies the choice of branch to be followed at the corresponding level of the tree. Thus the name /comp/405/subr/quadratic might identify a program for solving quadratic equations. Each node of the catalog is then implemented as a *directory* of the choices at that level. The directories at the bottom, or leaf, level of the tree contain only pointers to files. A pointer within a directory at any other level points either to a file or to a directory at the next lower level. The full name of a file is thus essentially the name of the path to the file from the directory at the root. Part of a typical tree of directories and files is shown in Fig. 6.1.

Different table construction and search techniques can be used at each level according to the expected size of directory for that level. For a multilevel catalog, whether tree-structured or not, it is not necessary that all directories be stored next to each other. Efficiency dictates, though, that the higher levels of the catalog be on-line. Levels that refer only to off-line files can reside on the same off-line volumes as those files.

Several systems, Multics and UNIX among them, associate with each process a *current* (or "working") directory. Names of other directories within the current directory's subtree are specified just by the path name within the subtree. Directories outside that subtree can be reached either by starting explicitly from the root or by following a branch *upward* in the tree. In UNIX, for example, ".." is the name of the parent of the current directory.

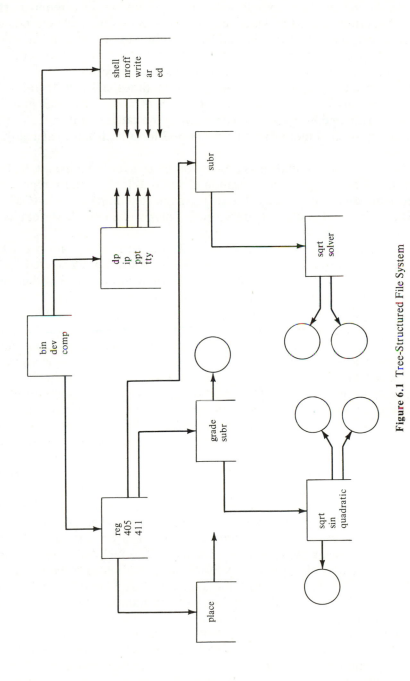

Figure 6.1 Tree-Structured File System

File sharing can be accomplished if one user knows, or can obtain, the name of another user's file. Once the name has been obtained, subsequent reference to the other user's file can be simplified by superposing arbitrary links on the tree structure. This is illustrated in Fig. 6.2, where either a file or a directory can be pointed to from more than one directory.

An alternative approach to sharing is sometimes called a "two-level" file. For each user, a directory translates each of his local names into the unique global name by providing pointers into the catalog. Illustrated in Fig. 6.3, this approach is more easily implemented for a hash-table catalog than for a tree.

The data structure known as a *B-tree* offers efficient manipulation algorithms together with efficient utilization of space. Widely used for representing an individual file, it is used in at least one operating system (OS/370 MVS) for the set of system file directories. This results in a file system itself organized as a B-tree.

Segmentation, introduced in Chapter 2 as a technique of main storage management, serves also for file management. Files are considered to be segments, and it is not even necessary to distinguish them from other segments. Because naming conflicts are resolved by the current process's segment table number held in the segment table register, nonunique file names cause no problem. Explicit translation from local file name to global file name is thus obviated. Moreover, the sharing of a file by several users is facilitated by the ability to record the same segment number in the segment tables of the sharing users, whether they refer to the shared file by the same name or by different names. The union of all the segment tables constitutes the catalog, and separate catalog maintenance routines are not required.

In the Multics system, files are indeed just segments and are not distinguished from other segments. A tree-structured catalog of all the segments in the system is maintained. Except for the leaves, all nodes of that tree are directory segments. In OS/360-370, the collection of files is organized into a tree of arbitrary branching ratios and depth. UNIX also permits such a tree, but distinguishes among three types of files: ordinary disk files; directories, which are maintained in a tree structure; and special files associated with I/O devices. This last group permits a user to execute I/O operations by merely using the appropriate file name. The PRIMOS V system provides a separate catalog for each volume, and distinguishes between two types of directories. The "user file directory" is like those previously described. The "segment directory" has a fixed number of entries, accessible by indexing rather than naming. It is designed for collections of files that are changing in size but not in number. TENEX organizes files into a tree having maximum depth five. The five levels are device name, user name, file name, extension field, and version number. The extension field is used to distinguish among different encodings of a program file (e.g., MAC for macro source, REL for relocatable, and SAV for binary image). The system creates and numbers a new version each time a file is written.

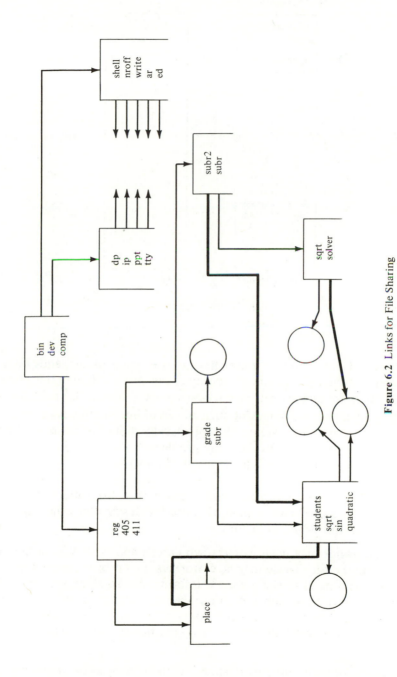

Figure 6.2 Links for File Sharing

153

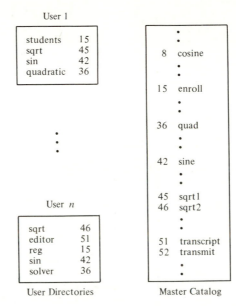

Figure 6.3 Multiple Entry into Catalog

6.1.3 Access Control

The degree of privilege that a user has in accessing a file depends both on the identity of the file and on the identity of the user. Although it is possible in theory to grant distinct sets of privileges to each (user, file) pair, the cost of storing, updating, and checking such a mass of information is not practical in any but the smallest systems. What is usually done instead is to identify *classes* of users, and to grant the same privileges to all users in a class. The most commonly encountered classes are the following.

1. The user most intimately associated with a file, often because he created it, is its *owner.* Two or more users can be designated as having owner privileges, but this is not often done.

2. The owner may have *partners,* who are supposed to collaborate with him in using the file. These may be coworkers on a project, or perhaps a set of persons who need to share certain information. In some systems, users who share an account or subaccount number are partners; in others, partnerships are defined explicitly. It may be possible for an owner to have one set of partners with respect to one file, and another set with respect to a different file.

3. Independently of partnerships, certain *designated users* may be granted access privileges not available to users generally. For example, a sociologist collecting data might give certain individuals the right to append their data to one of his files.

4. Users other than the owner, partners, and designated users constitute the largest class. We shall call its members the *public*.

The public generally enjoys fewer privileges than the partners, who in term enjoy fewer than the owner. Each designated user may be given privileges anywhere in the range.

Users in the foregoing classes may be permitted any of a number of different *access rights* to a file. The variety of possible access rights is extensive. The following list is representative, but not exhaustive.

1. *None.* It is possible in some systems for a user to have so little privilege with respect to a file that he cannot even learn of its existence.

2. *Knowledge.* The user can determine that the file exists and who its owner is. The user can then petition the owner for more extensive rights. Most systems permit public knowledge of files, and make the catalog available for browsing.

3. *Execution.* The user can load the program for execution, but cannot make a copy. Proprietary programs are often made available under this right.

4. *Reading.* The user can read the file for any purpose, including execution and copying.

5. *Appending.* The user can add data to the file, often only at the end, but can neither rewrite nor remove any of the file's content. This right is useful in collecting data from a variety of sources.

6. *Updating.* The user can rewrite the file's data. This normally includes writing the file initially, rewriting it completely or in part, and removing all or a portion of the data. Some systems distinguish among different degrees of updating.

7. *Changing protection.* The user can change the access rights granted to users. A partner of the owner, if given this right, can extend access rights to his partners in a different partnership. To prevent abuses of this extremely powerful mechanism, it is normally possible to specify which rights can be changed by the holder of this right.

8. *Deletion.* The user can delete the file from the file system.

The foregoing list of access rights can usually be thought of as constituting a hierarchy, with each right implying those that precede it. Thus the protection status of a file could be fully described by stating the highest access right for each class of user. A typical status might be that the owner may do anything (i.e., delete), the partners may append, and the public may read. This small amount of information can be kept in the catalog as part of the file description.

Exceptions can occur to treating the list of access rights as a hierarchy. In OS/360, for example, a user can be authorized to append to a file but not to read it. Such a restriction might be used by an instructor collecting input from students who are not to see each other's work.

The MPE III system for the HP 3000 classifies users and files in a more structured manner. Every file belongs to a group, every group to an account, and every account to the system. Every user belongs to an account and is identified with one of its groups. A group of files may be private to a user, shared by the users who belong to one account, or open to the public. The user classes include owner, group user, group librarian, account user, account librarian, and public. For each class, the owner specifies access rights. Most of these have already been described, but another is the accessing user's right to save the file into his own group.

A certain amount of access control can be achieved by the use of passwords. Different modes of access to a file can be contingent on the user's supplying a password originally assigned by the owner. One system provides for each file up to four different optional passwords, for execution, reading, appending, and writing. A fifth, master password is needed to set or reset any of the other four. As with all password schemes, the effectiveness of this one for sharing depends upon the sharing users not to divulge passwords intentionally or reveal them accidentally.

6.1.4   Data Integrity

Of the many hazards faced by a computer system, errors in data are among the most serious. How do data become unreliable? The three most common sources are *garbage, invasion,* and *malfunction.* Garbage data are those with errors present originally, for any of a variety of reasons. The application designer may have specified pressure gradient when wind velocity was desired, the velocity may have been entered in knots rather than in meters per second, or the wrong digits may have been entered. In any event, the results of the computation can be no better than the original data. The standard dictum is ''garbage in–garbage out'' (GIGO). It is virtually impossible for the operating system to do anything about this type of garbage, which should not be confused with the ''garbage'' data areas whose collection is discussed in Section 2.4.2. The burden of avoiding the GIGO trap falls on each user.

Invasion of one user's information resource by another, whether malicious or unintentional, can result in corruption of the data. Here the operating system can indeed provide protection, as discussed in Section 6.1.3. General approaches to protection not only of files, but of other system resources as well, are discussed in Section 7.1.

Malfunction comes in many forms. The user program may not have been designed to update all occurrences of an item in a multifile data base.

Lack of correct synchronization can result in the nullification of an update, as illustrated in Section 4.1. On a more elementary level, a new version of a user's program may perform an incorrect computation. Even the operating system can operate incorrectly, in ways too numerous to mention. Hardware malfunction contributes its share of errors. Although erroneous execution of processor instructions is not unknown, it is extremely rare. More frequent are malfunctions of the I/O subsystem. Disconnection of a terminal from the rest of the system occurs frequently. A dust particle present during magnetic surface recording can make the record unreadable. Far more severe is the head crash, described in Section 5.4.

What can be done to mitigate the effects of losing data? The best step is probably to anticipate that it might occur. The user can take snapshots periodically, perform occasional checks for data integrity, and provide for a *rerun* from the most recent checkpoint in the event error is detected. Just how to accomplish the foregoing is, of course, highly dependent upon the application.

A step that the operating system can take to guard against loss of information from disks and other high-risk devices is to make backup copies periodically, usually on magnetic tape, which can be securely stored off-line. Two types of backup are common, the *full dump* and the *incremental dump*. The full dump (sometimes called "periodic" dump) is just what its name implies. A duplicate copy of the entire on-line disk library is written on tape. Any file can later be recreated in the state it was in when the dump was taken. The full dump suffers from three disadvantages.

1. The file system may have to be withdrawn from service during the dump. Alternatively, the dump will have to omit files that are open for any form of writing.

2. The dump can easily take several hours, and represents a substantial workload for the system.

3. Because of the dump's long duration, it can be performed only infrequently, perhaps a few times per month. The information dumped may be badly out of date when it is retrieved.

The incremental dump is a copy of only those files and directories that have been changed since the previous dump. To determine which files are to be dumped, a flag is provided in the directory entry for each file. The flag is set when the file is altered, and reset when it is dumped. Recovery proceeds by mounting incremental dump tapes in *reverse* chronological order. The recovery process selects from each tape only those files it has not already restored. The final tape used is that of the most recent full dump. Incremental dumps can be used either to increase the interval between full dumps or to decrease the interval since the last backup of changed files. An advantage of the incremental dump is that it can be performed concurrently with other use of the file system. Its principal disadvantage is the complexity of the recovery procedure.

A third measure to enhance data integrity is provided as a service of some operating systems, and can otherwise be implemented by the user. It is the retention of *generation files,* which are chronologically successive versions of one file. At least three generations are kept, the *current, father,* and *grandfather* files, to have one available as backup if the two involved in a file maintenance operation are both corrupted.

6.1.5 Data Base Management Systems

The use of increasingly large on-line files accessed by several programs has created a number of problems in information management. The attempt to mitigate their effects has led to the development of more generalized systems of device and file management than have been discussed thus far. These systems are known as *data base management systems* (DBMS). Several problems typical of those that DBMS are intended to solve are sketched in the following subsection. The principal data models that are designed to help address those problems are presented briefly in the subsequent subsection.

Problems. An organization may have several application programs whose data requirements overlap in part. For example, a payroll program to compensate employees and a labor distribution program to charge the costs of compensation to different projects must both use the actual compensation data. The payroll program requires information about deductions from pay; the labor distribution program does not. The latter does require, however, a breakdown of each employee's time spent on different projects; the former usually does not. If separate files are maintained for the two programs, many items of data will be duplicated. Sometimes not just two but several programs manipulate the same data. It turns out in practice to be extremely difficult to guarantee that any change to one copy of the common data is faithfully made to every other copy. Moreover, multiple copies cost more to store, not only in space on the storage medium but potentially even in the provision of extra devices to hold the extra data on-line.

The programmer is really not interested in the engineering details of backing storage devices. The geometry of tracks and cylinders, and the non-linearity of seek time as a function of intercylinder distance are usually of little concern to the user. Nevertheless, the profound effect that these device characteristics can have on the efficiency of system operation forces the user to consider them in designing files and planning accesses. Particularly painful is the application redesign that may become advisable when new devices replace old.

The file user is often interested in accessing records on the basis of the values of fields that they contain. The collections manager for a public utility may desire a list of customers who have been in arrears for three or more months of the last six and who owe at least $50. Programming language facilities to specify the request directly can relieve the programmers of having to write a search program in terms of lower level primitives, such as reading records and comparing fields.

If the decision is made to avoid the problems inherent in duplicating fields, then other concerns arise. Different users or programs view a given item of information differently and may associate the item logically with different sets of other items. It may be a search key for some users but not for others. Completely different logical organizations of a file may be required by different users.

A change in one program may require a change in its data base. If the data base is shared with other programs, the change must be performed in such a manner as not to require corresponding changes in the other programs that access it.

A particularly touchy aspect of data base sharing is that different users may have different access rights. Some may be permitted to update a salary field, others only to inspect it, yet others only to inspect those below a certain amount, while the remainder may be denied access either to the salary field or to the entire payroll record.

Approaches. Three different types of models of data have been considered seriously. In a *relational* data base, the relations among different data fields are expressed by grouping them into ordered *n*-tuples of related fields. Thus the relation WAGE might be represented by a list of ordered pairs, each composed of employee number and hourly wage. The relation PAYMENT might be represented by a list of ordered triples: customer name, amount, and date. In a *hierarchic* (or "hierarchical") data base, items are organized into tree structures. Thus for a payroll, the employee name may stand at the root node, or top level of the tree; compensation, statutory deductions, and optional deductions at the next level; and so on. Values may be associated with nodes at any level, not just with leaves. In a *network* data base the items can be organized into arbitrary directed graphs. The sometimes artificial constraints imposed by tree structure are removed, but the processing is correspondingly more complex.

Whatever model of data is adopted for the DBMS, means are provided for referring to the data in higher-level terms than those found in COBOL, PL/I, or Pascal. *Data-definition* languages are provided instead; these may be either influenced by and built upon a programming language, or designed independently. The user describes data and specifies actions in a high-level language that may well relieve him from having to use, or perhaps even to learn, a standard programming language.

The mapping from the user's view of a file to its physical representation on a device now passes through an intermediate level, the data base as modeled by the DBMS. Different mappings are performed for different users. This process is not as simple as it might sound, because the requirements of different users may interact. A very simple example is a request to delete a record from a user's file. Because other users access the same fields as part of different logical files, it is possible that nothing may be deleted at all, yet the information must be skipped in subsequent processing of the requester's file. A crucial consideration, of course, is not to lose too much processing efficiency.

An operating system's file manager is not normally concerned with data values, except as the search key for a single record. Nor need it take into account the logical relationships among the fields of one record, or among several files. On the other hand, these issues are essential to a DBMS. Although the difference between a modest DBMS and a powerful file management system may appear small, there is a crucial distinction between managing a collection of separate files and managing an integrated collection of data fields. The issues of data base management are more specialized than our concerns in understanding operating systems. Because of the complexity of DBMS, another book the size of this one would be required to explain them adequately. For those reasons we leave DBMS essentially unexplored.

6.1.6 Implementation Techniques

The information known by the system about a file is collected into a file *descriptor*. The richness of the description varies from one system to another. At the very least, the file's identity and physical location are present. The following information fields are candidates for inclusion.

1. *Identification*. The descriptor includes both a symbolic name, such as the tree path name, and an internal name for ease of reference.

2. *Physical location*. If the entire file occupies a single contiguous extent in backing storage, it is sufficient to indicate where it begins and how long it is. If, however, the file's records are more widely distributed, the descriptor either contains explicitly the full set of location information or a pointer to a table where at least the beginning of that information can be found.

3. *Physical organization*. Related to physical location, this item describes the organization used to implement the file, as discussed in Section 6.2.

4. *Device descriptor*. This contains information about the physical device on which the file resides, and can be used to assist in constructing channel

programs for file operations. To obviate keeping a copy in the descriptor of each file on the device, a pointer to the device descriptor can be included instead.

5. *Access control information.* Included are identification of the owner, means of recognizing a partner, the list of designated users, and the access rights granted to each class of user. Passwords, if used, are part of this information.

6. *Type.* This item, sometimes incorporated in the file name, can include such information as the purpose of the file (e.g., data, Pascal source) and the encoding used (e.g., binary, ASCII, EBCDIC).

7. *Disposition.* This indicates whether the file is temporary, to be deleted upon termination of the using process, or permanent. For permanent files, it may indicate whether a generation file or other backup copy is to be made automatically.

8. *Administrative information.* Included are such historical and measurement information as time of creation, time of last modification, number of accesses, identity of using processes, and expiration date.

Although the file descriptor could be kept in the directory entry, this would restrict the file system to accessing each file through only one directory. Moreover, it would increase the size of all directory entries, thus retarding every search for a file. Common practice is to keep the descriptor with the file it describes and, in each directory entry for the file, to place a pointer to the descriptor.

When the file is to be active, it is convenient to place a copy of its descriptor in main storage, reducing the number of disk accesses by one for each reference to the file. The copy is typically made when a process issues an *OPEN* command for the file. Because the process may not have the right to read the entire descriptor, and surely not to rewrite it, the duplicate is normally written into a portion of the operating system's storage. This approach works well, too, when several processes are sharing access to a file.

It is convenient, particularly for a disk volume that is not permanently mounted, to include on that volume a directory of its contents. Such a directory is called a *volume directory* or, in at least one system, *volume table of contents* (VTOC). Volume directories constitute part of the system of multiple directories that extend from the top level of the catalog to the individual files.

How can backing storage be organized to hold files? Because the size of a file may vary during its lifetime, with its maximum size possibly never known in advance, backing storage for files is usually allocated dynamically.

Although free blocks could be linked into a single list, their number is usually so large that maintaining the list would be too slow. It is customary instead to use index tables to point to free blocks, often with one table per device or volume.

The backing storage allocated to a file normally need not be a single contiguous area. In fact, much time is saved by not recopying a large file to a new area when it becomes even larger. The price of that saving is to store the file in pieces and to keep track of the pieces. Of the many schemes that could be devised, three are fairly common. To avoid external fragmentation, and to make efficient use of devices, most file management systems use one block size for all files.

Block Chain.   One method is simply to link a file's blocks into a singly linked *block chain,* as shown in Fig. 6.4. This is particularly effective if the content of the file is to be processed in sequential order. File scan can be terminated by either of two mechanisms. A special word can be recorded to mark the end of the file, or the scanning process can compare a running length count with the file length stored in the file descriptor. The only storage overhead in the block chain is the pointer word in each block. Insertion or deletion of a block in the middle of the file affects only the immediately preceding block. For access to an arbitrary record, however, the time cost can be prohibitive.

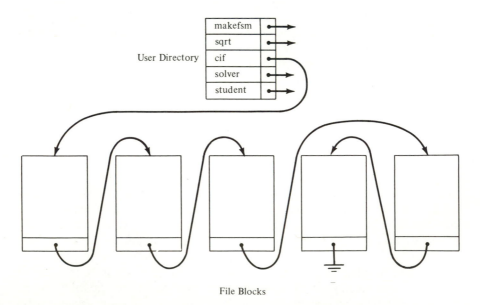

File Blocks

Figure 6.4 File System Structure Using Block Chains

Index Block. To increase speed of access to a point within the file, the chain block pointers can be removed from the chain and collected into a single table, called an *index block*. The order of the pointers within the index block is the same as that of the file blocks within the file. If the number of file blocks exceeds the number of pointer locations in an index block, multiple index blocks are used, linked in a chain. A link to the subsequent index block is distinguished from a pointer to a file block either by its position or by a flag bit. Any block can be accessed directly by specifying the file name and the offset within the index block. Storage overhead includes the index blocks, and can waste a significant portion of the last index block if it is not nearly full. Time overhead includes access to the index block, which need not be repeated for multiple accesses to the file. A major disadvantage of the index block organization is that insertion or deletion of a block in the middle of the file requires revision of the entire index block. Figure 6.5 illustrates the use of index blocks.

File Map. Replacing the linearly organized index block by a linked structure greatly simplifies the revision that would otherwise accompany

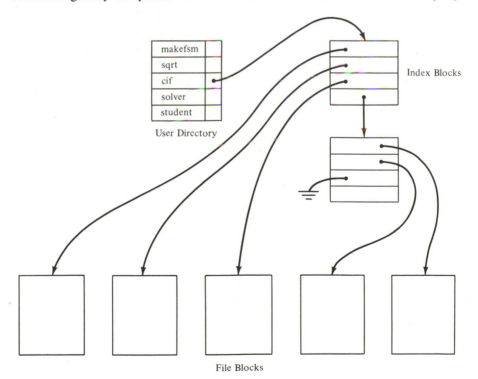

Figure 6.5 File System Structure Using Index Blocks

midfile insertions and deletions. This is most conveniently accomplished by establishing for all files simultaneously a *file map* of words in one-to-one correspondence with block locations in the file. The kth word in the file map represents the kth block location in the file system. Hence a pointer is not needed to find the block associated with a given file map word. The word corresponding to block j of a file is used instead to specify where block $j+1$ of the same file is to be found. It does so, again not by pointing to a file block, but by pointing to the file map word associated with that file block. A portion of a file map is shown in Fig. 6.6. File *cif*, for example, consists of blocks 10, 11, 12, 8, and 5, in that order. Storage overhead is again one word per block, with no waste for partially full index tables. Time overhead for a widely scattered file can be as high as one file map access per file block. It can be as low, for a file of contiguous blocks, as one file map access for the entire file. The file map itself can occupy several blocks without complications. It automatically holds not only the list of blocks for each file, but also the list of free blocks. Use of the file map permits easy insertion and deletion of blocks, but it forgoes the ability to find quickly block j of file i.

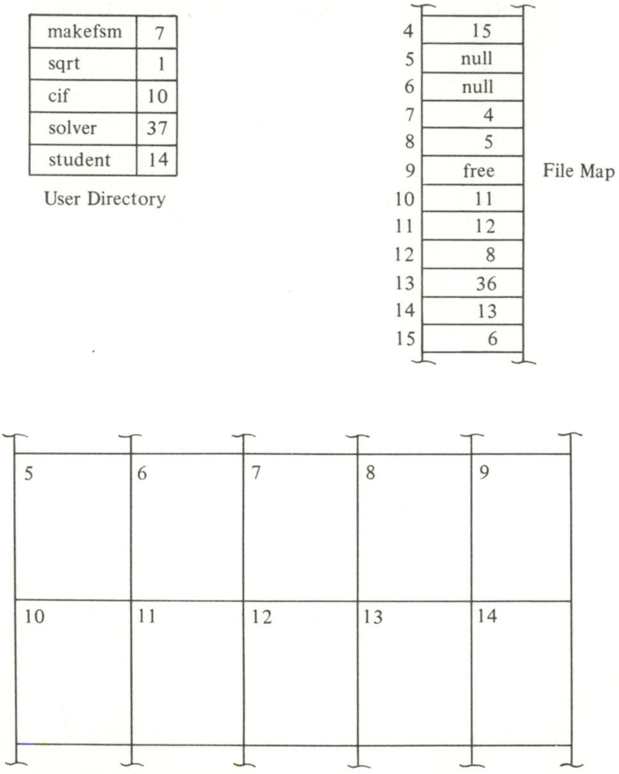

makefsm	7
sqrt	1
cif	10
solver	37
student	14

User Directory

4	15
5	null
6	null
7	4
8	5
9	free
10	11
11	12
12	8
13	36
14	13
15	6

File Map

5	6	7	8	9
10	11	12	13	14

File Blocks

Figure 6.6 File System Structure Using File Map

The choice of block size is an important implementation decision. If the blocks are large, buffer space will be more costly. Moreover, internal fragmentation of a file's last block will be high. This second effect is less severe for files in backing storage than for pages in main storage, both because the storage medium is cheaper and because the percentage loss is lower if a file has many blocks. If the blocks are small, time will be wasted in many I/O operations where fewer would suffice. Equally important as the number of I/O operations is the efficiency of each. To match the file system to the hardware devices, the block size is often chosen to equal the capacity of a sector or track on disk. Some operating systems, following the policy of maximizing the user's control over the hardware, permit the user to choose his own block sizes. Not only does this offer opportunities for gross inefficiency, but it also complicates the design of the file system.

An effective, simple implementation is that of the UNIX disk file system. This is treated as a randomly addressable linear array of 512-byte blocks. Starting at a fixed location on disk, each block contains eight 64-byte file descriptions. Called an ''i-node'', each description contains 13 direct addresses. The first 10 are those of the first 10 blocks of the file. If the file length exceeds 5120 (10 × 512), an eleventh address points to a second-level block that contains the addresses of the next 128 blocks. Thus 10 blocks can be accessed directly and 128 by one level of indirection. If the file length exceeds 70656 (138 × 512), a twelfth address points to a third-level block that has the addresses of 128 second-level blocks. This provides access to 16384 (128 × 128) more blocks by two levels of indirection. If the file length exceeds 8459264 (16522 × 512), a thirteenth address in the i-node points to a block that holds the addresses of 128 third-level blocks, for access by three levels of indirection to just over 1 gigabyte.

The foregoing set of files is accessed by means of a set of directories, which are themselves files, organized as a tree, but with extra links permitted. Each directory entry holds the 14-byte name of a file (or of another directory) and the 2-byte address of its i-node relative to the start of the i-nodes.

The addresses of free blocks are themselves packed 50 to a block, and those blocks of addresses are chained into a linked list. Thus a single I/O operation suffices to obtain 50 blocks and a pointer to the addresses of another 50. Neither compaction nor garbage collection is required, because (1) all allocations are of the same size, (2) there is no need for contiguity, and (3) freeing is explicit.

The system maintains a table of all active i-nodes, and a current I/O pointer into each open file. These I/O pointers are kept in an ''open file table'' in main storage. Each sharing user has a pointer, in his own swappable file table, to his own I/O pointer (in the open file table) for the shared file. The user is unaware of pointers and i-nodes, because all file access is by path name in the directory tree. The conversion of path name into an active i-node table entry is performed by *OPEN,* which places a pointer to that entry in a newly created open file table entry. *CREATE* first creates a new active i-node table entry and writes its relative address into a directory, before proceeding similarly to *OPEN. READ* and *WRITE* access the file through the active i-node table entry, and *SEEK* resets the I/O pointer, thus performing a logical seek without seeking physically. *CLOSE* frees the structures built by *OPEN* and *CREATE.*

6.2   INDIVIDUAL FILE ORGANIZATION

The way information is organized into a file can have a profound effect on the cost of storing, accessing, and using it. We have already seen the advantages that may accrue from blocking records, and the cost of blocking. Other aspects of organization are dictated by the intended sequence of use of different records. In *sequential* access, each record of a file is accessed in order by the values of a record field designated as the *key.* It may or may not be necessary to use each individual record, but in normal sequential processing that decision is not made until the record has been accessed and its key examined. In *random* access, the order in which records are accessed is not predictable. It must be possible to access two records consecutively without examining all records whose keys are intermediate in value between the keys of those two records. Before considering how the operating system assists in handling an individual file, we review a few of the more important file organizations.

6.2.1   Sequential Organization

The earliest computer backing storage, cards and tape, permitted program-controlled access only in sequence by physical adjacency. Although modern storage devices facilitate access in random sequence, many applications do not benefit from random access. Moreover, sequential access is less costly than random if the fraction of records to be accessed is high. Sequential files continue, therefore, to hold great importance.

Although successive records of a sequential file can be linked in a list structure, efficient access normally dictates that they be stored in physical order by key. Typical keys might be employee name or number for payroll, meter location for electric utility billing, or part number for inventory control. Outputs such as paychecks, customer bills, and stock level reports are usually produced for all records with regular frequency. Changes to file record fields, such as employee name, address, or wage rate, customer payments or meter readings, or additions to and withdrawals from stock, arrive more or less irregularly. Such *transactions* can be accumulated into batches, sorted into file order and processed against the file in a single pass, which is normally one of the passes regularly scheduled for output. A sequential file should be distinguished from a *serial* file, whose records may follow in arbitrary order.

It may or may not be possible to update a sequential file without recopying the unchanged information. If the medium is punched cards, or nonaddressable magnetic tape, it is not possible to rewrite the information into the same cards or onto the same tape. Even on other storage media, there may be no room to update records in place, if the transactions result in increasing the length of variable-length records. If new records are added to the file, or old ones deleted, it may for that reason be necessary to copy the file. Even if copying is not necessary it may be wise. If a transaction is later discovered to be in error, the easiest way to undo its effect may well be to recopy the record as it existed before the transaction was applied. If updated records are written to a new file, the old version of the file will still be available after updating.

To permit access to a sequential file, the control program must be able to translate the user's file name into a physical starting location. This latter may be, for example, the identification of a magnetic tape reel, or the address of a track on a permanently mounted disk. If a disk is used for a sequential file that is to be copied during updating, arm motion can be greatly reduced by careful allocation of space for the two versions. An obvious approach is to use adjacent cylinders for the old and new files. More attractive is to split each cylinder into a group of tracks for the old file and another group for the corresponding portion of the new file.

One fairly common form of sequential access is the reading of a program into executable storage. At least one system provides a file organization, the *partitioned* file, intended chiefly for program storage. A partitioned file is essentially a collection of sequential files grouped together under a common name.

6.2.2 Random Organization

For some applications, batching transactions for an eventual pass against a master file causes an intolerable delay. A case in point is airline reservations, for which the potential traveler is often unable or unwilling to wait a week, or even a day, to learn on what flight space is available. Because the sequence in which records need to be examined cannot be predicted, means are required for inexpensive random access to the files. The advent of disk storage made random access to large files economically feasible.

The records of a file designed for random access are accessed by key, as are those of a sequential file, but the records are no longer required to be in order by key. To permit access to a direct file, the control program must be able to translate the pair composed of user's file name and key value into the physical location of the corresponding record if it exists. This is customarily implemented as a two-stage process. The file name is translated into the address of a table, usually called an *index,* in which the keys are stored sequentially, each with the address of the corresponding record. If a variable-length record grows too large, overflowing its storage allotment, it can be moved to wherever space is available, perhaps at the end of the file. If a record has been moved because of overflow, the index entry may or may not have been updated. If not, a pointer to the new record location replaces the record at its previous location. A new record can be appended to the end of the file, and its key inserted in sequence into the index. A deleted record need not be removed, but merely rendered inaccessible. This is done either by deleting its index entry or by setting a marker bit either in the index entry or in the record itself. Because access is made directly to a specified record, without reading intervening records, a file designed for random access is sometimes called a *direct* file.

The phrase "random access" is applied to devices as well as to files, and it is important to distinguish between the two contexts. A random-access file is one that is intended to be accessed at random. A random-access device is one that is perceived as being suitable for the storage of a random-access file. Strictly speaking, it is a device whose random-access time is as low as its sequential-access time. Magnetic core storage is an example. A more liberal interpretation requires only that the random-access time be acceptably low. For most applications, disks and drums would be classified as random-access; tapes would not. A random-access device is not restricted to storing direct files; it is quite able also to store sequential files.

6.2.3   Other Organizations

Provision of both sequential access and random access to the same file is desirable in some applications. Electricity bills are generated most economically by passing the customer file sequentially. Prompt answering of customers' telephoned inquiries dictates random access. A file organization is required that permits random access without scanning undesired records, yet also permits sequential access without repeated consultation of an index table of keys. A direct file whose records are actually stored consecutively in key order meets the requirements. But for how long? As soon as record overflow occurs or the need for insertion or deletion arises, key order cannot be maintained.

Deletion poses an easy problem. A single bit near the start of the record can be used to control skipping, and the corresponding index entry can easily be flagged, or even removed. The provision of extra space and some pointers allows for modest amounts of overflow and insertion. Blank space is set aside every few records to allow for insertion of new records that have keys in the range of those few original record keys. This extra space is typically on the same track, or another track of the same cylinder, although it may be on a neighboring cylinder. When a record is inserted, either some records are moved to allow insertion in the proper sequence, or the new record is placed in the free space and a pointer to it is appended to its predecessor in key order. The originally unoccupied space can also be used to handle overflow from a growing record. Extra overflow tracks can also be provided to hold records once the primary overflow areas become filled. Pointers to and from those records will consume space and, more important, will generate extra disk accesses to nonadjacent cylinders. Ultimately, sequential processing becomes so adversely affected that it becomes necessary to reorganize the file.

The details of implementation of such an *indexed sequential* file vary from one system to another. File organization that permits both sequential and random access has two major costs. From the outset, extra space is required for inserted records, whether new or overflowed. As file modification continues, more and more time in sequential processing is spent in indirect access to records. Eventually, the file needs to be recopied into sequential order.

The list of possible file organizations does not stop here. Other useful organizations include: *inverted* files, for records with multiple key fields; *multilists* having arbitrary pointer structures; and *tree-structured* files, which are often, although not always, implemented as linked lists. Among trees, the B-tree is assuming increasing importance as an implementation of different file organizations.

6.2.4 Access Methods

Some operating systems provide for one or more of the foregoing organizations; others leave their implementation to the user. Although a few important systems provide no assistance with file organization, most large systems do provide for sequential and direct files, and for simultaneous sequential and random access.

The way information is accessed by the I/O supervisor depends both on the details of file organization and on whether blocking is provided. The combination of file organization and blocking discipline chosen is referred to in OS/360-370 as an "access method". This is in two ways a misnomer. The file organization may constrain possible methods of access, but it does not dictate the method. On the other hand, the choice of buffering discipline is also an essential part of the access mechanism, but is not connoted by the phrase. In many other contexts, the term "access method" is used to mean what it says.

In the UNIX system, a disk file is treated by the system as comprising a sequence of fixed-length blocks for each of which an index entry can be established. Other structural details and means of access must be programmed by the user.

At the other extreme, IBM's OS/360 and VM/370 [Seawright and MacKinnon, 1979] provide directly for a large variety of file organizations. When the user creates a file, he specifies the desired conceptual organization, and when the user programs, he writes commands that reflect the chosen organization. The language and operating systems together convert the user's requests into the appropriate I/O operations.

6.3 HIERARCHY OF FUNCTION

The efficient management of files is not really separable from that of the devices on which they reside. In some systems (e.g., Multics), the two are closely interlinked; in others (e.g., OS/360, EXEC 8, CDC's SCOPE) the various facets are interdependent but separately identifiable. The functions range from file manipulations at a symbolic level to the actions of physical devices. It is often convenient to organize the collection of functions into a linear hierarchy in which operations at any one level can be implemented without knowledge of the details of implementation at lower levels. This means that the design and understanding of the I/O control program can be effected with the aid of the programming technique known as *hierarchic modularity*. Control program modules at each level obtain the services of lower-level modules, communicating with them only by calls and the associated parameters.

With the diversity of function that we have seen both in the preceding chapter and in this one, it should be no surprise that there is more than one way to organize the many operations into a hierarchy. One possible organization is shown in Fig. 6.7 and discussed here; many different organizations can also be developed. Typical names of software modules are "basic file system", "logical file system", and "physical file system". Unfortunately, the functions of the "basic file system" module, for example, of two different operating systems can be rather dissimilar. There appears to be little agreement as to what the names mean. Consequently, the present discussion stresses module function over title.

At level 1 in our sample hierarchy the logical file name is translated to find the physical location of the file. If the file is not on-line, a mounting message is issued. Once the file is on-line the descriptor information is stored in a table for immediate access as required by the process; level 1 is normally not reentered.

At level 2, various specifications are incorporated into the routines that will perform commands to access the file. The specifications include logical file organization (e.g., sequential, random, inverted), buffer disciplines, and whether blocking is to be used. Typical commands at this level are *OPEN* and *CLOSE*. The level 2 routines are usually invoked only at the start and end of file use. In some situations, such as recording information on a

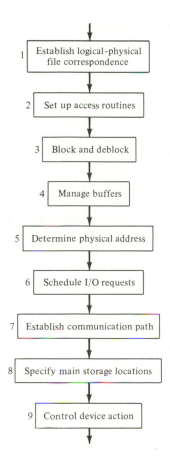

Figure 6.7 One Hierarchy of File and Device Management

scratch file and subsequently reading it, multiple use will occur. In the example cited the scratch file may be first opened for output, then closed, later opened for input, and finally closed again.

Level 3 is omitted if blocking is not in use. Otherwise, it interprets commands such as *GET* and *PUT,* assembling logical records into physical blocks and disassembling physical blocks into logical records.

Level 4 appears in all but the crudest systems. Commands such as *READ* and *WRITE,* issued either directly by the user or by the level 3 routines, request the movement of physical records into and out of buffers, according to the disciplines in effect. Although the description of blocking and buffering is most readily understood in the context of sequential files, other logical file organizations use blocking and/or buffering. Inverted files may require both, whereas random organization uses blocking but not buffering.

At level 5 begins the process of preparing an actual device access when an input buffer is empty or output buffer is full. For file organizations such as direct, the ultimate physical address required is not determinable in advance of making the first access to consult the index. The address of that initial access, however, can be determined. Knowledge is required of the block's key or position within the logical file and of the physical file layout in terms of device parameters such as track length.

At level 6 the many requests that may be competing for access to device, control unit, or channel are enqueued in priority order. The channel programs for each request are built at this stage. These incorporate a specification of the initial main storage locations to be accessed.

The device has been identified, and the channel program to control it constructed. The direction of data flow has been specified. At level 7, a communication path must be established between the device and main storage. This function is performed typically by hardware. If there is a choice of potential paths, it may be necessary to select one of several. This may be accomplished in part by hardware, although selection by the control program is more common.

The specification of all main storage locations is shown at level 8 in the hierarchy chiefly because the implementation is in hardware. The actual storage locations to be used could have been determined as high as level 4.

Finally, at level 9, the channel program is executed and the specified device action and data transmission occur.

The foregoing hierarchy has ignored allocation of devices, which is presumed to have taken place statically prior to first mention of the file in the program. In some systems, just the contrary occurs. When the file is first mentioned, the device allocation request is generated and the allocation is made dynamically. This critical distinction is discussed in Section 5.2.

It should be remembered, too, that the logical division of the resource management tasks into a hierarchy of functions does not automatically entail the packaging of each such function into a hierarchy of modules. Although some systems may maintain close correspondence between the functions identified here and the parts of the program, other systems may be differently organized. The functions that they must perform, however, are basically the same.

FOR FURTHER STUDY

Good general treatments of file management are to be found in Watson [1970, Sec. 6.1], Shaw [1974, Chap. 9], Tsichritzis and Bernstein [1974, Chap. 6], and Lister [1975, Chap. 7]. A deeper treatment of the implementation of file operations is presented in Sec. 9.3 of Habermann [1976].

The tutorial by Dodd [1969] offers a good introduction to ways of organizing an individual file. A much more thorough treatment is contained in Chaps. 2 and 3 of Wiederhold [1977].

Alternative hierarchies of I/O function are presented by Shaw [1974, Sec. 9.6] and by Tsichritzis and Bernstein [1974, Sec. 6.1]. The article by

Dependahl and Presser [1976] also illustrates hierarchical I/O, with particular reference to two commercial system implementations.

EXERCISES

6.1 A volume mounting message can be issued as soon as the need for the volume is known, often before the job is scheduled. Volumes mounted before the process becomes ready are said to be *premounted*. Compare the advantages of, and requirements for, premounting as opposed to demand mounting.

6.2 Why is a B-tree potentially more attractive than an arbitrary tree for implementing a file system?

6.3 Why is file creation not listed among the access rights in Section 6.1.3?

6.4 Explain how the owner of a file can lose all protection by granting the right to change protection status.

6.5 What information would you need to determine the optimum frequency at which to take checkpoint dumps?

6.6 Making an incremental dump requires the checking of flags in directory entries. Devise a scheme for tree-structured directories that limits flag checking to only those directories that have flags set.

6.7 In recovery from an incremental dump, what is the advantage of proceeding in reverse rather than forward chronological order?

6.8 During file system recovery, it is sometimes decided to compact the files. What is the benefit, and what is the cost?

6.9 Explain the effect of each physical characteristic of a disk drive on the performance of a disk-based file system.

6.10 For each of the three file system implementation methods described in Section 6.1.6, explain the changes that occur when the file
(a) grows at the end;
(b) shrinks at the end;
(c) grows in the middle;
(d) shrinks in the middle.

6.11 Suggest a file system implementation method suitable for user-specified block sizes.

6.12 Although UNIX file storage never needs to be compacted, there is a benefit in compacting it occasionally. Explain why.

6.13 A serial file differs from a sequential file in that the order of the records is arbitrary. For what kinds of application might a serial file be useful?

6.14 A random file with many records has a very large index. Access time increases with increasing index size. Propose ways to counter the increase.

6.15 Develop hierarchies of I/O function that are alternative to that of Fig. 6.7.

Chapter 7

SYSTEM MANAGEMENT

Each of the five preceding chapters has focused on the management of one particular system resource. By now it has become obvious that the several resources and their management are hardly independent, but rather are related by such obvious links as the nearly ubiquitous time–space trade-off as well as by more subtle links. For purposes of exposition, however, it has been convenient to discuss several major resource classes separately. Some important topics in resource management are not so easily identified with a particular resource type; rather, they apply more to the collection of resources as a whole, and are considered here in a separate chapter.

7.1 PROTECTION OF RESOURCES

The hardware, software, and data resources of a computer system, some shared by the entire community of users, some by a few, and others proprietary to an individual member, constitute a treasure trove that represents a substantial investment of money, time, and effort. Any treasure may become lost, strayed, or stolen. Computer systems need to be protected not only against the encroachments of the outside world, but also against internal pressures. After all, the members of a multiuser community often have no inherent reason to guard each others' treasures; they are merely joined in a *mariage de convenance* aimed at reducing the economic cost of using a computer. Consequently, the system managers, both human and program, must bear primary responsibility for protection of system resources, and they normally accept much of the responsibility for protecting user resources as well.

7.1.1 Types of Dangers

One type of threat to resources is *loss* of data or of the integrity of data. The most extreme form is, of course, total loss, but even partial losses, especially if unknown to the user, can be insidious. The causes of loss of integrity include accidents, control program failure, hardware failure, and the user's own mistakes. The perpetration of fraud is often based on intentional tampering with data. The integrity of data has already been discussed in Section 6.1.4.

Another threat is the misuse or *misapplication* of resources. The disclosure of information in a person's medical record for nonmedical purposes may constitute a violation of the physician's confidentiality. Leaving a printout of a payroll master file in a public place can lead to abuses by employees not authorized to read it. The examination of proprietary data by a competitor who has obtained access, perhaps legitimately, to the same service bureau system as the data's owner can result in an unfair business advantage. Application of a computer system to purposes perceived as contrary to public policy also constitutes a misapplication of resources. Many cases of crime by computer have been reported. According to Parker [1976], the average loss per incident is of the order of $500,000.

Unauthorized access is another threat. Even if not malicious it can result in the destruction of programs and data. Malicious penetration may be for the purpose of violating privacy restrictions, or it may be only a means of obtaining cost-free computing services. Prevention of unauthorized access is sometimes called *restriction*.

A fourth threat is the leakage of information, access to and use of which are permitted, but further transmission of which is not. An example is a service bureau program attempting to extract information from a customer program and transmit it to its owner. Prevention of this leakage is known as *confinement*.

As is evident from the discussion, the foregoing classes of threats are not mutually exclusive, nor are they rigidly defined. The classification is intended chiefly to indicate the major types of dangers against which protection may be desired. Observe that privacy of information is involved in most of the classes.

There are a number of fairly standard protection problems that must be considered by system designers. One is that of mutual suspicion between a calling and a called procedure. The caller seeks protection against being damaged by the called procedure. The called procedure seeks to exclude the caller from information files private to the called procedure. A second problem is to guarantee to a calling procedure that an object passed as an argument to another procedure will not be modified. A third problem is to limit the propagation of access rights. One procedure may wish to share data with a second, but prohibit the second from sharing them with a third. An extension of that problem is to revoke rights previously granted.

Many important protection problems do not admit of technical solution. Misapplication is almost invariably not a technical problem, at least not at the level of hardware and operating system design. Administrative, legal, and social safeguards must be invoked to guard against misuse of computer systems. Even for problems that appear to be technical, the most effective solutions, albeit not always the most palatable, may be nontechnical. One way to prevent unauthorized access, for example, is to enclose the computer system, including terminals, in a physically secure area and to control physical access by any person. Many technical approaches to protecting computer resources do exist, however, and they are surveyed in the following section.

7.1.2 Protection Mechanisms

The impairment of integrity, if not due to accident, or to hardware or software system failure, is most often due to contamination resulting from unauthorized access. The provision of restrictions to access, to be discussed later, protects against this contamination. Another cause of data disintegration is error in the program of a user who accesses the data legitimately. Although treating data of one type as though they were of another (e.g., a string of digit characters as though it were a decimal number) can poison those or other data, the type matching enforced by some compilers limits that source of error. Errors in the operation of concurrent processes, as discussed earlier, although considered until recently to be far more subtle, may be suppressed similarly by checking for violation of critical regions. This can be provided in compilers of languages that have been designed for writing concurrent programs.

Physical protection against electromagnetic radiation, fire, flood, earthquake, and bombing can help assure the integrity of a computer system. Maintaining backup copies of critical programs and data sets at a secure, remote location is sometimes used to mitigate the effect of a potential accident. A common guard against failure of electrical power is the so-called "uninterruptible power supply".

One way to render data unlikely to be misused is to make them too expensive to use by persons not equipped with a special tool. The data may be *encrypted* by algorithm or *encoded* with the aid of a codebook, and the transformed data left safely in sharable files. This approach is effective if it is considerably easier to restrict access to the decryption algorithm or to the codebook than to the data, which may be portions of a file other parts of which are legitimately needed by many users. It is assumed, of course, that the potential value of the information is less than the cost of breaking the cipher or discovering the code.

In implementing restrictions to access, a particularly important problem is that of *authentication* of the identity of a user at a terminal. Once the user is admitted to use of the system there is still, to be sure, the problem of restricting his access to specific resources. What concerns us now, however, is determining whether the user is who he says he is. The traditional solution is to issue to each user, or group of users, a *password*. A control program known sometimes as the *protection monitor* maintains a list of the identities and passwords of all authorized users. A common method of concealing password lists within the computer system is called *one-way encryption*. Passwords are encrypted by an algorithm that is not easily reversed. Only the encrypted form of a password is stored in the computer. Whenever the user enters a password, it is immediately encrypted and compared with the stored version. Even knowledge of the encryption algorithm together with the encrypted password is insufficient to yield the associated user password.

Passwords can be disclosed, however, by wiretapping or by electromagnetic pickup, as well as by examination of discarded ink ribbons or printouts, or even by peeking over a user's shoulder. The image left on a screen or in a terminal's local buffer may also reveal passwords. Several guards can be supplied against password disclosure at the terminal. The PLATO system for computer-assisted instruction displays the character "X" for each password character entered. Moreover, an extra "X" is occasionally inserted at random, making it impossible to tell even the length of the password. More effective yet is simply to disable display of the password. A method sometimes used on printing terminals is for the system first to overprint several characters (e.g., "X", "O", and "A") in each position where the user may subsequently type a password character.

Allowing the user to change the password decreases further the danger of disclosure. So does the use of *one-time* passwords. The protection monitor maintains for each authorized user a list of randomly selected passwords, which have previously been disclosed to the user. Each time the user desires access, he enters the next password on the list. An alternative that has been proposed is for the computer to transmit to the user a pseudo-random number x to which both the computer and user apply a simple transformation T. The user replies by transmitting $T(x)$ and, if that reply matches the computer's value, the user is admitted to service. A potential infiltrator who knows both x and $T(x)$ is unable to determine T, if it is well chosen, and consequently does not know how to reply to the different pseudo-random number y that is transmitted when the user attempts to sign on. Neither the one-time password nor the transformation scheme is proof, however, against an infiltrator who can attach his own terminal to the authorized user's line after authentication.

Unsuccessful threats to penetrate a system's access restrictions can be monitored and reported to the system managers. This information may be of use in tightening the defenses and perhaps even in identifying would-be infiltrators. The B7000/B6000 MCP, for example, logs all security errors on a standard file. Successful penetration can be signaled to the user if the response to his login includes a copy of the previous login or logout that used the same identification.

Physical protection of the system can be used to guard not only against damage due to accident but also against efforts at penetration. Protection of a centralized computer facility against entry by unauthorized persons is not too difficult to enforce, although it may present direct or indirect monetary or other costs that are not felt to be acceptable. On the other hand, protection of arbitrarily located terminals and of dial-access telephone communication lines against electronic or electromagnetic invasion is not possible.

We have discussed thus far the problem of whether a user is authorized to access a system at all. Another problem is that of restricting the user's access to specific resources, thus preventing the destruction of code, disintegration of data, degradation of service, and dissemination of information, whether malicious or not. Those entities to which access is desired are called *objects* and include, for example, files, pages, segments, processes, main storage extents, backing storage extents, and entire I/O devices. The entities that may access objects are called *subjects,* and can usually be thought of as being processes. Some of those are control program processes; others are user processes. The form of access that a subject may exercise with respect to an object is an *access right*. We saw in Section 6.1.3 that, for a file object, typical access rights are read, write, append, and execute. For a process object, typical access rights are invoke, block, and restart. Some access rights may be designated as transferable. As subjects enter and leave the system, it is necessary to create and delete access rights. The rights to perform these operations are themselves access rights to objects that are in fact the subjects in question. Consequently, every subject is also an object.

Access to each type of object is usually controlled by the control program that manages the resource represented by the object. Access to an I/O device is restricted by the I/O controller; access to a process is managed by a separate protection monitor. In controlling access, this diffuse protection subsystem makes use of a conceptual *access right matrix,* which records for each subject–object pair which particular access rights apply. A row corresponds to each subject, and a column to each object. The access rights held to an object by a subject are entered at the intersection of the corresponding row and column. A portion of such a matrix is shown in Fig.

		Objects						
	Subjects			Files			Devices	
	subj1	subj2	subj3	file1	file2	file3	dev1	dev2
subj1		block		delete		execute		
Subjects subj2	delete		restart		append			write
subj3				write	write		read	

Figure 7.1 Conceptual Matrix of Access Rights

7.1. The access right matrix is usually much too large to occupy main storage, and too sparse to search efficiently. At any given moment, moreover, most of the matrix is not of interest. Furthermore, it is dynamically changing in both size and content. Storing the access right matrix in matrix form is therefore impractical.

The information in that conceptual matrix must nevertheless be represented in some practical implementation. Three approaches are commonly considered. One is to maintain for each subject a *capability list* of the objects that it is authorized to access. Each entry in the list is a *capability* or *ticket,* and admission to the object is by ticket only. In fact, one refinement is to issue consumable tickets, one of which is needed for each instance of access, thus limiting the amount of access by each subject. Capability lists of inactive subjects do not occupy valuable space. For each access request, the capability list must be searched. Subdividing the list into a list for each access right may shorten this search. One disadvantage of capabilities is the difficulty of revoking access to a particular object. Another is the difficulty of constructing a user list for a protection audit. Yet another is the cost of modifying potentially many capability lists when an object is created. A major problem is to prevent a subject from modifying its own capability list, all the while associating the list with the subject. Nevertheless, capabilities are useful in some contexts. An example is the page table described in Section 2.3.3.

A second implementation is orthogonal to the first. With each object there is associated an *authorization list* of the subjects that are authorized to access it. Use of authorization lists present several disadvantages. For each access request the list must be searched. The many authorized processes that are not currently active contribute to the length of the list. A mechanism must be provided for permitting a subject to add or delete rights without accessing the entire list. The access control information incorporated in a file descriptor is a simple form of authorization list.

A compromise between the two foregoing implementations is the following. Each object has a list of *locks,* which represent access rights by unspecified subjects. Each subject has a list of *keys,* which represent access rights to unspecified objects. Access is permitted if a key fits a lock. Each subject's keys are, of course, inaccessible to itself. This implementation is sometimes used to protect main storage extents. (In IBM 360-370 storage protection the "protection key" is the key and the "storage key" is the lock.) Another mechanism for storage protection is the use of hardware *limit registers* in conjunction with implicit base registers. When a relocatable segment is loaded into main storage, its origin is placed by the operating system into a base register and its highest location (physical address) is placed into an associated limit register. The base and limit registers then hold the lowest and highest locations that may be accessed by the associated program. All storage references are checked by the processor to ensure that they lie between those bounds. In a system that uses segmentation, the segment table can be used to hold access rights, which can be enforced by the segmentation hardware.

A rather different type of mechanism that aids in restricting access is incorporated in the hardware of many processors. This is the provision of two or more states or *modes* with respect to what instructions can be executed. There are usually two modes, *user* mode and *supervisor* mode. In user mode, for example, it may be impossible to execute I/O instructions. This forces a user program to route its I/O requests to a control program that runs in supervisor mode. A mode-switching instruction executed in user mode is *trapped* by hardware detection, and control given to the requested program by the interrupt handler.

A generalization of the user and supervisor modes is offered by *levels* (sometimes called "rings") of protection. Each segment in a system is assigned to one of a sequence of two or more successive levels. A process executing on a given level can access any procedure segment or data segment on its own level or on a level higher than its own. It has no direct access to a data segment on a level lower than its own, and strictly controlled access to a procedure segment on a level lower than its own. Such access is via special procedure entry points that cause either a hardware trap or equivalent control by software.

Mechanisms for enforcing confinement of processes can be devised, but they are generally either technically or economically unattractive, and will not be discussed here. If the foregoing methods for enforcing restriction of access appear complicated, do not be dismayed. Most of them are indeed complicated, and necessarily so because a protection system that offers partial protection provides in a sense no protection. Moreover, protection is particularly difficult when sharing is extensive. An operating system that provides total protection against unauthorized access at a price acceptable to the community of users is an elusive goal.

An interesting approach to implementing extensive protection is embodied in the M.I.T. Multics system. The policy underlying Multics is the following.

Access should be based on permission rather than exclusion; the default is that access is not permitted.

Every access should be checked.

The design of the protection system should not be secret; its success must not depend on the users' ignorance.

A process should be granted the least privilege necessary to accomplish its objective.

The protection system should present a natural interface to the human user, even at the cost of increased complexity in meeting uncommon needs for protection.

The Multics system combines highly general sharing with extensive protection, using the segment as the unit of protection. Each segment entry in a directory includes a list of authorized using processes together with the types of use—read, write, execute, append—authorized for each. Almost all of the protection responsibility is handled by the storage system. Process identifications embody three components: name, project, and "compartment". In an authorization list, one or more of the components of an entry can be left unspecified. This allows such authorizations as read access by any user on a given project plus write access by specifically named users. Protected subsystems can be built using eight levels of protection, numbered from 0 to 7. Level 0 is reserved for the Multics supervisor. A subsystem can use descriptor segments that contain protected subsystem numbers greater than or equal to the using subsystem's own number.

At the opposite extreme from Multics is Venus, which offers no protection. The reason is the basic design premise that its users are expected all to be cooperating. Most systems fall somewhere between the extremes of Multics, for which special trapping hardware was built, and of Venus. Protection is usually based on segments, as in Multics, or on files. Typical degrees of file access are listed in Section 6.1.3. Two implementations are briefly summarized in the following paragraphs.

Associated with each file in the UNIX system are seven protection bits. Six specify whether the file's owner may read, write, or execute it and whether a non-owner may read, write, or execute it. If the seventh bit, known as set-user-ID, is on, a current user who is executing the file has the same access rights as the file's creator, but only during that execution. For example, a user can thus be permitted to execute a program that accesses data to which the user does not have access.

In the TENEX system, each user is identified by a 36-bit word. Any two users are considered to belong to the same group if the bitwise **and** of their identifier words is nonzero. A job that attempts to access a file may be its owner, in the same group as its owner, or independent of its owner. For each of those three categories of ownership, five types of access are separately protected: read, write, execute, append, and directory listing. A 15-bit matrix therefore defines the protection status of each file.

7.2 SYSTEM PERFORMANCE

7.2.1 Overview

A question of great importance is how well the system is serving its community of users. Influencing the answer are the users' programs, the control programs that are intended to serve them, and the underlying hardware on which everything runs. If the user community is growing, or if the needs of individual users are growing, it may be necessary to expand the capabilities of the system in order to handle an increased workload. To the extent that system software is more readily changed than system hardware, it may be possible to increase the productivity of the hardware by making changes in the programming system, or in specific user programs. In seeking to improve performance or to reduce costs, or perhaps both, two types of changes can be made, *reconfiguration* and *tuning.* The two terms do not really refer to clearly distinguishable activities; they are applied rather to the two ends of what is more fruitfully regarded as a continuous spectrum of the degree of change. Thus a reconfiguration, or change in system configuration, might be the addition of extra main storage capacity or another I/O channel, or the provision of a control program that automatically batches together short jobs requiring the same language translator. Examples of tuning might include a change of parameters in the job dispatching algorithm, or moving a backing storage device from one channel to another.

The interdependence of user program, system program, and hardware injects complexity into the determination of present performance and the prediction of performance changes due to proposed system changes. Even stating precisely what is meant by performance makes implicit appeal to the users' expectations. Several different performance measures will be discussed. In determining the values of these measures, both hardware and software measuring devices can be employed. It is often convenient to incorporate the latter into the operating system. In that event the control programs help both to influence system performance and to measure it. To predict the effect of major or minor system changes on performance it is necessary to model the system and its workload. Both analytic and simulation models have been used.

7.2.2 Measures

Four measures of system performance are of primary interest. *Throughput* measures the volume of work turned out by the system, usually under steady-state load. It is expressed in units such as jobs processed per day, transactions handled per hour, or messages switched per minute. Throughput is of particular importance to the system manager, because it measures the productivity of the system as a whole.

A measure of greater importance to an individual user is *response time,* the delay between presentation of a request to the system and the receipt of service from it. For batch processing, this is usually taken to mean the *turnaround time* between the arrival of a job and the production of output. Turnaround is clearly dependent not only on the system, but also on the particular job. The distribution of turnaround times for all jobs depends less on any one job, and more on the system and its total workload. For interactive processing, as for batch processing, the response time depends upon the nature of the request. One measure commonly used because it is easily defined is the delay in responding to a *trivial* request such as an empty message (e.g., entering nothing but the end-of-message character).

Availability expresses the likelihood that the desired service is available at a given moment. This may be as simple as the fraction of time the system is operating normally. On the other hand, it may involve probability distributions for different services that are subject to withdrawal as total system capacity is reduced by partial failures. For an interactive system, availability might mean the probability that there exists a free port to which a user terminal can be connected. This number is clearly influenced not just by the computer system, but also by the behavior of other users.

Utilization is less a measure of what the system is doing for users, or can do, than it is a measure of the extent to which different system components are contributing to the over-all operation. Utilization is usually quoted in percent of time spent by a component or larger subsystem in a specified activity. Examples of activities are processor busy or waiting, disk mechanism seeking, and simultaneous occurrence of I/O transmissions on two channels. The balance among components, such as whether a system is I/O-bound or processor-bound, is a major aspect of utilization.

These measures of performance refer, of course, to the system being described, but they also refer to a particular *workload.* The measures of performance of a given system will vary from one workload to another. Thus, performance independent of workload is not a meaningful concept. Consequently, it is important to characterize workloads if one wishes to make general statements about computer system performance. For reconfiguring or tuning a particular system, however, one needs to know only the particular workload that it must handle. Measurements on a running system characterize the interaction of system with workload.

7.2.3 Measurement

Systems at work can be measured by either hardware or software. The earliest software measurement device was the program trace. Although it provided some useful information, it typically slowed the subject system by a factor of perhaps 20 to 50. This made its use very expensive. Moreover, timing relationships were completely destroyed. As attention turned from gathering statistics on execution frequency of individual instructions to measuring frequency and duration of file operations, the full trace gave way to *software monitors,* programs that record these much less frequent, and really more important, actions. The incorporation of such measurement programs in the operating system offers two advantages. First, the user is relieved of the burden of preparing his own software monitor. Second, measurement within the control programs simplifies the acquisition of system information often not accessible to a user program. Measurement by software still distorts what is being measured, but the distortion, often termed measurement *artifact,* can usually be held to a few percent. Another disadvantage of software measurement is that the measurement tool must be developed for the specific system and is often difficult to transport to another system.

The hardware measurement tool can be anything from an ordinary stopwatch, coupled to the system by a person's eye and brain, to an elaborate *hardware monitor* composed of comparators, counters, and clocks, and coupled to the system electronically. Hardware monitors can record processing and I/O subsystem utilization, the amounts of time spent executing instructions in different sets of locations, the extent of I/O overlap, and even the frequency of use of different instructions. Unlike the software monitor, the hardware monitor does not degrade the performance it seeks to measure. It does not introduce artifact. Its use does present some difficulties, however. Changeover to measurement of different quantities can be time-consuming. The monitor must be connected physically to the subject system in such a manner as not to impair the latter's operation. The interpretation of hardware monitor data is sometimes difficult.

Both software and hardware monitors are capable of collecting substantial volumes of data. With either, there is a choice of how much raw data should be recorded and to what extent the data should be summarized before recording. Summarization during measurement reduces the recording requirement, and hence the burden on measurement analysis programs. It may also reduce the artifact introduced by software monitors, which usually use standard system devices and control program services in recording data. Hardware monitors typically have private devices for data recording. The chief disadvantage of summarization is the potential value of the raw data. Tuning a system for maximum performance may be much easier with a knowledge of time distributions of certain activities or conditions than from knowledge only of averages or total values.

The amount of measurement routinely performed by most operating systems is not extensive. An interesting exception is TENEX, designed primarily for the support of multiple terminal users. TENEX measures the fraction of real time spent by the processor in each of four states: idle, wait, core, and trap. The first three are states of the dispatcher; in "trap", the processor is handling paging system traps. In "wait", all processes are waiting for page fault completion. In "core", main storage management is being performed. TENEX also maintains integrals, over time, of three quantities: the number of processes with pages in main storage, the number of paging transfers between main and backing storage, and the number of terminal interactions. Of direct interest to the user are three exponential averages of the number of runnable (i.e., running or ready) processes. The three time constants are 1, 5, and 15 minutes. This collection of averages permits the user to predict trends as well as to assess local variations.

7.2.4 Modeling

To predict performance changes due to system changes or to workload changes, it is necessary to have a model of the behavior of system and workload. The most accurate model is the system itself, and this can actually be used, in trial-and-error fashion, if the changes are inexpensive and reversible. When it is not advisable to experiment with the system itself, either an *analytic* model or a *simulation* model can be used.

An analytic model is essentially a set of equations that relate one or more measures of performance to one or more system or workload parameters. One example is determination of the time to execute the instructions corresponding to a *kernel,* a carefully prescribed, frequently occurring processor task. Another is determination of overlap between processor and I/O subsystem as a function of hardware cycle times, disk drive characteristics, and the activity ratio of records in an application program master file.

A simulation model represents the operation of the system being modeled, by performing actions abstracted in both time and complexity from those of the real system. In determining the effect of changing the number of job streams in a batch processing system, one might abstract from each job only its arrival time, storage requirement, and run duration. In a few minutes of execution, the model could represent operation over a day of simulated time. A special case of simulation model is the *benchmark,* a job whose real or simulated execution is considered typical of the work to be performed by the system. Simulation models can often be built for predicting quantities for which no suitable analytic basis has been devised. It is necessary, however, to avoid the extremes of too much abstraction, and of too little. If the level of simulation is too fine, the model will be too costly to run. If the level of simulation is too coarse, not enough information will be gleaned.

7.3 ACCOUNTING AND PRICING

We now turn our attention briefly to the realm of management. Most of the present section is not about computers per se, but management needs may impose requirements on the design of computer hardware and software. Economic considerations are important in almost all activities; computer use is no exception.

Computer system resources must be paid for. Costs of disposables, such as printer paper, are incurred only in proportion to actual use. For most resources, however, the costs are independent, or nearly independent, of utilization. Thus the main storage must be paid for (whether by lease or by amortization of purchase price) regardless of how fully it is occupied or how frequently it is accessed. The terms "cost" and "price" are not synonymous. In this discussion the former is the expense to the system manager of providing service; the latter is the amount charged to recipients of the service.

The total cost of system operation must be shared by the sharing users. In some organizations, the policy is adopted of paying for all costs centrally, as is customary for libraries. This is most often the case when a computer is operated by an organization and used by its members, perhaps even only by members of a single department. Then the costs of performing resource accounting and of preparing and issuing bills can be obviated. Even if there is no need to issue bills, however, the information about resource utilization can help individual users to improve the efficiency of their programs, and the installation manager to improve the efficiency of the system. Resource use accounting may be incorporated in the operating system for this reason alone. If the funds that support different users come from different sources, then resource use accounting becomes necessary.

If users are to be billed separately for their shares of the resources, then a pricing policy is required. The complexity of computer systems engenders complexity not only in resource use determination, but also in selection of a suitable policy. Many legal, economic, and social considerations, as well as technical, affect the choice of pricing policy, which, in turn, influences what resource use measurements are needed.

7.3.1 Resource Use

Resource use accounting is a natural extension of the system performance measurement discussed in Section 7.2.3. The microsecond-level measurements that require a hardware monitor are not particularly necessary for accounting, nor do many systems come provided with a hardware monitor. On the other hand, it is important to know with which user a particular resource allocation is associated. That information is readily accessible to the operating system. Consequently, the information required for resource use accounting is almost invariably collected by a control program.

What kinds of measurements are worth while? The answer depends, of course, on the pricing policy, the cost of making the measurements, and the utility to the user of knowing the measured values. The following are among the quantities most often measured.

Elapsed time from job submission to job completion.

Connect time, during which an interactive user's terminal is connected to the system.

Processor time (often called "CPU time"), during which the instruction counter is assigned to the job.

Main storage occupancy (sometimes called "core residence") in units of time, or of storage (typically the maximum allocated), or of storage multiplied by time. Thus 120K words allocated for 3.5 seconds followed by 200K words allocated for 6 seconds might be represented as 9.5 seconds, or 200K words, or 1620 kiloword-seconds. In a paging system, the occupancy might be reported in units of page-seconds.

Backing storage occupancy during execution, in units of storage, time, or both.

Backing storage occupancy when not executing, both on-line and off-line, in units such as maximum number of disk tracks allocated during the billing period.

Frequency or duration of use of system programs such as utilities or translators.

I/O transmission time: channel, control unit, or device.

Number of I/O operations, often distinguished by class of device.

Time spent waiting for I/O completions.

The number of input records (punched cards, credit card slips) read and of output records (lines or pages of print) written.

The foregoing measures will typically be reported for the job as a unit; indeed, "job" is defined in at least one system to be the unit of work for accounting purposes. These measures may also be reported for identifiable subparts of a job, often called "job steps". In a paging system, I/O traffic due to paging will usually be recorded separately to help assess the performance of the paging mechanism. Each user may or may not be billed directly for the paging traffic his job incurs.

7.3.2 Pricing Policy

One of three major goals, and some minor goals, may be incorporated in a pricing policy. One major goal is *simplicity*. The total cost of accounting and billing, especially for a large number of short jobs, can be substantial. This cost must ultimately be borne by the users. They may decide that the cost outweighs the advantages of detailed accounting. Probably the easiest mechanism for implementing simple pricing is to charge each member of the user community a fixed fee independent of his extent of system use. If this is perceived as inequitable, the price could be based on a single measurement, such as elapsed time.

A second goal is *reproducibility*. Many users feel that the price should be determined solely by the service they receive, independently of the cost of providing service. Not only does this knowledge impart psychological comfort; it also enhances the user's ability to predict the cost of a computation. It matters not whether the user's job is the sole occupant of a lightly loaded system, or whether it is waiting in processor queues and I/O queues with a large number of competing jobs. The price is the same.

A third goal is *fairness*. What is perceived as fair by one user may not be by another, and solutions may need to be negotiated. It may well be agreed that users should pay for the costs of providing the services they receive.

But how should control program costs be allocated among users? Should dispatcher time be charged to the process that has ceased to run, to the process that has begun to run, to both, to all ready processes, to all processes in the system? How about the costs of paging, both hardware and software? There is clearly a limit to how many resources should be devoted to determining what is fair. The policies of reproducibility and fairness are difficult to implement because of the fundamental problem that the extent of use of a computer system is highly variable over periods of time during which the cost of operation is essentially fixed.

Pricing policies can also be used to achieve lesser objectives than simplicity, reproducibility, and fairness. Users can sometimes be persuaded to use scarce resources more efficiently, or to shift their use from scarce resources to plentiful. Substantial savings in the cost of printer paper can ensue from high charges for each line printed. A high price for each I/O transfer can encourage the use of larger blocking factors, thus reducing both contention for disk arm movement and demands on the I/O supervisor. The incremental charge for the larger buffers required must be lower than the saving in I/O charges. Uneven distribution of workload throughout the day may be alleviated by charging less at off-peak hours than at peaks. A deep discount for overnight batch service can be very effective in redistributing the workload.

Users willing to pay for special treatment can be granted higher priority in return for higher prices. The easiest mechanism is to multiply the entire bill by a factor that reflects the degree of extra priority in the competition for resources. By permitting that factor to be less than unity, the user is allowed to give up priority in return for savings in money.

One pricing policy is to charge for the use of each resource in proportion to the cost of providing it. Thus a lightly used device will be priced higher than a heavily used one of equal cost. Although this may tend to reinforce existing usage patterns by application of positive feedback, it has the merit of making each system component self-supporting.

During execution of a user's process, the recording of resource use is mandatory, the calculation of price is optional, and the issuance of bills is rare. Performing the accounting (price calculation) at job execution time gives the user a timely report of what it is costing him to run. If the billing records are on-line, the accounting program can also update the user's balance and report how much the user now owes or, if he has paid in advance, how much is left. Another advantage of maintaining billing records on-line is that they may be checked for financial status before the user's process is enqueued for execution. Maintaining billing records off-line is cheaper, however, and makes them less vulnerable to contamination. Deferring use of the accounting program to when the system is lightly loaded saves the space and time required during periods of high load.

7.4 SYSTEM CONTROL

7.4.1 User, Operator, and System

A major impetus to the development of "operating" systems was the desire to eliminate operator activity between jobs, thus achieving nonstop operation. It is true that the operating system was much more efficient than the operator and much less likely to commit errors. The operator, however, offered one major redeeming feature—intelligence. A major policy question is whether to harness this intelligence routinely in the functioning of the operating system. As most programmers have discovered, it frequently requires as much effort to prepare application program sections to handle unusual or error cases as to handle the main-line cases for which the program is basically written. Since this can be true of control programs as well, it can be very tempting to rely on the system operator to furnish guidance or to take action in the event of malfunction or of such unusual system activity as a high rate of paging, abnormally slow response, or deadlock. To the extent that preplanned judgement is required for the successful continuance of operation, this is a dangerous policy. To the extent that the system designers can capitalize upon human intelligence available at execution time, it is a fruitful policy. Thus in some systems the operator turns the system on, mounts volumes, handles card decks, and watches for smoke, whereas in others the operator reconfigures storage regions, preempts jobs, makes long-term scheduling decisions, and generally guides the operating system. For example, the CDC SCOPE system places rather greater reliance on the operator than does OS/360-370.

The user must, of course, communicate with the facility, whether operator or system, that is serving him. Early operating systems and system operators usually received their instructions from the user partly in writing, but chiefly on punched cards added at the front of the user's job deck. These were called *job control* cards and typically specified such relatively simple matters as what compiler, if any, was required and whether to load and execute the object deck. As systems became more and more complex, the volume and detail of the user's instructions grew until the deck of job control cards could be rather substantial. The variety of possible instructions constitute what is widely known, and often maligned, as a *job control language* or system *command language*.

7.4.2 Command Languages

The purpose of a command language (CL) is to permit the user to request those control program actions that are under his control, rather than being performed automatically. Typical actions include the allocation and release of resources, such as main and backing storage, devices, and files, including the establishment of the correspondence between a logical file and a physical file. A particularly important request is that for the allocation of a processor, whereby the user requests the execution of a program. The user may supply argument values for the program's formal parameters. A user's request for control program action may depend upon some condition, such as the successful fulfillment of an earlier request.

Command languages are used in both batch and interactive environments. In batch mode, most of the actions specified in a CL occur after translation and before execution, although in many systems certain of the actions (e.g., device allocation) may be deferred until execution has begun. The time at which these actions are performed may thus be either fixed or distributed over an interval. We shall refer to that time as *scheduling time* because the bulk of these actions involve the scheduling of resource allocations. The user specifies all of his requests to the operating system at scheduling time. Because of this early binding, the user must decide all needs in advance, including what actions to take conditionally. If some of the actions involve standard CL sequences that can be specified in advance, then invoked at scheduling time, it may be fruitful to compile those sequences. Even in batch mode, however, it is not uncommon to execute CL statements interpretively.

In interactive mode, the user specifies requests before, during, and after execution. Because of this late binding, he need not decide anything in advance. The user's requests are processed upon receipt, by a *command language interpreter,* sometimes called a *shell.* A common form of CL interpreter implementation is to treat each command as the name of a file to be executed.

It is now recognized that a command language (CL) is more than a collection of control cards. It is indeed a language, by means of which the user instructs the operating system to perform certain actions, thus programming the "virtual machine" (a concept explored in Section 8.4) represented by the hardware and operating system together. Some requested actions are more commonly described in terms of their results than of the mechanism by which they are accomplished. For example, the loading of a compiler's run-time library may be nowhere requested explicitly, but rather deduced from a request to execute an object program produced by that compiler. Because of the widespread use of assemblers when control cards were commonly used, the syntax of early job control languages was similar to assembler-language syntax. This assembler-language orientation has persisted longer in instructing the operating system than in writing application programs. Such languages are particularly unappealing for interactive use, and recent CLs have more of a programming-language orientation. Although some attention is now directed to designing CL extensions to existing programming languages, virtually all commercial operating systems use a CL that is distinct from its programming languages. Although many systems provide separate CLs for the batch and interactive modes, the use of a single CL for both is becoming more widespread.

The characteristics usually desired in a CL are not unlike those prized in programming languages. A command language should be friendly to the users, powerful in its expressive capability, and inexpensive in its operation. Ease of use demands a simple syntax, and a mnemonic vocabulary of reasonable size. Default values should be understood, but not for so many variables as to burden the user. Economy of expression is also helpful and saves lots of time in using an interactive system. Of great value in an interactive CL is the ability to ask the system for help in using the system. A corollary is that the system should actually provide the help requested. Few system messages are as aggravating as "help not available".

Expressive power requires appropriate data types and data structures, although there appears not to be general agreement upon which ones are appropriate in a CL. It also requires control structures, or at least a means of specifying conditional execution of a request. A way to produce and invoke a named sequence of commands is invaluable. The assembler-language orientation of early CLs led naturally to the provision of macro facilities for this purpose. Macro generators are particularly useful in producing command sequences for more than one system, thus enhancing the portability of programs from one system to another. The programming-language orientation of later CLs has led to the *command procedure*. The ability to pass parameters to a command procedure, or to an invoked process, obviates much rewriting of command sequences.

The third characteristic posited for a CL is that it be inexpensive to use. We would like both the CL program and its interpreter to be small, and we would like translation to be fast. These desires are not wholly consistent with those for a user-friendly and expressive system. A balance must therefore be struck between the capabilities provided in the CL and the resources devoted to providing them.

The classic example of an awkward command language is the OS/360 Job Control Language (JCL), which includes basically only three verbs: JOB, EXEC, and DD. By means of parameters, their subparameters, and subparameters of subparameters, all embedded in a ghastly syntax which is partly keyword and partly positional, these verbs can be extended to express virtually all scheduling-time requests. There is, fortunately, a facility for the insertion of open subroutines ("catalogued procedures"). Although no branching is provided, execution can be made conditional on the success of prior executions.

At the opposite extreme is the simplicity of the command language provided at Manchester University by the MU5 operating system. Only two commands appear for each process. A batch process is controlled by

> ***A process-name user password
> lines of input
> ***Z

where the lines of input are interpreted by the named process. Control of an
interactive process is distinguished by use of "M" instead of "A", and the
input lines are sent to the interpreting process one at a time. What this
means, of course, is that users or groups of users define their own CLs and
write their own CL interpreters. In practice, one simple command interpreter is used widely.

Less artificially simple command syntax and vocabulary are offered by
an APL interactive system. Any line whose first nonblank character is a right
parenthesis is considered to be a system command. No command has more
than two parameters, which are positional. Here are some examples.

)LOAD MATH:SESAME	activate a copy of the stored workspace *MATH* protected by key SESAME
)COPY MEMOS LEAVE	copy into the active workspace the object *LEAVE* from workspace *MEMOS*
)VARS	report a list of global variables in the active workspace
)OFF	terminate the interactive session

The Univac EXEC command language offers a reasonable syntax for its
$28+n$ verbs, where n is the number of language processors. Statement labels
are provided. They permit a limited branching capability in the form of an
unconditional forward branch, and a skip conditioned primarily by error
status.

Many interactive systems provide help to the user unfamiliar with his
system. Two forms of adaptation to different user skill levels, introduced in
the TENEX system, are incorporated in its commercial successor, the DEC
TOPS-20 system. One is a choice among three input styles for commands.
Each command begins with a keyword which may be followed by further
keywords, parameters, and "noise words" that make the command more
readable. One input style is to enter a command complete with all words
present. A second is to omit noise words and to abbreviate each keyword by
using any *unique prefix* (initial substring long enough to distinguish it from
other keywords). A third input style is to type part of a command followed
by a special character that causes the system to expand abbreviations and
print any following noise words as a prompt. The second form of adaptation
to users is special assistance to novices beyond even that provided by the
third input style described. If a substring entered by the user is not a unique

prefix, the system rings a bell on the terminal and awaits more characters. If the substring is not recognizable, the system asks the user to reformulate the command. If the user still does not know what to do, he can enter "?" to request a list of all options available at that point.

The Hewlett-Packard MPE III offers on-line assistance through use of the command HELP, which displays portions of the operating system manuals. That system also provides user-defined command procedures, and conditional execution by means of IF, THEN, ELSE, and ENDIF.

One of the richest CLs is that of the ICL 2900 series systems. Both scalar and array variables are provided, of integer, boolean, and string types. Block structure is used to delimit the scope not only of variables and labels, but also of resources. The automatic release of resources upon block exit is an aid in the prevention of deadlock. Command procedures can be defined and called. Conditional execution is controlled by an IF..THEN..ELSE structure, and also by an interrupt function module introduced by WHENEVER.

Perhaps the most widely admired command language is that of UNIX, processed by a command line interpreter known as the UNIX shell. Both a command language and a programming language, it provides control-flow primitives and string-valued variables. The shell executes commands entered either from an interactive terminal or from a batch file. Command lines entered by the user, whose login normally invokes the shell automatically, are interpreted as requests to execute other programs. Command syntax places the command name first, followed optionally by positional parameters. The command name is treated as that of a file to be executed. If the name is not found in the user file directory, it is sought in a system directory of commands intended to be generally used. Standard command names are very short (e.g., ed for editor and pr for printer). Standard input and output files (the user's keyboard and screen) are provided, but user-specified file names override the choice of standard files. Thus command > filename redirects output to the named file, and command < filename redirects input from the named file. The ability to direct the output of one command as input to another obviates the need to define temporary files. This facility is provided by the pipe, illustrated in Section 4.4.

In executing a command, the shell normally creates a new process and waits for the process to finish. The character "&" following a command instructs the shell not to wait for completion of the command but to return and handle the next command concurrently. Thus the sequence

```
cat apl | grep APL > file1 & cat file2
```

requests the shell to write into file1 all lines of file apl that contain the string "APL" and concurrently to list file2. The shell is itself a command. It can be invoked recursively to execute a file of commands, thus providing a subroutine facility. The command sh map vol1 instructs the shell to execute the commands filed in map, passing the string vol1 as an argument value. A return code permits conditional execution. The sequence cmnd1 && cmnd2 causes cmnd2 to be executed if the execution of cmnd1 was successful, whereas cmnd1 || cmnd2 causes cmnd2 to be executed if the execution of cmnd1 was unsuccessful. Other facilities include WHILE, CASE, and indexed FOR control structures.

7.4.3 Job Initiation and Termination

What are some of the actions that occur at scheduling time? The answer will vary from system to system, and for some it may be convenient to subdivide scheduling time into different epochs. In general, however, the following actions are accomplished. The CL program is read to determine what resources and actions the user job needs. The job and data accompanying the job are enqueued. Requests for mountable volumes are transmitted to the operator, and mounting instructions are issued as soon as the corresponding devices are made available. Input/output devices and other resources requested by the job (all resources if full preallocation is enforced) are allocated. Considerable time may elapse, of course, in waiting for devices to become available. Eventually, executable storage is allocated and the user's program is loaded and relocated. Ancillary programs, such as utilities, compilers, and run-time libraries, are loaded and relocated, except those already present. Finally execution is begun, often by calling the user program as a subroutine of the operating system.

Although most of the actions specified, directly or indirectly, in CL occur prior to execution, some may be performed upon termination. Obvious examples are the release of resources no longer required and the issuance of volume dismounting messages. Some systems (e.g., Honeywell 66) check first whether resources about to be released will be required by a subsequent process, in which event the resources are saved. Actions immediately prior to termination may include generating a code to control conditional branching in subsequent commands, closing open files, and entering newly created files into a system catalog. If job termination was abnormal, further system-specified and user-specified actions, such as storage dumps, may occur.

In many systems it is necessary to decide at the time the program is written what I/O devices will be used. In others, it is possible to defer the choice until scheduling time. This permits different devices to be used for the same purpose on different runs. Such *device independence* can aid program development by permitting a program to be tested first with a small collection of data on cards and later with a large disk data set, without rewriting and recompiling the source language program. The cost of this late binding is that construction of the channel program must be deferred from translation time until later, and performed once for each execution. The user needs to rewrite only the job control program, and the binding of the I/O devices to file names is another action that can occur at scheduling time.

7.5 SYSTEM STARTUP

Throughout the discussion thus far it has been assumed that there were running programs already in the computer. These include at least the nucleus of the operating system and usually one or more user programs as well. The user programs were brought in by the loader. Any extensive loader could itself have been loaded by a simple loader. But how did *that* loader come to be in place? The question of how to start the system initially arises under two different sets of circumstances. One occurs when the system is first turned on after manufacture, after intentional shutdown, or after withdrawal from service for a hardware repair that might affect the content of storage. The other occurs when a software error destroys the operator's confidence in the content of storage, perhaps as a result of encountering difficulty in continuing operation by less drastic means. The number of such occurrences in a day's operation is often taken as a measure of the stability of an operating system.

A very simple absolute loader can be written to start loading the control program nucleus into fixed locations in main storage. This loader can be recorded on punched cards or paper tape, or on a mountable magnetic tape or disk volume. Many computers embody provision for executing an arbitrary instruction entered manually by the operator. If that instruction reads the beginning of the simple loader into storage, a second manual instruction can transfer control to the newly read first instruction of the loader. As long as one instruction can cause the reading of more than just one more instruction, a net gain is possible whereby the simple loader, called a *bootstrap* loader, can load itself and begin normal execution. To preclude the need for entering the same instructions manually whenever this *initial program loading* or *cold start* is to take place, the instruction sequence is often built into the hardware and invoked by pressing a single button.

One mechanism for cold start combines the relative simplicity of card reading with the higher speed of disk reading. A single read instruction in the cold start sequence reads an entire card from the card reader. The several intructions on the card are sufficient to control further reading from a backing storage volume. The Burroughs B6700 MCP is started in the following manner. The program in hardware reads in one card and transfers control to the instructions read in. These instructions read in the object deck (about 50 cards) of a simple loader. That loader reads a parameter card containing a tape name and a file name. It then searches the system for a matching tape, and searches that tape for the designated file, which is a full loader. The simple loader loads the full loader, and the full loader loads the MCP.

An alternative approach is to incorporate in the hardware a read-only storage with enough program in it to perform at least enough of the cold start to bring in a full loader. Whether or not such hardware assist is used, another function sometimes incorporated into the cold start sequence is the clearing of storage locations, typically to binary zeros.

FOR FURTHER STUDY

Privacy issues are treated in Chap. 5 of Gotlieb and Borodin [1973] and in Hoffman [1977], which also contains much material on protection in general. Many fascinating cases of computer crime are related by Parker [1976]. Many aspects of computer security are discussed in the tutorial monograph by Hsiao, Kerr, and Madnick [1979].

The subject–object model of protection was first proposed by Lampson [1971], and extended in the survey articles by Graham and Denning [1972], and by Popek [1974]. Saltzer and Schroeder [1975] present a more comprehensve tutorial, and the chapter by Jones [1978] is still more advanced.

Elementary textbook treatments of protection are offered by Watson [1970, Sec. 5.4], by Tsichritzis and Bernstein [1974, Chap. 7], by Lister [1975, Chap. 9], and by Wilkes [1975, Chap. 6], who outlines an implementation of authorizations. Watson [1970] presents an implementation of capabilities in Sec. 5.4.5 and discusses some problems with levels of protection in Sec. 5.4.4. The treatment in Habermann [1976, Secs. 9.4 and 9.5] is deeper.

Performance evaluation is surveyed by Lucas [1971]. Analytical tools are stressed in the book by Hellerman and Conroy [1975], whereas those by Drummond [1973] and Ferrari [1978] are more general.

The collection of articles edited by Unger [1975] is a good source of information on command languages. In particular, the article by Gram and Hertweck [1975] provides an excellent overview of the issues. Frank [1976] propounds the advantages of a minimum command language, whereas Brunt and Tuffs [1976] present the ICL 2900 approach of richer function. The UNIX shell is described by Bourne [1978].

On the issue of getting started, Madnick and Donovan [1974, Sec. 2-5.1] present as an example a cold start program readable by those familiar with IBM 360-370 architecture.

EXERCISES

7.1 If a shared stack is used for parameter passing (see Section 4.7.2), what protection problem can arise?

7.2 Suppose that a system permits the deletion of an object to which access rights are held, followed by the creation of a new object having the same name. What problems can arise? What measures can be taken to forestall such problems?

7.3 The "lost object" problem occurs when all copies of some capability are overwritten, rendering the object inaccessible. The fact of inaccessibility is hard to discover, and the space used by the object may remain unreclaimed. Explain how this pitfall can be avoided.

7.4 Investigate uninterruptible power supplies, and report how they work, what they cost, and what limitations they have.

7.5 Methods to guard against terminal password disclosure depend upon whether the terminal communicates with the computer in half-duplex or full-duplex mode. Explain.

7.6 A B7000/B6000 MCP file can have the attribute SENSITIVEDATA. When such a file is deleted, the operating system overwrites its storage area with garbage. Why might such a precaution be necessary?

7.7 Describe carefully the introduction of measurement artifact caused by the summarization performed by a software monitor.

7.8 How easy is it to bill a user for higher priority in accessing only certain resources?

7.9 What advantages and what disadvantages lie in having a command language that is an extension of a programming language?

Chapter 8

SYSTEM CONFIGURATIONS

The foregoing chapters have been concerned chiefly with describing some of the more common approaches to coping with the many problems of resource and system management. This chapter examines the design and configuration of operating systems. To place those topics in perspective, the chapter opens with an examination of the historical context from which modern operating systems have evolved. It continues with a presentation of multiprocessing operating systems, emphasizing the opportunities and problems they present. Although this book does not seek to make the reader capable of designing an operating system, several issues that are central to the design process are discussed next. Finally, some other types of system configuration are surveyed. They include (1) systems in which a single programming language serves all users, (2) systems designed to support a single application, (3) systems that are virtual rather than real, and (4) systems intended for only one user.

8.1 EVOLUTION

The earliest computers, even those considered large at the time, executed single programs written in raw machine language. Debugging was performed on-line with limited aids all controlled manually by the operator, who also directed the hardware in loading the program prior to execution. Input/output operations were not overlapped with processing. Final output could be produced on as slow a device as an electric typewriter while the rest of the hardware waited. No system software was provided.

Computers became larger and faster. When main storage reached a thousand words or so, the programmer's manually produced "memory map" with absolute addresses became unwieldy, and was replaced by the facilities of elementary symbolic assembler programs. Self-loading programs were commonly produced, and the operator had then only to initiate program loading. As machine capability increased, so did concern for using it efficiently. Debugging was forced off-line to preclude its consuming valuable resources. The tool that permitted off-line debugging was the storage dump, made feasible by faster printers. To ensure that all information on the dump came from the current program, it was not uncommon to precede loading by a storage-clearing process. This might be accomplished by a short program or by a hardware feature, but woe betide the operator who pushed the storage clear switch at the wrong moment! Not only did computer efficiency concern system designers; so did the increasing complexity of the programmer's task. As a result, further aids were developed which became components or precursors of modern programming systems.

A key class of aids was the translators. One early machine [the Harvard Mark IV (1952)] had a macroexpander embodied in separate hardware, but almost all translators, then as now, were programs. Symbolic assemblers became widespread; a particularly useful variant provided optimization of instruction and data placement in magnetic drum main storage, where random-access time was much greater than serial. This was SOAP (ca. 1955), the Symbolic Optimizing Assembly Program for the IBM 650. Interpreters, especially for floating-point computation using fixed-point arithmetic units, assumed considerable importance. The most popular of these was the Bell Interpretive System (1956), also for the 650. The first compilers were also developed starting at about the same time. Among these were Univac's B0, the Purdue Algol compiler, and IBM's Fortran.

Punched cards, with some manual handling, served as backing storage both before and after the advent of magnetic tape. They often served as the medium for compiler output, whence the term "object deck" which is still used even when cards are not. Magnetic tape drives, card readers and punches, and printers were for a long time the principal peripheral devices attached to computers. Although rewinding magnetic tape was almost the only overlapped operation on the earliest machines, it was not long before further degrees of I/O overlap became common. The full utilization of overlap capability was very burdensome for the programmer. Timing was often crucial, particularly in using devices with cyclic mechanical components, such as the feed knives and propulsion rollers of a card reader. An entire cycle might be missed if the programmer failed to observe minimum and maximum numbers of instructions that could be executed between successive attentions to the device. Moreover, it was necessary to assemble and disassemble computer words in correspondence with successive frames on tape or successive rows or columns on cards. Collections of I/O subroutines were written to perform these complex and frequently recurring tasks, and they were typically shared by all users of the computer.

Magnetic tape served both as backing storage and as a speed buffer between the computer on one hand and the card reader, punches, and printers on the other. The use of separate hardware subsystems for medium conversion from card to tape, tape to card, and tape to print became common. Anticipatory tape reading to minimize the program's wait for data led to buffering. The economics of magnetic tape use led to blocking. The management of buffering and blocking was also assigned to the I/O subroutines, as were the writing of labels on tape and the checking of those labels to ensure correct mounting.

It was not only these shared subroutines for I/O, but also mathematical subroutines for translators, that led to the provision of programming systems maintained by the computer operations staff for the benefit of the user community. Utility programs were also furnished. They provided medium conversion, program editing, and both sorting and report-writing programs tailored to each user's specific needs by a process of generation. One of the earliest of these systems was Univac's Generalized Programming (1958).

How did the role of the computer operator evolve? He read and followed the programmer's instructions regarding where to load the program and how to initialize storage locations and control registers. The operator mounted tape reels, at first on specific physically numbered tape drives and later on any free drives whose logical addresses he set by switches or plugboard wiring to correspond to the program. This representation of a logical tape drive by an operator-selected physical tape drive constituted the first implementation of a virtual resource. When separate peripherals were used for medium conversion, the operator moved tape reels as necessary, or switched tape drives between "mainframe" and off-line units. The operator also set various console switches according to instructions. Their settings could represent run-time variables, conditions, or initialization. Often there was no guarantee that the switch settings would be recorded by the program, an omission that could markedly heighten the difficulty of debugging.

An important duty was to load each program to be executed, a task considerably lightened by the advent of self-loading programs. For short jobs, the tape setup and program load time often exceeded the running time, and constituted a source of great inefficiency. To reduce tape handling, the operator would group the card decks for a number of separate jobs into a single *batch*, which was then converted to tape. Another tape was used to record output from the batch processing of all the jobs, and was converted to print after all the jobs in the batch had run.

Recovery from errors (unreadable tape, programmed check failure, malfunction in the processing unit) was another responsibility of the operator. In this the operator would again follow instructions prepared by the programmer. Typical action would be to restart at an earlier point in the computation, a programmer-provided checkpoint at which results were "known" to be correct. One installation provided excellent motivation for the programmer to plan for all possible errors. If, during the execution of a production program, an error occurred for which the programmer had not left specific instructions, the operator was required to ask the programmer immediately what to do next, whether at three o'clock in the afternoon or at three in the morning.

Small wonder it was, with these many duties of device allocation, job scheduling and loading, and error recovery, that operators made mistakes. Even in the absence of operator error, the skill of the operator often determined, more than did any other factor, the efficiency of the entire installation.

The first programming systems (early 1960s) were intended to relieve the operator of some of this burden, and acquired naturally the designation "operating systems". Their control programs, often also called "monitors", resided partly in main storage, and operated in response to commands from both operator and programmer. By automating between-job operations and providing batch processing, they greatly improved efficiency of operation. This was especially true in installations that ran many short programs, whose instruction decks were stacked together, under a "stacked-job" monitor.

The translators provided in these programming systems initially emphasized machine-oriented languages rather than human-oriented programming languages. Symbolic assemblers were the mainstay, but these were soon extended into compiler-like programs with translation-time variables, conditional generation, and macroinstructions. Linkers were furnished for joining separately assembled routines, thus providing the advantages of modularization in programming. Early user acceptance of programming languages forced operating system designers to provide compilers, sometimes even by retrofitting. Both assemblers and compilers led to managing libraries of programs: translators, their run-time routines, and the users' own source and object programs. Error recovery was effected by interrupt subroutines to which control was transferred automatically by the hardware upon its detection of certain types of errors, such as invalid instructions or arithmetic overflow, thus "trapping" the errors.

The control of peripheral devices led ultimately to two developments of major importance.

1. The card-to-tape, tape-to-card, and tape-to-print converters all had to provide for control of two I/O devices and for conversion between data formats. Eventually (1961), the three types of conversion were combined in a single converter that controlled three types of device, rather than a total of six. Moreover, it embodied a small computer, the IBM 1401, which could execute simple programs for the required conversions. The programs already existed to accept input from cards and to direct output to a printer. Furthermore, the small computer had extensive facilities for character manipulation as well as arithmetic capability. It could perform all of the functions of the punched-card tabulator, the mainstay of commercial data processing. The new high-speed line printers developed for computer systems permitted one peripheral computer to do the work of three tabulators at less cost, and provide unused computer power besides. The exploitation of this excess computer capacity was the beginning of widespread computer use in

business data processing.

2. In a large computer system, some tape drives would be connected to the peripheral computer and some to the central computer. After a batch of program or data cards had been converted to tape, the operator would physically move the tape reel from a drive on one machine to a drive on the other. The operator would also move output tape reels back from the central to the peripheral machine. Later, means were provided for manually switching the connection of a tape drive from one computer to the other, obviating the dismounting, carrying, and remounting of reels. Eventually, the manual switching was replaced by switching under computer control.

After it was recognized that I/O conversions and device control could be performed economically by a computer, appeal was made to the observation that computer service was cheaper on a large machine than on a small one. The peripheral computer was discarded, the conversion and device control programs were allocated space in the central computer, and spooling was provided. This was the first form of multiprogramming. In this original form, only one of the multiple programs was a user program, but multiprogramming was soon extended to accommodate more than one user program. One particularly interesting hardware design was embodied in the Honeywell 800, which executed in turn one instruction from each of as many as eight programs. Whether a computer system provided multiprogramming or not, the interjob delay could be appreciably shortened if extra tape drives were available, by mounting tapes for the new job while its predecessor was running. As long as the operator specified the job schedule, he knew what to mount. Once the monitor took over job scheduling, premounting was impossible until monitors were enabled to issue anticipatory tape mounting messages. Their I/O subroutines had to be extended also to allow the attachment of an increasingly large selection of devices, including tapes with various speeds and recording densities, optical as well as electrical card readers, curve plotters, and magnetic disks.

Whereas magnetic drums, which had been used from very early computers onward, required one recording head for each track, magnetic disks needed only one head per disk surface with a hundred or so tracks. Despite the cost of the head-moving mechanism, disk storage was much cheaper than drum storage, and indeed became the first economically feasible "random-access" backing store. The first disks were an integral part of the disk drive. Later came single removable disks, and then removable multiple-disk packs. The first applications of disks were essentially sequential processing plus random inquiry, as in public utility customer billing, inventory control, and payroll. Disk-based dedicated systems were later developed for such essentially random-access applications as air defense and airline reservations. For both the purely random access mode and the mixed sequential and random-access mode, data organizations had to be designed and data access programs were added to the control program facilities. These random-access applications introduced further requirements, such as the control of terminals, the use of communication lines, and a different mode of multiprogramming. There is in a sense only one application program, but its interaction with each terminal transaction can be considered a distinct process. Each of these requirements led to an expansion in operating system function. The use of terminals coupled with multiprogramming, incidentally, led to a return from off-line to on-line debugging, because the on-line debugger no longer monopolized access to the computer resources.

The foregoing facilities evolved into three major areas of batch-oriented operating systems. These areas are not defined precisely, and the three overlap not only pairwise but jointly. A brief review of their evolution will help to explain both their names (in IBM terminology, at least) and their composition. The I/O subroutines, with their device control, error recovery, blocking and buffering, and data access facilities, became the *input/output control system* (IOCS). Although the IOCS is by and large unglamorous, it alone can easily constitute nearly half of the bulk of a complete operating system. Job scheduling was originally performed by the stacked-job monitor, which introduced the concepts of the job queue and of priority. Anticipatory tape mounting led to device allocation, and program loading to storage allocation. These functions were grouped into the *scheduler.* When an interrupt occurs, control is passed to interrupt routines, or exception handlers, by a program that supervises the allocation of processor cycles. This *supervisor* handles all allocations of time to both system and user programs. Because a job not in main storage cannot be given access to the processor, the supervisor has also become involved, together with the scheduler, in storage allocation. Intentional interrupts can be used to request the supervisor to provide miscellaneous system services. Input and output are handled in many systems by normal, rather than exceptional, interrupts, and some of the required functions are shared by the supervisor and the IOCS.

The use of multiple processors in a single system arose from three different desires. One was to increase operating efficiency by specialization. The dedication of multiple peripheral processors to I/O in the CDC 6000 series is one example. Another is the use of a "front-end" processor to handle communication with the external world and a "back-end" processor to do number crunching or other processing. In that collaboration the two computers could be functionally similar. Mapping their division of labor into the operating system led to semi-independent front-end control programs, such as the Houston Automatic Spooling Priorities system (HASP) developed for use with IBM operating systems.

A second objective is the throughput increase that is statistically expected if a stream of diverse jobs is processed by more than one processor. Suppose that some I/O-bound jobs and some processor-bound jobs are run on two uniprocessor systems. Almost any division of the jobs between the two processors will result in an excess of one type of job on each processor. But a two-processor system can handle the collection of jobs without imbalance.

The third incentive toward the use of multiple processors was the desire for high system reliability, as exemplified by duplicated and even triplicated processors for such critical applications as air route traffic control. The associated operating systems have had to be ready to substitute one processor for another. A natural generalization is the maintenance of correct operation following the loss of *any* type of hardware unit.

As processors became faster, storage larger, and systems cheaper, interactive use became more and more feasible, both technically and economically. The earliest interactive systems supported interactive users only, and provided them all with the same language. Subsequently, resources left idle during user think time were harnessed to provide a batch service in the background. Larger systems made it possible to offer a choice of languages. One outcome of these trends was the "computer utility", of which Multics is a prime example. Another outcome was the development of interactive monitors for many minicomputer systems. An interactive dialog between programmer and system has once again become the mode of choice for program development. Now, however, a single user need no longer monopolize the hardware.

Grosch [1953] first observed that processor power rose approximately as the square of processor price. For twice the money, a user could obtain twice the power from doubling the number of units, but four times the power from doubling the size of units. A trend toward ever larger computer systems was the natural consequence. Even if the operating system claimed substantial overhead resources, the net power available to the user community per unit price increased markedly with system size. Multiprocessor systems were introduced despite an economic disadvantage. Grosch's Law, as his observation was called, was widely accepted well into the 1960s, and continued to influence computer system design for a long time. More recently, however, the exponent on processor price began to fall, and now stands much closer to unity than to two. Not only does this make multiprocessing more attractive, but it also makes a small computer economically competitive with a share of a large one. Even as the relative cost of small computers has fallen in comparison with that of large, the absolute cost of computing has also fallen. Consequently, microprocessors are becoming more widely used both as uniprocessors and as components of multiprocessors. The user accustomed to the services of a programming system does not want to lose them in the transition to smaller processors. As a result, we now have programming systems that support even the sole use of a microprocessor.

8.2 MULTIPROCESSING OPERATING SYSTEMS

As the economic disincentive to multiprocessing has decreased, interest in solving the technical problems has increased. Not only experimental operating systems, but commercial ones as well, are being designed for multiple-processor configurations. In this section we explore the issues that distinguish multiprocessing operating systems from uniprocessing systems, which have engaged our attention in the previous chapters. A brief review of the underlying hardware configurations leads to a discussion of operating system design approaches. The section closes with an examination of resource management mechanisms specific to multiprocessing.

8.2.1 Hardware

There are many ways to interconnect two processors. A communications multiplexor on each can be connected to a communication line. This is one possible basis of a computer *network*. An I/O channel on each can be connected to its counterpart on the other, making each processor appear to the other as an I/O device. A disk or drum shared between the two can serve as a buffer for asynchronous transfer of information.

None of the foregoing modes of interconnection, however, satisfies the most widely accepted definition of a multiprocessing system. What is required instead is that two or more processors share main storage. Thus not only can data in that storage be accessed by more than one processor, but programs in it can be executed by more than one.

Wide variability characterizes the configurations that qualify as multiprocessors. Although there may be a score of processors, a pair is far more common. Each processor may possess a private, or *local*, storage in addition to being able to access the common storage *global* to more than one processor. The configuration may be symmetric, with identical processors each connected to identical local storage and devices. Or it may be asymmetric, with considerable differences in the facilities available at each processor site. The degree of physical coupling among the processors can also vary, particularly in the nature of the switches and buses used to connect the processors to the storage modules.

8.2.2 Approaches

Three types of operating system configurations for multiprocessing are common. The *master–slave* configuration gives one processor, the master, principal responsibility for managing the system. The master alone performs storage management and processor scheduling, and may well execute all the control programs. This highly asymmetric configuration is readily implemented as an extension of a uniprocessing operating system. Many front-end/back-end systems follow this organization, which is well suited to asymmetric hardware configurations and to a straightforward division of labor among a small number of processors (e.g., two). Advantages include simplicity and the ability to use a single copy of each control program, which need not be reenterable. The master maintains all the job queues for all the processors and frees the others, the slaves, from the burdens of scheduling.

A major cost is the increase in interrupt handling; many an interrupt to a slave processor will have to be transmitted as an interrupt to the master as well. Not only will there be more total interrupts claiming overhead resources; the frequency of interrupting the master may be so high that it can accomplish little other than job switching. Indeed, the master–slave mode can be carried to the extreme of using one processor only as a scheduling master that does not run user jobs. A serious disadvantage of master–slave mode is that malfunction of the master can bring the entire system to a halt. This is particularly unfortunate in that multiprocessing is sometimes adopted to enhance over-all system reliability, not to jeopardize it. Another disadvantage is that the inflexibility of this approach can lead to considerable inefficiency in resource management.

Less sensitive to catastrophic failure is an organization in which each processor executes the operating system. This mode, sometimes termed *loosely coupled* multiprocessing, results in a collection of semi-independent processors. The control programs must be either reenterable, to permit concurrent execution by several processors, or else made available in multiple copies. Although each processor maintains its own process queues and many tables, especially for I/O management, some global tables must be shared. This sharing raises the standard problems of data integrity and process synchronization. Detection of processor failure can be difficult under this configuration, as can restarting a processor. A process normally remains associated with only one processor throughout its life. Careful initial allocation of processors to processes can make this approach particularly suitable for throughput improvement.

Further improvement in efficiency comes from considering processors, as well as storage units and I/O devices, to constitute a pool of resources. Rather than being replicated in the different processors, the operating system is distributed over the processors. Any processor can execute the dispatching algorithm, resulting in a symmetric configuration that we shall call *democratic.* All queues and tables are held in global storage, as is a single reenterable copy of the operating system. Because processors are treated as pool resources, a process need not be assigned to the same processor each time it is selected. Better load balancing can result, as can graceful degradation of performance in the event of failure. Because of the central storage of control program code and information, contention problems are more severe. Because all resources are treated as pooled, the danger of deadlock is greater. This configuration is most easily implemented if all the processors are identical.

Whatever approach to multiprocessing is used, an important function of the operating system is to shield the user from asymmetry in the hardware or software. This includes not only asymmetry present in the original system configuration, but also asymmetry induced by component failure. Protection against failure is often sought by decentralizing control of the system. The multiple-copy and democratic modes offer different degrees of software distribution.

Where should the locus of control of a computer system lie? This question has gained increasing prominence with the increase in importance of communication-based systems, and with the decrease in cost of providing control function elsewhere than in one central processor.

Decentralized, or _distributed_ control, offers two major advantages. Many actions, such as I/O device error handling, can be accomplished without access to centrally located information. Communication facilities, as well as processor time, are saved by performing those actions under local control. Incorporating some of this function into a microprocessor in the device or control unit may prove economically attractive. The other major advantage of distributed control is that it may be possible to render hardware failure less likely to engender operating system failure. The idea is that by distributing operating system components appropriately, no hardware unit is critical, and system operation continues in the event of hardware failure, albeit degraded in performance. This capability is sometimes described as _fail-soft_, and is generally restricted to multiprocessor configurations. It is important to note, however, that mere physical separation of software components does not guarantee a logical distribution that will permit continued operation with a component inoperative.

Centralized control saves the costs of the control program redundancy, however modest, that must be built into a fail-soft system. Centralization may also offer economy of scale if the unit cost of providing control function remotely exceeds the cost of providing it centrally. Finally, central control obviates the need for any information to be held in duplicate at different locations, with the attendant costs and dangers (see Section 6.1.5). A major design issue therefore is the extent, if any, to which control should be decentralized.

8.2.3 Mechanisms

The availability of multiple processors, as compared with uniprocessor systems, injects complexity into the management of certain resources. We now review a few of the issues that arise.

Storage Management.   The key issue here is efficiency, both of system operation and of storage assignment. The cost of accessing storage, both in time and in interprocessor contention, often depends upon which processor is accessing which storage module. Main storage local to a processor may be either faster or slower than global main storage, and it can guarantee access without contention. Even homogeneous global storage can be accessed at different costs by processors in an asymmetric hardware configuration. Moreover, it is not necessarily the case that _all_ processors share access to _all_ of the shared storage. As long as any two processors share access to some main storage, we consider the system to be a multiprocessor. Where to locate both code and data can therefore have an important effect on over-all operating efficiency. The best known algorithm for determining optimal storage allocations requires time that increases exponentially in the number of requests to be satisfied simultaneously.

Processor Management.   A system with n processors offers to its users a run state capable of holding n processes rather than 1. The simplest way to manage such a system is to make only once the decision as to which processor is to serve a given process. Then each processor has run, ready, and blocked states independent of those for other processors. This mode is typical of loosely coupled multiprocessing. The processors are not totally separate, of course, because they share executable storage. The assignment of a new process to a processor can be based on the current workload of each processor, the translator requested by the process, or other relatively simple criteria. The decision may even be made manually by the operator if the required information is presented in human-readable form. Otherwise, a program in one of the processors can perform the assignment. Such loosely coupled multiprocessing is particularly convenient for, although by no means restricted to, systems with two processors.

More efficient utilization of the hardware can be provided by not binding the assignment of each process to a fixed processor. If dynamic changes in workload free a processor, it can be assigned to any ready process rather than only to a process that used it to begin with. Determination of the optimal allocation of processors to processes is another task of exponential complexity. It is usually avoided in practice by making simple decisions, such as assigning the next available processor to the highest-priority ready process. Some of the potential loss of efficiency may be recouped by the use of *group scheduling.* This technique, still experimental, assigns groups of related processes to execute simultaneously and allocates storage to related objects simultaneously.

Where to process an interrupt is another choice offered by multiple processors. It is nearly universal practice to process an internal interrupt on the processor within which it originated. An external interrupt, on the other hand, can reasonably be sent to any processor. In a master–slave system all external interrupts are routed to the master. This is the method adopted by the Honeywell 66 multiprocessor. Although the hardware implementation is simple, the response time can be long. An alternative is to let all processors share external interrupts. This is done, except for I/O interrupts, on the Univac 1100 Model 80 system. Each interrupt is offered in turn to every processor during a predefined time slot. The first processor to respond during its time slot handles the interrupt.

Process Management.   The mechanisms presented in Chapter 4 for process interaction do not depend on there being only one processor. Some differences in mechanism are possible in a multiprocessor system, however, because two or more interacting processes can be in execution simultaneously. One new mechanism that multiple processors make available is the *interprocessor interrupt (IPI),* whereby one process can notify another of its desire to synchronize. The IPI is used by the HYDRA system as a component of the *kernel lock,* which is used primarily to provide mutual exclusion for operations on queues. A processor mask word keeps track of which processors are waiting to obtain the lock, and enables a relinquishing processor to signal all waiting processors, one of which succeeds in obtaining the lock. A process that blocks on a kernel lock does not give up its processor, which remains unavailable to other ready processes. Because of the potential withdrawal of such a valuable resource for a long time, the kernel lock is made available only to control programs, not to users.

The implementation of semaphores in multiprocessing is more complex than in uniprocessing. Figure 4.20 presents uniprocessor implementations of *P* and *V* for a counting semaphore. Simultaneous access to the semaphore *s* by two processes is precluded by disabling interrupts to the lone processor. This mechanism is inadequate for a multiprocessor system, because it does not prevent two or more processors from accessing the semaphore concurrently. Because access to the semaphore must be implemented as a critical region, hardware-based mutual exclusion of multiple processors is necessary. One solution, shown in Fig. 8.1, is to use an indivisible read–write instruction such as test-and-set. The two-component semaphore is extended by inclusion of a third component, the boolean flag *mutex.* The initial value of *s.mutex* is **true** to show that no process executing $P(s)$ or $V(s)$ is inside its critical region. The initial value of *s.count* is zero before any process has executed either $P(s)$ or $V(s)$, and the initial value of *s.ptr* is **null**, because the list of processes blocked on *s* is empty. The local boolean variable *permission* is used, as in Fig. 4.7, to hold the value read by executing the *TS* instruction.

Interprocess communication can employ any of the mechanisms described in Section 4.4. Recent experimental multiprocessor systems have tended to use message-based communication, because of its symmetric treatment of processes.

An important consideration is how well the process interaction mechanisms work in the presence of errors. A waiting process can become deadlocked if the signal for which it is waiting is never sent or, once sent, becomes lost. One way to break such a deadlock is to incorporate time limits into the interaction mechanisms. An alternative is to provide a control program capable of waking up a blocked process whose awaited condition has not been satisfied. An error indication would be attached to a process resumed under either of these approaches.

Error Recovery. Most issues of error recovery are not appreciably affected by the presence of multiple processors, but there is one exception. Failure of a processor is more likely, but potentially less serious, than in a uniprocessor system. It is more likely because there are more processors. It is potentially less serious because the processors that have not failed can aid

```
procedure P(s)
    record s (integer count; pointer ptr; boolean mutex)
    boolean permission
    process p
    begin
        disable interrupts
        repeat permission ⟵ TS(s.mutex)
        until permission = true
        s.count ⟵ s.count−1
        s.mutex ⟵ true
        if s.count < 0 then insert calling process on s.ptr↑
                            p ⟵ some ready process
                            s.mutex ⟵ true
                            DISPATCH p with interrupts enabled
                       else s.mutex ⟵ true
                            enable interrupts
    end

procedure V(s)
    record s (integer count; pointer ptr; boolean mutex)
    boolean permission
    process p
    begin
        disable interrupts
        repeat permission ⟵ TS(s.mutex)
        until permission = true
        s.count ⟵ s.count + 1
        if s.count ⩽ 0 then p ⟵ remove some process from s.ptr↑
                            WAKE UP p

        s.mutex ⟵ true
        enable interrupts
    end
```

Figure 8.1 Multiprocessor Implementation of P and V

in recovery. A multiprocessor system is not necessarily more reliable than a uniprocessor system, however, any more than a multiengine airplane is necessarily more reliable than a single-engine airplane, especially when operating system (or pilot) capability is taken into account. Jones and Schwarz [1980] characterize multiprocessing system reliability by two measures. *Availability* measures the ability of the system to respond to requests, whereas *integrity* measures the ability of the system to maintain its state accurately. Failure of a hardware or software component can degrade availability, reducing the system's performance and functionality. Failure can also compromise integrity, resulting in incorrect output and damaged file information. Experience has shown that it is easier to maintain availability than integrity.

The key to reliability is to maintain a logical distribution of the responsibility for performing work, and of the authority for making decisions. This requirement for logical distribution is imposed on both hardware and software. If processor and storage modules are interconnected by a single switch whose failure can disconnect all processors from global storage, the physically distributed processors are not logically distributed. If several processors perform scheduling by executing a single copy of the scheduler, the scheduling function is not logically distributed. Techniques for the logical distribution of responsibility and authority in a multiprocessor operating system are the subject of intense study and development.

Continued operation in the presence of a fault requires that the fault be detected, its cause diagnosed, and recovery effected. One fault-detection tool particularly suitable for multiprocessors is the timer, which can signal an error if it is not reset by some deadline. In the HYDRA system a timer is used to assist in the detection of processor halts and endless loops. Each processor is assigned one bit in a word in global storage. When correctly using HYDRA, it will set its bit frequently. Every 4 seconds each processor checks whether all other processors have set their bits. Thus any processor that does not set its bit at least once every 4 seconds will be detected as malfunctioning. Mechanisms for diagnosis and recovery have also been developed, and the reader is referred for details to more specialized works.

An interesting approach to reliability is found in the Tandem system, designed for commercial transaction processing. There are two processors, each with its own local main storage, but not sharing global main storage. An interprocessor bus is provided for direct communication. The entire operating system is duplicated, and user programs may optionally be duplicated. The "backup" copy of an active process lies inactive in the processor that is not running the primary copy. At fixed checkpoints, process state information is transmitted from the primary to the backup copy by means of a message-based communication system. Upon detection of a failure, the backup copy is activated, and it resumes processing from the most recent checkpoint.

8.3 DESIGN ISSUES

8.3.1 Goals

It may appear fatuous to declaim that understanding a system's goals is prerequisite to a satisfactory design. Nevertheless, more than one system has proved unsatisfactory because its goals were either not clearly understood, or not taken properly into account during the design phase. It is essential that the goals be explicitly stated and that the designers ask consciously to what extent they are meeting those goals.

In Chapters 2 through 7 the goals of an operating system were presented, somewhat simplistically, in terms of requirements to manage a collection of resources in accordance with certain policies. What needs to be made clear at this point is that different groups of users will desire to follow different policies because their needs are different, or will need to implement different mechanisms because their circumstances are different.

The difference in needs is reflected chiefly in the uses to which the system is to be put. Parnas has proposed a classification [1969, unpublished] based on two variables: whether the sequence of job completion is dictated by priority or by deadline; and whether or not a user must communicate with the system during execution of a job. This latter distinction is sometimes characterized by the terms "interactive" and "batch", although "batch" no longer implies the grouping of jobs into batches, either by the operator or by his automatic successor. Figure 8.2 names the four resulting types of multiuser systems. Note that the terms "time sharing" and "multiprogramming" do not appear. This is not because those terms are inaccurate, but because they do not distinguish among the four types of systems, all of which can be multiprogrammed, thereby permitting users to share time. The four types are not meant to be mutually exclusive, because a system of broad scope may offer more than one class of service. A computer utility system may provide all four.

Other differences in goals relate to the extent to which the workload is either controllable or predictable. A process control system usually has the right to reject a user job. It may just not be prepared to initiate yet another operation in the oil refinery, nuclear reactor, or blast furnace to which it is attached. The designers of an operating system intended for a community of conversational users of a single programming language can safely make much more restrictive assumptions about user demands than can those of a broad computer utility.

The difference in user circumstances refers in part to how much function the users are willing to pay for, and in part to the underlying hardware system. The nature of the hardware interrupt mechanism, for example, will help establish which control program functions can reasonably be interrupt-driven. The storage device provided to hold the bulk of the operating system, the so-called *system residence* device, has a profound effect that permeates the design of the entire programming system. The replacement of

User's Relation to System

		In communication	Not in communication
Job Ordering	Deadline	Real-time	Deadline batch
	Priority	Conversational	Priority batch

Figure 8.2 Classification of Operating Systems

tapes by disks for this purpose caused a revolution in how operating systems were built. A second such revolution may result if cheap, electronic backing storage replaces disks, as may well occur in the near future.

8.3.2 Policy Choice

Competing policies are available to the designer for managing many system resources. This does not mean, however, that the designer is free to select policies for different resources independently of each other. A free choice here may constrain another choice there. For example, a policy of not requiring users to state resource needs in advance precludes the selection of avoidance as the policy for coping with deadlock. Implementation mechanisms can also be constrained. The same policy of not stating resource needs eliminates SJN as the dispatching mechanism for enforcing the policy of equal service. The operating system designer must therefore take a global view and make policy decisions that are not independent, but interdependent.

It can be very tempting to treat the choice of policies, and of mechanisms, as an exercise in optimization. A mathematical model of the operating system is constructed, system and workload parameters are estimated, and numerical results calculated to determine an "optimal" design. The foregoing process is more easily described than performed. One reason is that it can be extraordinarily difficult to construct a model that reflects with sufficient precision both which variables are crucial to performance and how those variables are interrelated. Another reason is that, for many of the necessary parameters, estimation may be little better than guesswork. Once the operating sytem is running, of course, measurement can be used to suggest incremental improvements. Until then, the designer's best advice may well be that of C. A. R. Hoare: "Avoid pessimisation."

8.3.3 Flexibility

Although different user communities have different sets of needs, sometimes those sets of needs are related to each other, and can be served by operating systems that, similarly, are related to each other. Occasionally, different sets of needs may be felt by a single community of users at different points in time, typically because of changes in hardware configuration, but perhaps for other reasons. Because of the substantial cost of writing an operating system for each distinct set of users and each distinct configuration of hardware, a common solution is to design and implement several *variants* of one operating system. The required tailoring is often performed through the agency of *system generation*, in which the generator program accepts user-supplied parameters and produces the specified variant.

Different variants may incorporate, for example, different sizes of program modules. More than one operating system has been designed with small modules to permit its being run on a computer with limited main storage. This restriction to small modules has caused inefficiency that was avoidable when the same operating system was run on a computer with larger main storage. Different variants may offer or withhold certain facilities, such as management of off-line data sets, control of nonstandard I/O devices, maintenance of generation data sets, or authentication of user identification. Another difference among variants may be in the binding time of variable information. A case in point is device independence. The ability to specify actual I/O devices as late as execution time can be provided at the cost of greater size and slower operation of the I/O management routines.

The flexibility provided by different variants of the operating system may be the result of making changes to the original operating system as circumstances dictate. Because of the interdependence of policies and mechanisms relating to various resources, this approach has often led to the necessity of making minor modifications to many parts of the operating system, even if only one function was to undergo major change. A frequent result was the introduction of errors, some of them quite subtle.

A far better approach is to derive the different variants from a common ancestor that is designed with a number of decisions not yet taken, and is therefore not fully enough specified to implement. Different choices for the remaining decisions lead to different variants, which can then be implemented without incurring the dangers of undoing decisions already embodied, perhaps quite deeply, in another variant. This planning for variety, planning for change, leads then to the development of *families* of related operating systems.

A third approach is exemplified by the protection facilities of HYDRA and the command language for the MU5. The implementation is intentionally incomplete. Each installation is expected to implement the desired policies by using the mechanisms provided. Different variants are thus expected to be designed and implemented independently of each other.

8.4 VIRTUAL MACHINES

We have seen how one user can appear to use that which does not exist and how several users can appear to use simultaneously that which cannot be shared concurrently. Virtual storage is an example of the former deception; virtual processors and virtual devices, of the latter. A natural extension of these ideas is to put at the user's disposal an entire *virtual machine*. An operating system can be constructed to make it appear to the user that he has exclusive use of a personal copy of an entire hardware system. The first operating system to provide a virtual machine was CP67. Running on an IBM 360 Model 67, it presented each user with a virtual 360 Model 65 complete with I/O devices. The commercially available IBM VM/370 operating system is its descendant.

The provision of such a facility costs both storage and speed of execution. This cost can be kept lowest by selecting, as the hardware system to be provided, a copy of the hardware system on which the operating system is itself running. This restriction is not essential, but unless the simulation of different hardware is of interest per se, it is usually not provided in the virtual machine.

Why would a user pay the cost of having the exclusive use of a machine that he is sharing with other users, presumably because the user cannot afford the cost of exclusive ownership? The question is actually overstated, because he is not paying for the full-time use of the full set of real resources. The user is merely permitted, while in virtual machine mode, to execute programs written for the entire hardware system, and the real resources are in fact diluted by increased running time. Why, then, would a user be willing to pay a penalty to access a hardware system that is available without penalty by using the control program facilities whose description has filled most of this book? For the very privilege of *not* using those control programs!

On his virtual machine the user can run his own control programs, either exclusively or in cooperation with some of the standard control programs. One use of virtual machines is to provide a facility for experimental research on operating systems. Another use is as a vehicle for testing new control program implementations in an environment that prevents their hurting other users of the real systems. The "user" of the virtual system can of course be a group of individuals who are using the new control program, giving it a shakedown cruise before it is incorporated in the actual operating system. A third use of virtual machines is to ease a user's burden of converting from one operating system to its successor. If the new one can provide a virtual machine, a person can use the old operating system on that machine to run applications that have not yet been converted for the new operating system. An alternative is to implement the same virtual machine on both the old system and the new.

The virtual machine is not just an artifact intended to facilitate the actions of a user who does not want to run with the crowd. In one sense, every user of an operating system is presented with the virtual machine defined by the system-provided interface between the user and the hardware. One fruitful way to design an operating system is to think in terms of providing a suitable virtual machine to each user. The provision of identifiable virtual machines can be used to enforce policies governing interactions among users. In particular, protection mechanisms can be implemented by running control programs on each user's virtual machine.

8.5 RESTRICTED-DOMAIN PROGRAMMING SYSTEMS

Our attention has been devoted thus far to operating systems that support a wide range of user activities. Many computers, however, are used in programming environments that are restricted to a subset of the activities we have considered. We bring the book to a close with a brief examination of three different restrictions of the programming system domain.

8.5.1 Single-User Systems

The advent of the personal computer has been responsible for the development of a number of programming systems designed to serve a single user at a time. Many different types of single-user systems have been developed. OS6 was implemented on the virtual machine provided by an interpreter running on a small minicomputer. Two microprocessor-based systems are CP/M, oriented to assembler language, and UCSD Pascal, oriented to a programming language. The Pilot system was written for a powerful minicomputer. The CMS system runs on a large, shared computer, but is really a single-user system, because each user has a private instance of CMS on the virtual machine provided to him by VM/370.

All of these systems provide an environment intended for the development and execution of programs. Typical components include one or more translators, a filing system, device control routines, and an editor suitable at least for line-oriented programming and sometimes also for arbitrary text. Other components may be provided in some systems. A desk calculator mode is offered by UCSD Pascal, a symbolic debugger by CP/M, and a text formatter by CMS.

The single-user programming system may not satisfy our definition of an operating system, because it does not serve a community of users. To the extent that the single human user initiates multiple processes, however, and to the extent that he is competing with the programming system for resources, it is nevertheless reasonable to view the control program portion of such a system as an operating system. A few simplifications of the operating system's design ensue from the restriction to a single user. One is that there is no need to protect the user from interference by another user. It is necessary only to protect the integrity of permanent information in the system. Another simplification is that the resource allocation effort can be much reduced. The designers of OS6 claim that the control of resources reduces to the problem of storage allocation.

A feature that is more likely to be provided in a personal computer system than in a multiuser system is *advice-taking*. The system takes from the user advice that assists it in optimizing its activities. An example is provided by some of the operations available in the Pilot system. These refer to

216

"spaces", sets of contiguous pages. One operation advises the system that a particular space will be needed soon and should be swapped in as soon as possible. Another advises the system that a space is no longer needed in main storage, and can safely be swapped out at any time. A third advises the system that a space will no longer be needed, and can be overwritten without first being swapped out. By taking the proferred advice, the system's ability to optimize paging traffic is improved.

8.5.2 Single-Language Systems

We shall use the term *single-language* to characterize a programming system that provides ony one programming language for all users. Such a system may be restricted to a single user, or to a single application, but often it is not. Examples include systems dedicated to providing interactive APL or BASIC service.

In a single-language programming system, the language system can often be restricted to a single translator. Particularly if the translator is interactive, the user communicates freely with both the translator and the operating system. The distinction between the two need not be held firm. The design of the operating system can be optimized to match the language. For example, a garbage collector might well be incorporated in an operating system dedicated to LISP. In any multiuser single-language system, the translator would probably be permanently resident in main storage, together with the operating system nucleus. Ease of use is enhanced by having a command language that is similar to the unique programming language.

Several features are commonly found in single-language systems, although none is exclusive to such systems. One is that the principal translator is an interpreter or an incremental compiler. To save space, it is normally reenterable. The translator often serves as the agent that recognizes commands to the operating system, and passes them on. Another feature, found in many interactive multilanguage systems as well, is the provision of an active *workspace* for each user connected to the system. This is an unnamed region of storage, dedicated to that user, and containing whatever objects he is working with. When a user logs in, he is allocated a workspace. When the user becomes inactive, the workspace may be swapped out. When the user logs out, the workspace is freed. In APL, a copy of the active workspace can be saved into the file system, which is a collection of named workspaces. An alternative used in other systems is to save program and data objects under their own names.

8.5.3 Single-Application Systems

Yet another form of programming system is restricted to serving a single application. Examples include systems for word processing, engineering design, and process control. There may be one user or several; there may be several programming languages or one, or even none at all. In a typical word-processing system, for example, the users do not write programs. Instead, they call for editing, formatting, and filing services, and so on, by means of commands presented directly to the system. The operating system used in a single-application environment can stress the management of resources required by the application, while ignoring others. In a process-control system, deadline scheduling and interrupt handling will be emphasized, but spooling, device independence, and a hierarchic file system may well be omitted. An engineering design system, on the other hand, will devote more attention to file management and to supporting interactive graphics. And so on.

Restricting the domain of a programming system in any of the ways described here often results in an operating system that is simpler to build, to understand, and to use. With decreasing dependence upon economies of scale, we can expect to encounter more and more computer systems that are specialized in one manner or another. Their operating systems can be viewed as restricted forms of the general-purpose operating systems that have constituted the major subject of this book.

FOR FURTHER STUDY

The historical development of operating systems is reviewed briefly by Kurzban, Heines, and Sayers [1975, Sec. 1.1]. An alternative view is given in Chap. 1 of Sayers [1971], whose Chaps. 7 to 9 survey a number of operating systems of the 1960s. The journal, *Annals of the History of Computing*, established in 1979, is a growing source of historical information.

Multiprocessing systems are treated briefly by Kurzban, Heines, and Sayers [1975, Sec. 2.4] and by Enslow [1977], who discusses further the approaches to operating system design. Two works by Satyanarayanan [1980a, 1980b] discuss multiprocessor hardware. Jones and Schwarz [1980] discuss many operating system problems in detail, and report the results of experience with some experimental systems. The Tandem approach to fail-soft design is presented by Levy [1978], with further details in Katzman [1978] and Bartlett [1978].

The textbooks by Shaw [1974] and Habermann [1976] are devoted principally to the design of operating systems. Design issues are also considered by Watson [1970, Sec. 1.4], Tsichritzis and Bernstein [1974, Chap. 8], and Kurzban, Heines, and Sayers [1975], whose Chap. 7 presents a good overview of the system development process.

The use of virtual machines for operating system portability is described by Hall, Scherrer, and Sventek [1980]. Their use to enforce isolation of users for protection is discussed in Jones [1978]. Interesting restricted-domain systems include APL\360, described by Breed and Lathwell [1968]; OS6, described by Stoy and Strachey [1972]; and Pilot, described by Redell et al. [1980].

EXERCISES

8.1 Cite instances of the interdependence of the management of storage, processor, processes, devices, and files.

8.2 What are the causes of change in the specification of operating system function?

8.3 Give an example of the information that might be stored in global tables by a loosely coupled multiprocessing operating system.

8.4 Why is processor redundancy needed in a fail-soft system?

8.5 Is the Tandem system a multiprocessor?

8.6 Why is it easier to provide, as a virtual machine, a copy of the host machine rather than of an arbitrary machine?

8.7 Why might a single-language programming system incorporate more than one language translator?

8.8 What advantage follows from having all user workspaces the same size?

BIBLIOGRAPHY

ARMS, W. Y., J. E. BAKER, AND R. M. PENGELLY [1976]. *A Practical Approach to Computing.* Wiley, London.

ARNOLD, J. S., D. P. CASEY, AND R. H. MCKINSTRY [1974]. Design of Tightly-Coupled Multiprocessing Programming. *IBM Syst. J.* **13**(1): 60–87.

ATWOOD, J. WILLIAM [Oct. 1976]. Concurrency in Operating Systems. *Computer* **9**(10): 18–26.

BARRON, D. W. [1972]. *Assemblers and Loaders*, 2nd ed. Macdonald, London.

BARRON, D. W. [Aug. 1974]. Job Control Languages and Job Control Programs. *Comput. J.* **17**(3): 282–286.

BARTLETT, JOEL F. [1978]. A "Nonstop" Operating System. *Proc. 11th Hawaii Int. Conf. Syst. Sci.*, January, Vol. 3, pp. 103–117.

BAYER, R., R. M. GRAHAM, AND G. SEEGMÜLLER (EDS.) [1978]. *Operating Systems—An Advanced Course.* Springer-Verlag, Berlin.

BAYS, CARTER [Mar. 1977]. A Comparison of Next-fit, First-fit, and Best-fit. *Comm. ACM* **20**(3): 191–192.

BELADY, L. A. [1966]. A Study of Replacement Algorithms for a Virtual-Storage Computer. *IBM Syst. J.* **5**(2): 78–101.

BELADY, L. A., R. A. NELSON, AND G. S. SHEDLER [June 1969]. An Anomaly in Space–Time Characteristics of Certain Programs Running in a Paging Machine. *Comm. ACM* **12**(6): 349–353.

BENSOUSSAN, A., C. T. CLINGEN, AND R. C. DALEY [May 1972]. The Multics Virtual Memory: Concepts and Design. *Comm. ACM* **15**(5): 308–318.

BOBROW, DANIEL G., JERRY D. BURCHFIEL, DANIEL L. MURPHY AND RAYMOND S. TOMLINSON [Mar. 1972]. TENEX, a Paged Time Sharing System for the PDP-10. *Comm. ACM* **15**(3): 135–143.

BOURNE, S. R. [July-Aug. 1978]. The UNIX Shell. *Bell Syst. Tech. J.* **57**(6): 1971–1990.

BREED, L. M., AND R. H. LATHWELL [1968]. The Implementation of APL\360. In M. Klerer and J. Reinfelds (eds.), *Interactive Systems for Experimental Applied Mathematics*. Academic Press, New York, pp. 390–399.

BRINCH HANSEN, PER (ED.) [1969]. RC 4000 Software Multiprogramming System. A/S Regnecentralen, Copenhagen, April.

BRINCH HANSEN, PER [Apr. 1970]. The Nucleus of a Multiprogramming System. *Comm. ACM* 13(4): 238–241, 250.

BRINCH HANSEN, PER [July 1972]. Structured Multiprogramming. *Comm. ACM* 15(7): 574–578.

BRINCH HANSEN, PER [1973a]. *Operating System Principles*. Prentice-Hall, Englewood Cliffs, NJ.

BRINCH HANSEN, PER [Dec. 1973b]. Concurrent Programming Concepts. *Comput. Surveys* 5(4): 223–245.

BRINCH HANSEN, PER [June 1975]. The Programming Language Concurrent Pascal. *IEEE Trans. Software Eng.* SE-1(2): 199–207.

BRINCH HANSEN, PER [1977]. *The Architecture of Concurrent Programs*. Prentice-Hall, Englewood Cliffs, NJ.

BROOKS JR., FREDERICK P., AND KENNETH E. IVERSON [1969]. *Automatic Data Processing*, System/360 ed. Wiley, New York.

BROWN, H. [1978]. Recent Developments in Command Languages. In *Information Technology* (Proc. 3rd Jerusalem Conf. Inf. Technol.). North-Holland, Amsterdam, pp. 453–460.

BRUNT, R. F., AND D. E. TUFFS [Jan.-Mar. 1976]. A User–Oriented Approach to Control Languages. *Software—Practice and Experience* 6(1): 93–108.

BULL, G. M., AND S. F. G. PACKHAM [1971]. *Time Sharing Systems*. McGraw-Hill, London.

BUNT, R. B. [Oct. 1976]. Scheduling Techniques for Operating Systems. *Computer* 9(10): 10–17.

CALINGAERT, PETER [1979]. *Assemblers, Compilers, and Program Translation*. Computer Science Press, Potomac, MD.

CLARK, W. A. [1966]. The Functional Structure of OS/360 Part III: Data Management. *IBM Syst. J.* 5(1): 30–51.

COFFMAN JR., E. G., M. J. ELPHICK, AND A. SHOSHANI [June 1971]. System Deadlocks. *Comput. Surveys* 3(2): 67–78. Reprinted in Freeman [1975, pp. 153–167].

COFFMAN JR., EDWARD G., AND PETER J. DENNING [1973]. *Operating Systems Theory*. Prentice-Hall, Englewood Cliffs, NJ.

COLIN, A. J. T. [Nov. 1968]. The Lancaster University Operating System. *Comput. Bull.* 12(7): 247–255.

COLIN, A. J. T. [1971]. *Introduction to Operating Systems*. Macdonald, London.

COMER, DOUGLAS [June 1979]. The Ubiquitous B-Tree. *Comput. Surveys* **11**(2): 121–137.

CONWAY, MELVIN E. [July 1963]. Design of a Separable Transition-Diagram Compiler. *Comm. ACM* **6**(7): 396–408.

CORBATÓ, F. J., AND V. A. VYSSOTSKY [1965]. An Introduction and Overview of the MULTICS System. *Proc. AFIPS Conf.* (FJCC) **27**, Part 1: 185–196. Reprinted in Rosen [1967].

COURTOIS, P. J., F. HEYMANS, AND D. L. PARNAS [Oct. 1971]. Concurrent Control with "Readers" and "Writers". *Comm. ACM* **14**(10): 667–668.

CUTTLE, G., AND P. B. ROBINSON (EDS.) [1970]. *Executive Programs and Operating Systems.* Macdonald, London.

DENNING, PETER J. [May 1968]. The Working Set Model for Program Behavior. *Comm. ACM* **11**(5): 323–333.

DENNING, PETER J. [Sep. 1970]. Virtual Memory. *Comput. Surveys* **2**(3): 153–189.

DENNING, PETER J. [Dec. 1976]. Fault-Tolerant Operating Systems. *Comput. Surveys* **8**(4): 359–389.

DENNING, PETER J. [Jan. 1980]. Working Sets Past and Present. *IEEE Trans. Software Eng.* **SE-6**(1): 64–84.

DEPENDAHL JR., ROBERT H., AND LEON PRESSER [Oct. 1976]. File Input/Output Control Logic. *Computer* **9**(10): 38–42.

DIJKSTRA, E. W. [1965]. Cooperating Sequential Processes. EWD123, Mathematics Department, Technological University, Eindhoven, The Netherlands, September. Reprinted in F. Genuys (ed.) [1968]. *Programming Languages.* Academic Press, London, pp. 43–112.

DIJKSTRA, EDSGER W. [May 1968]. The Structure of the "THE" Multiprogramming System. *Comm. ACM* **11**(5): 341–346.

DIJKSTRA, E. W. [1971]. Hierarchical Ordering of Sequential Processes. *Acta Inf.* **1**(2): 115–138. Reprinted in Hoare and Perrott [1972, pp. 72–93].

DODD, GEORGE G. [June 1969]. Elements of Data Management Systems. *Comput. Surveys* **1**(2): 117–133. Reprinted in Freeman [1975, Sec. 8.3].

DORAN, R. W. [Oct. 1976]. Virtual Memory. *Computer* **9**(10): 27–37.

DRUMMOND JR., MANSFORD E. [1973]. *Evaluation and Measurement Techniques for Digital Computer Systems.* Prentice-Hall, Englewood Cliffs, NJ.

ENSLOW JR., PHILIP H. [Mar. 1977]. Multiprocessor Organization—A Survey. *Comput. Surveys* **9**(1): 103–129.

FERRARI, DOMENICO [1978]. *Computer Systems Performance Evaluation.* Prentice-Hall, Englewood Cliffs, NJ.

FOSTER, CAXTON C. [Mar. 1971]. An Unclever Time-Sharing System. *Comput. Surveys* **3**(1): 23–48.

FRANK, G. R. [May 1976]. Job Control in the MU5 Operating System. *Comput. J.* **19**(2): 139–143.

FRASER, A. G. [Feb. 1969]. Integrity of a Mass Storage Filing System. *Comput. J.* **12**(1): 1–5.

FREEMAN, PETER [1975]. *Software Systems Principles.* Science Research Associates, Palo Alto, CA.

FULLER, SAMUEL H. [1975]. Computer Structures. In Freeman [1975, Chap. 2].

GOTLIEB, C. C., AND A. BORODIN [1973]. *Social Issues in Computing.* Academic Press, New York.

GRAHAM, G. SCOTT, AND PETER J. DENNING [1972]. Protection—Principles and Practice. *Proc. AFIPS Conf.* (SJCC) **40**: 417–429.

GRAHAM, ROBERT M. [1975]. *Principles of Systems Programming.* Wiley, New York.

GRAM, CHR., AND F. R. HERTWECK [1975]. Command Languages: Design Considerations and Basic Concepts. In Unger [1975, pp. 43–67].

GROSCH, H. R. J. [Apr. 1953]. High Speed Arithmetic: The Digital Computer as a Research Tool. *J. Opt. Soc. Amer.* **43**(4): 306–310.

HABERMANN, A. N. [July 1969]. Prevention of System Deadlocks. *Comm. ACM* **12**(7): 373–377, 385.

HABERMANN, A. N. [1976]. *Introduction to Operating System Design.* Science Research Associates, Palo Alto, CA.

HALL, DENNIS E., DEBORAH K. SCHERRER, AND JOSEPH S. SVENTEK [Sep. 1980]. A Virtual Operating System. *Comm. ACM* **23**(9): 495–502.

HAVENDER, J. W. [1968]. Avoiding Deadlock in Multitasking Systems. *IBM Syst. J.* **7**(2): 74–84.

HELLERMAN, HERBERT, AND THOMAS F. CONROY [1975]. *Computer System Performance.* McGraw-Hill, New York.

HOARE, C. A. R. [1972]. Operating Systems: Their Purpose, Objectives, Functions and Scope. In Hoare and Perrott [1972, pp. 11–19].

HOARE, C. A. R. [Oct. 1974]. Monitors: An Operating System Structuring Concept. *Comm. ACM* **17**(10): 549–557. Erratum in *Comm. ACM* **18**(2): 95 [Feb. 1975].

HOARE, C. A. R., AND R. H. PERROTT (EDS.) [1972]. *Operating Systems Techniques.* Academic Press, London.

HOFFMAN, LANCE J. [1977]. *Modern Methods for Computer Security and Privacy.* Prentice-Hall, Englewood Cliffs, NJ.

HOLT, R. C., G. S. GRAHAM, E. D. LAZOWSKA, AND M. A. SCOTT [1978]. *Structured Concurrent Programming with Operating Systems Applications.* Addison-Wesley, Reading, MA.

HOLT, RICHARD C. [Sep. 1972]. Some Deadlock Properties of Computer Systems. *Comput. Surveys* **4**(3): 179–196.

HORNING, J. J., AND B. RANDELL [Mar. 1973]. Process Structuring. *Comput. Surveys* **5**(1): 5–30.

HSIAO, DAVID K., DOUGLAS S. KERR, AND STUART E. MADNICK [1979]. *Computer Security.* Academic Press, New York.

ISLOOR, SREEKANTH S., AND T. ANTHONY MARSLAND [Sep. 1980]. The Deadlock Problem: An Overview. *Computer* 13(9): 58–78.

JONES, ANITA K. [1978]. Protection Mechanisms and the Enforcement of Security Policies. In Bayer, Graham, and Seegmüller [1978, Chap. 3.C].

JONES, ANITA K., AND PETER SCHWARZ [June 1980]. Experience Using Multiprocessor Systems—A Status Report. *Comput. Surveys* 12(2): 121–165.

KATZMAN, JAMES A. [1978]. A Fault-Tolerant Computer System. *Proc. 11th Hawaii Int. Conf. Syst. Sci.*, January, Vol. 3: pp. 85–102.

KILBURN, T., R. B. PAYNE, AND D. J. HOWARTH [1961]. The Atlas Supervisor. *Proc. AFIPS Conf.* (EJCC) 20: 279–294. Reprinted in Rosen [1967].

KILBURN, T., D. B. G. EDWARDS, M. J. LANIGAN, AND F. H. SUMNER [Apr. 1962]. One-Level Storage System. *IRE Trans. Electron. Computers* EC-11(2): 223–235.

KNUTH, DONALD E. [1973]. *The Art of Computer Programming*, Vol. 1: *Fundamental Algorithms*, 2nd ed. Addison-Wesley, Reading, MA.

KURZBAN, STANLEY A., THOMAS S. HEINES, AND ANTHONY P. SAYERS [1975]. *Operating System Principles.* Petrocelli/Charter, New York.

LAMPSON, BUTLER W. [1971]. Protection. *Proc. 5th Annu. Princeton Conf. Inf. Sci. Syst.*, pp. 437–443. Reprinted in ACM *Operat. Syst. Rev.* 8(1): 18–24 [Jan. 1974].

LEVIN, R., ET AL. [1975]. Policy/Mechanism Separation in HYDRA. *Proc. 5th Symp. Operat. Syst. Principles*, Austin, TX, pp. 132–140.

LEVY, JOHN V. [Oct. 1978]. A Multiple Computer System for Reliable Transaction Processing. ACM *SIGSMALL Newslett.* 4(5): 5–22.

LISKOV, BARBARA H. [Mar. 1972]. The Design of the Venus Operating System. *Comm. ACM* 15(3): 144–149.

LISTER, A. M. [1975]. *Fundamentals of Operating Systems.* Macmillan, London.

LOWE, THOMAS C. [Apr. 1969]. Analysis of Boolean Program Models for Time-Shared, Paged Environments. *Comm. ACM* 12(4): 199–205.

LUCAS JR., HENRY C., [Sep. 1971]. Performance Evaluation and Monitoring. *Comput. Surveys* 3(3): 79–91.

MADNICK, STUART E., AND JOHN J. DONOVAN [1974]. *Operating Systems.* McGraw-Hill, New York.

MCKEAG, R. M., AND R. WILSON [1976]. *Studies in Operating Systems.* Academic Press, London.

MCKELL, LYNN J., JAMES V. HANSEN, AND LESTER E. HEITGER [June 1979]. Charging for Computing Resources. *Comput. Surveys* 11(2): 105–120.

MEALY, G. H. [1966]. The Functional Structure of OS/360 Part I: Introductory Survey. *IBM Syst. J.* 5(1): 3–11.

MENZEL, REINHARD G. [July 1976]. Concurrent SP/k: a Language Supporting Concurrent Processes. M.Sc. thesis, Department of Computer Science, University of Toronto.

MUNTZ, R. R. [1975]. Scheduling and Resource Allocation in Computer Systems. In Freeman [1975, Sec. 7.4].

PARKER, DONN B. [1976]. *Crime by Computer.* Scribner, New York.

PARNAS, D. L. [1974]. Betriebssystem-Strukturen. Lecture notes, Technische Hochschule Darmstadt, Fed. Rep. Germany.

POPEK, GERALD J. [June 1974]. Protection Structures. *Computer* 7(6): 22–23.

PRATT, TERENCE W. [1975]. *Programming Languages: Design and Implementation.* Prentice-Hall, Englewood Cliffs, NJ.

PRESSER, LEON [Mar. 1975]. Multiprogramming Coordination. *Comput. Surveys* 7(1): 21–44.

PRESSER, LEON, AND JOHN R. WHITE [Sep. 1972]. Linkers and Loaders. *Comput. Surveys* 4(3): 149–167.

REDELL, DAVID D., ET AL. [Feb. 1980]. Pilot: An Operating System for a Personal Computer. *Comm. ACM* 23(2): 81–92.

RITCHIE, DENNIS M., AND KEN THOMPSON [July 1974]. The UNIX Time-Sharing System. *Comm. ACM* 17(7): 365–375. A later version appeared in *Bell Syst. Tech. J.* 57(6): 1905–1929 [July-Aug. 1978].

ROSEN, SAUL (ED.) [1967]. *Programming Systems and Languages.* McGraw-Hill, New York.

ROSIN, ROBERT F. [Mar. 1969]. Supervisory and Monitor Systems. *Comput. Surveys* 1(1): 37–54.

SALTZER, JEROME H. [July 1974]. Protection and the Control of Information Sharing in Multics. *Comm. ACM* 17(7): 388–402.

SALTZER, JEROME H., AND MICHAEL D. SCHROEDER [Sep. 1975]. The Protection of Information in Computer Systems. *Proc. IEEE* 63(9): 1278–1308.

SATYANARAYANAN, M. [1980a]. *Multiprocessors: A Comparative Study.* Prentice-Hall, Englewood Cliffs, NJ.

SATYANARAYANAN, M. [Oct. 1980b]. Commercial Multiprocessing Systems. *Computer* 13(5): 75–96. Condensed from: A Survey of Multiprocessing Systems, report RC 7346, IBM Research Center, Yorktown Heights, NY, Oct. 10, 1978.

SATYANARAYANAN, M. [Oct. 1980c]. Multiprocessing: An Annotated Bibliography. *Computer* 13(5): 101–116.

SAYERS, ANTHONY P. (ED.) [1971]. *Operating Systems Survey.* Auerbach, Princeton, NJ.

SEAWRIGHT, L. H., AND R. A. MACKINNON [1979]. VM/370—A Study of Multiplicity and Usefulness. *IBM Syst. J.* 18(1): 4–17.

SEVCIK, STEVEN E. [1975]. An Analysis of Uses of Coroutines. M.S. thesis, Department of Computer Science, University of North Carolina at Chapel Hill.

SHAW, ALAN C. [1974]. *The Logical Design of Operating Systems.* Prentice-Hall, Englewood Cliffs, NJ.

SHORE, JOHN E. [Aug. 1975]. On the External Storage Fragmentation Produced by First-Fit and Best-Fit Allocation Strategies. *Comm. ACM* 18(8): 433–440.

STONE, HAROLD S. [1972]. *Introduction to Computer Organization and Data Structures.* McGraw-Hill, New York.

STOY, J. E., AND C. STRACHEY [May,Aug. 1972]. OS6—An Experimental Operating System for a Small Computer. Part 1: General Principles and Structure. *Comput. J.* **15**(2): 117–124. Part 2: Input/Output and Filing System. *Comput. J.* **15**(3): 195–203.

TEOREY, T. J., AND T. B. PINKERTON [Mar. 1972]. A Comparative Analysis of Disk Scheduling Policies. *Comm. ACM* **15**(3): 177–184.

TSICHRITZIS, DIONYSIOS C., AND PHILIP A. BERNSTEIN [1974]. *Operating Systems.* Academic Press, New York.

ULLMAN, JEFFREY D. [1976]. *Fundamental Concepts of Programming Systems.* Addison-Wesley, Reading, MA.

UNGER, C. (ED.) [1975]. *Command Languages* (Proc. IFIP Working Conf., 1974). North-Holland, Amsterdam.

WARWICK, MARTIN [1970]. Introduction to Operating System Concepts. In Cuttle and Robinson [1970, Chap. 1].

WATSON, RICHARD W. [1970]. *Timesharing System Design Concepts.* McGraw-Hill, New York.

WEGNER, PETER [1968]. *Programming Languages, Information Structures, and Machine Organization.* McGraw-Hill, New York.

WIEDERHOLD, GIO [1977]. *Database Design.* McGraw-Hill, New York.

WILKES, M. V. [1975]. *Time-Sharing Computer Systems,* 3rd ed. Macdonald, London.

WIRTH, N. [Jan.-Feb. 1977]. Modula: a Programming Language for Modular Multiprogramming. *Software—Practice and Experience* **7**(1): 3–35.

WITT, B. I. [1966]. The Functional Structure of OS/360 Part II: Job and Task Management. *IBM Syst. J.* **5**(1): 12–29.

WULF, W., ET AL. [June 1974]. HYDRA: The Kernel of a Multiprocessor Operating System. *Comm. ACM* **17**(6): 337–345.

Appendix

SUMMARY OF PROGRAM NOTATION

The programs in this book are intended for the human reader, and do not need to be executed by a computer. Their presentation has been simplified by taking some syntactic and semantic liberties with the notation, as compared to a real programming language. The following summary of the program notation, which is strongly influenced by Algol and Pascal, should enable it to be read by anyone who has experience with a procedure-oriented programming language. Keywords are in boldface, procedure names in uppercase italics, and other identifiers in lowercase italics. Comments are enclosed between "/*" and "*/".

A procedure declaration contains **procedure,** followed first by the procedure name and then by an optional list of formal parameters enclosed in parentheses. Procedures may be defined within a monitor, whose name is preceded by **monitor.**

A parameter or variable is declared by the use of its name preceded by one of the following attributes.

boolean	**global**	**pointer**	**record**
condition	**integer**	**process**	**semaphore**
event	**local**	**queue**	**shared**

Individual fields of a record may be declared within a parenthesized list following declaration of the record. The constants **true** and **false** (for variables of type **boolean**) and the constant **null** (for variables of type **pointer**) have the usual meanings, as do numeric constants.

Most statements are represented by English text in roman font. Exceptions are **read**, **write,** assignment, and procedure call. Assignment is indicated by an arrow pointing left. Arithmetic and logical expressions are formed in a conventional manner. A procedure call is indicated by use of the procedure name followed by the list of actual parameters.

Sequential execution of a set of statements is indicated by placing them between **begin** and **end.** Concurrent execution is indicated by **cobegin** and

227

coend. The prefix **co** of **cobegin** and **coend** indicates that the enclosed state-ments are executed concurrently, independently of each other, hence may be overlapped in time. The order in which their executions begin is unspeci-fied; so is the order in which their executions end. Program execution does not proceed beyond **coend** until execution of each enclosed statement is complete.

Iteration constructs are "**while** condition **do**" and "**repeat** statement **until** condition". For indefinite repetition, the **until** clause is omitted. The alternation construct is "**if** condition **then** statement **else** statement". The **else** clause can be omitted. The scope of **do**, **repeat** (without **until**), **then**, and **else** is indicated by indentation. There is one exception: an empty loop body may be represented by **begin end**. The **region** construct is explained in Section 4.2.

Qualified names may be used for record fields, with a period joining the field name to the record name. A pointer name followed by an arrow point-ing up is equivalent to the name of the entity pointed to by the named pointer. The addressing function A returns the address of its argu-ment as a pointer value. Thus assignment of the value $A(q)$ to the pointer p sets p to point to q, after which "$p\uparrow$" and "q" name the same entity.

Given the declarations

record a (**integer** b, **pointer** c)
record x (**boolean** b, **integer** y)

$a.b$ is an integer, whereas $x.b$ is a boolean. Let the assignment $c \leftarrow A(x)$ be executed. Then $a.c\uparrow$ is the record x, and $c\uparrow.y$ is the integer field in that record.

To simplify the appearance of programs, several omissions are permit-ted. A sequence of statements not otherwise enclosed is understood to be preceded by **begin** and followed by **end**. Two dots are used for elision of one or more list elements, statements, procedures, or other entities.

INDEX